AVID

READER

PRESS

ALSO BY ROSS DOUTHAT

To Change the Church:
Pope Francis and the Future of Catholicism

Bad Religion:
How We Became a Nation of Heretics

Grand New Party:
How Republicans Can Win the Working Class and
Save the American Dream
(with Reihan Salam)

Privilege:
Harvard and the Education of the Ruling Class

The
Decadent Society

America Before and After
the Pandemic

ROSS DOUTHAT

Avid Reader Press

New York   London   Toronto   Sydney   New Delhi

For Gwendolyn, Eleanor,
Nicholas . . . and Plum

AVID READER PRESS
An Imprint of Simon & Schuster, Inc.
1230 Avenue of the Americas
New York, NY 10020

Copyright © 2020 by Ross Douthat

The Decadent Society was previously published with the subtitle,
"How We Became the Victims of Our Own Success."

First Avid Reader Press trade paperback edition March 2021

AVID READER PRESS and colophon are trademarks of Simon & Schuster, Inc.

For information about special discounts for bulk purchases,
please contact Simon & Schuster Special Sales at 1-866-506-1949
or business@simonandschuster.com.

The Simon & Schuster Speakers Bureau can bring authors to your live event.
For more information or to book an event, contact the Simon & Schuster Speakers Bureau
at 1-866-248-3049 or visit our website at www.simonspeakers.com.

Manufactured in the United States of America

1   3   5   7   9   10   8   6   4   2

Library of Congress Cataloging-in-Publication Data has been applied for.

ISBN 978-1-4767-8524-0
ISBN 978-1-4767-8525-7 (pbk)
ISBN 978-1-4767-8526-4 (ebook)

The crisis consists precisely in the fact that the old is dying and the new cannot be born; in this interregnum a great variety of morbid symptoms appear.

—Antonio Gramsci

pity this busy monster, manunkind, not. Progress is a comfortable disease . . .

—e. e. cummings

Contents

Contents

PART 3
THE DEATHS OF DECADENCE

The Closing of the Frontier

The peak of human accomplishment and daring, the greatest single triumph of modern science and government and industry, the most extraordinary endeavor of the American age in modern history, occurred in late July in the year 1969, when a trio of human beings were catapulted up from the earth's surface, where their fragile, sinful species had spent all its long millennia of conscious history, to stand and walk and leap upon the moon.

"Four assassinations later," wrote Norman Mailer of the march from JFK's lunar promise to its Nixon-era fulfillment, "a war in Vietnam later; a burning of Black ghettos later; hippies, drugs and many student uprisings later; one Democratic Convention in Chicago seven years later; one New York school strike later; one sexual revolution later; yes, eight years of a dramatic, near-catastrophic, outright spooky decade later, we were ready to make the moon." *We were ready*—as though the leap into space were linked, somehow, to the civil rights revolution, the baby boomers coming into their own, the transformation in music and manners and mores, and the hopes of utopia percolating in Paris, Woodstock, San Francisco.

Mailer's was a mystical take on history, but one well suited to its moment. For the society that made it happen, the Apollo landing was both a counterpoint to the social chaos of the 1960s and the culmination of the decade's revolutionary promise. It proved that the efficiency and techno-optimism of Eisenhower-era America could persist through the upheavals of the counterculture, and it represented a kind of mystical, dizzy, Age of Aquarius moment in its own right. As much as anything that happened here on earth, the fire on the moon helped make the summer of '69 seem like a beginning, not a peak—an opening into a new era, in which the frontier would no longer be closed, the map no longer filled in, and human beings would expand their explorations, their empires, their arguments and imaginations and ambitions into the very stars.

This was the space age, which lasted for about thirty years: from Sputnik in 1957 to the space shuttle *Challenger* explosion in 1986. And we who live in its aftermath have forgotten just how confidently it was expected to continue. In *The Heavens and the Earth: A Political History of the Space Age*, his magisterial narrative of the period, Walter McDougall runs through the expert predictions of the 1960s and 1970s: that soon reusable spacecrafts would be constantly "ascending and descending like angels on Jacob's ladder" into space; that by the year 2000, both superpowers would have lunar colonies; that human missions to Mars would begin within a decade of the moon landing; that space would soon become the site of revolutions in energy production, weather control, and more. Likewise with Apollo-era pop culture: *2001: A Space Odyssey* promised a manned mission to Jupiter in its eponymous year, while the timeline of the future on *Star Trek* assumed that space exploration and colonization would follow as naturally from the Apollo program as sailors and settlers had followed the course discovered by Columbus.

This dream did not quite die with *Challenger*, but it had lost adherents across the disappointingly earthbound seventies, and from the Reagan era onward, it became a fond and somewhat fantastical hope, invoked as a flourish by presidents seeking to inspire and pursued by the sort of eccentric billionaires who also invested in cryonics. As it became clear that we would not master the vastnesses of space as easily as explorers crossing the Atlantic, the public's attention waned, political support diminished, and science fiction lost its gee-whiz edge and turned dystopian. The movies especially began to treat the infinite spaces differently—as a zone of terrors where no one hears you scream (*Alien* and its imitators), a source of sinister invasions and a home of malignant demigods (the UFO craze, *The X-Files*), or as a purgatory to be escaped by a safe return to earth (*Apollo 13*, *Gravity*, *The Martian*, *Ad Astra*). Where *Trek* had confidently blended sixties liberalism with the frontier spirit of *Wagon Train*, its successors *Star Wars* and *Battlestar Galactica* were not even visions of the human future at all: they were dispatches from a stellar prehistory; a vision of far away or long ago.

Meanwhile, unmanned spaceflight expanded, robots reached distant worlds, astronomers discovered planets that might well be earthlike—but none of it kindled the popular imagination as the giant leap for mankind had done. For the most part, humanity had decided that whatever might be up there, it would probably remain indefinitely out of reach.

This resignation haunts our present civilization. Across human history, the most dynamic and creative societies have been almost inevitably expansionary, going outward from tribes and cities and nations to put their stamp upon a larger world. Sometimes this has meant settlement and sometimes conquest, sometimes it has meant missionary zeal, sometimes simply exploration for the sake of commerce and curiosity. In the case of the modern West, the first world civilization, it meant all of them: God and gold and glory, settler societies and far-flung imperial rule, races to the poles and to the peaks, and the sprawl of roads and railways and steamship lines and airline routes and communication networks that bound the world's peripheries into a universal web.

"Behind institutions, behind constitutional forms and modifications, lie the vital forces that call these organs into life and shape them to meet changing conditions." The American historian Frederick Jackson Turner wrote those words in 1893, opining on how the idea and reality of the Western frontier shaped American history. There is a sense in which Turner's frontier thesis can be usefully applied to the entire modern project, whose institutions and forms and bedrock assumptions—the sense of historical mission, the expectation of perpetual progress—have been ordered around the permanence of exploration, expansion, and discovery.

Indeed, because the deep forces of modern history—industrialization, political centralization, secularization—so often disrupted the rhythms of lives lived in stability and place and continuity, the *ideology* of exploration and discovery has been much more necessary than in many past civilizations, offering a new form of consolation to replace what faith and tribe and family and hierarchy had once supplied. In modernity, the former world is always passing away; the solidity of the past always melting into air. But the promise is that tomorrow will bring something new; that a better life is just a long sea voyage or wagon train away; that ours is an age of ever-unfolding wonders that more than compensate for what's been lost.

As the crimes committed by Western empires amply attest, this is a morally ambiguous way of ordering a civilization, and the peoples being "discovered" and displaced and sometimes exterminated have particular reasons to doubt that it represents any sort of high perfection. But an order animated by the dream of progress is now the order in which most human beings live and move and have their being, and the destination toward which all human societies seem to be advancing, including inhabitants of societies that were once victims of its ruthless logic. (There is no society more modern, further out on the edge of history, than the nation of Japan, which just seventy-five years ago was brought to its knees by a weapon that was as much an apotheosis of modernity's spirit of discovery as the moon landing.) From Ireland to sub-Saharan Africa, Amazonia to China, the great modern wave has rolled across cultures and regions and societies that seemed to preserve something premodern or hold something undiscovered in their hearts. And in the Western nations where it all began, it remains a central cultural assumption that unexplored frontiers and fresh discoveries and new worlds to conquer are not just desirable but the very point of life.

So it is a significant factor in our era's anxieties, in the sense of drift and stagnation and uncertainty with which this book is principally concerned, that the actual physical frontier has been closed for a generation or more—that for the first time since 1491, we have found the distances too vast and the technology too limited to take us to somewhere genuinely undiscovered, somewhere truly new. It is not a coincidence that the end of the space age has coincided with a turning inward in the developed world, a crisis of confidence and an ebb of optimism and a loss of faith in institutions, a shift toward therapeutic philosophies and technologies of simulation, an abandonment of both ideological ambition and religious hope.

Of course, this shift might have happened anyway, even if Mars were closer and more habitable or light-speed travel a more realistic possibility. The existence of a frontier does not guarantee that it will be a destination, and past civilizations have given up on exploration for essentially internal reasons, even when new horizons were very much in reach. (The abandonment of major sea voyages by China's Ming dynasty, in the same era as Columbus, did not come about because the world's oceans were too wide but because of the empire's changing intellectual fashions and political priorities.) Already when Neil Armstrong took his first small step, there were many voices making the case for the wastefulness of NASA's voyages, for the pointlessness of "whitey on the moon," and some of the turn toward pessimism preceded the realization that we would not be sending astronauts to Jupiter by the year 2001. A great deal of post-1960s thought—postcolonial, environmentalist—is premised on the idea that Western expansion was mostly cancerous, and this critique has been extended even to the idea of galactic colonization, with the exact same sort of ideological language applied. When the nonagenarian space optimist Freeman Dyson wrote hopefully about stellar exploration in a 2016 issue of the *New York Review of Books*, three letter writers chastised him for not counting the ecological cost and warned that "a human-designed outer space 'teeming with life and action' sounds like a nightmare out of Joseph Conrad."

Still, sometimes this application of anti-imperialist and environmentalist ideas to space travel feels like a kind of excuse making—that like the fox in Aesop's fable, we enjoy telling ourselves that we wouldn't want the fruit anyway, or that eating it would be immoral, so as to soothe the pain of knowing that it's there but out of reach.

Either way, whether the closing of the stellar frontier somehow caused the West's post-1960s turn toward pessimism or simply interacted with trends already at work, it remains a turning point in the history of the modern world. Before Apollo, it was easy to imagine that "late" was a misnomer for our phase of modernity, that our civilization's story was really in its early days, that the earthbound empires of Europe and America were just a first act in a continuous drama of expansion and development.

Since Apollo, we have entered into decadence.

In our culture, the word *decadence* is used promiscuously but rarely precisely—which, of course, is part of its cachet and charm. The dictionary associates it with "having low morals and a great love of pleasure, money, fame, etc.," which seems far too nonspecific—Ebenezer Scrooge was immoral and money loving, but nobody would call him decadent—and with cultures "marked by decay or decline," which gets us a little closer but also leaves a great deal undefined. In political debates, it's often associated with a lack of resolution in the face of external threats—with Munich and Neville Chamberlain, with W. B. Yeats's line about the best lacking all conviction. In the popular imagination, it's often associated with sex and gluttony; if you shop for something *decadent* on Amazon, the search algorithm will mostly deliver pornographic romances and chocolate strawberries. It can be a term of approbation—"I love this cake, it's so decadent"—as well as disparagement; it can refer descriptively to a particular nineteenth-century aesthetic and philosophy; it can refer judgmentally to any style that the critic deems to represent a falling-off from a previous aesthetic high. It hints at exhaustion, finality—"the feeling, at once oppressive and exalting, of being the last of a series," in the words of the Russian poet Vyacheslav Ivanov—but a finality that hasn't yet arrived, so why not eat, drink, and be merry in the meantime?

In trying to distill a useful definition from all these associations, there's a tendency to end up with what might be called "higher" and "lower" understandings of decadence. The low definition, the one familiar from advertising and lazy cultural criticism, basically defines the term to mean "inordinately pleasurable experiences with food and sex and fashion"—from the extreme (orgies, bondage bars, opium dens) to the rather less adventurous (four-star meals, weekends in Vegas)— and empties out the moral and the political elements entirely.

The high definition, on the other hand, tries to make the aesthetic and moral and political all fit together in a comprehensive civilizational indictment—in which moral decay goes hand in hand with overripe aestheticism and rampant hedonism, which in turn connects to a cowardly failure to make the sacrifices required to protect civilization from its enemies. This sort of decadence is an overture to a catastrophe in which the barbarians sweep in, the orgies are canceled, and the overdecorated palaces are all put to the torch.

The problem with this definition is that history doesn't work that neatly. Neither the trajectory of morals nor aesthetics yields to simple narratives of rise and fall, and their connection to political strength is likewise highly contingent. Empires can fall at the height of their political and cultural vigor if they face a potent-enough enemy, and cultures can give in to appetitive excesses without necessarily seeing their political stability undone. (It was more than four hundred years from Nero's reign to the actual fall of Rome.)

But there might be a useful middle ground: a definition of decadence that's neither empty of any judgment nor excessively deterministic. This definition would follow in the footsteps of the great cultural critic Jacques Barzun, who begins his massive survey of Western cultural history—titled, of course, *From Dawn to Decadence*—by passing a clinical judgment on our own era:

> Borrowing widely from other lands, thriving on dissent and originality, the West has been the mongrel civilization par excellence. But in spite of patchwork and conflict, it has pursued characteristic purposes—that is its unity—and now these purposes, carried out to their utmost possibility, are bringing about its demise.

This sense of an ending, Barzun goes on, need not mean "stoppage or total ruin." And this will be crucial to my own argument in this book: that for all its association with decay and decline, a society can be decadent without necessarily being doomed to soon collapse.

> All that is meant by Decadence is "falling off." It implies in those who live in such a time no loss of energy or talent or moral sense. On the contrary, it is a very active time, full of deep concerns, but peculiarly restless, for it sees no clear lines of advance. The forms of art as of life seem exhausted; the stages of development have been run through. Institutions function painfully. Repetition and frustration are the intolerable result. Boredom and fatigue are great historical forces.
>
> It will be asked, how does the historian know when Decadence sets in? By the open confessions of malaise. . . . When people accept futility and the absurd as normal, the culture is decadent. The term is not a slur; it is a technical label.

At the risk of being presumptuous, let me try to refine Barzun's definition a bit further. Decadence, deployed usefully, refers to *eco-*

nomic stagnation, institutional decay, and cultural and intellectual exhaustion at a high level of material prosperity and technological development. It describes a situation in which repetition is more the norm than innovation; in which sclerosis afflicts public institutions and private enterprises alike; in which intellectual life seems to go in circles; in which new developments in science, new exploratory projects, underdeliver compared with what people recently expected. And, crucially, the stagnation and decay are often a direct consequence of previous development. The decadent society is, by definition, a victim of its own significant success.

Now, all this—both Barzun's meditation and my own attempted definition—may still sound impossibly vague: Isn't "sclerosis" in the eye of the beholder? Who decides what constitutes "the absurd"?

But really it narrows things in quite useful ways. First, emphasizing the *economic* element limits the scope of decadence to societies that are actually stagnating in a measurable way and frees us from the habit of just associating decadence with anything we dislike in rich societies or with any age (Gilded, Jazz) of luxury, corruption, and excess. Emphasizing the decay of *institutions*, likewise, frees us from the trap of regarding an individual case—whether a Nero, or a Bill Clinton, or a Donald Trump—as a synecdoche for a civilization as a whole. Focusing on *repetition* in the cultural and intellectual realm frees us—well, a bit—from the problems of individual intellectual and aesthetic taste and lightens the obligation of deciding exactly which literary style or intellectual shift constitutes the tipping point into decadence.

In each case, the goal is to define decadence as something more specific than just any social or moral trend that you dislike. A society that generates a lot of bad movies need not be decadent; a society that just makes the same movies over and over again might be. A society run by the cruel and arrogant might not be decadent; a society where even the wise and good can't legislate might be. A poor or crime-ridden society isn't necessarily decadent; a society that's rich

9

and peaceable but exhausted, depressed, and beset by flares of nihilistic violence looks closer to our definition.

Most important, the emphasis on stagnation means that we can talk about decadence without implying that some kind of collapse is necessarily looming on the horizon. It makes the word compatible with the reality of nondecadent civilizations falling in a historical heartbeat while decadent civilizations go on and on. It frees us from the assumption that there's some iron logic that links orgies in the capital to barbarian invasions on the frontier, weak-kneed leaders to bombed-out cities, corruption in high places to wars that lay those high places low. It lets decadence be decadence without the implication that the "falling-off" leads inexorably to a truly catastrophic fall. And even if certain features of decadence do make a Götterdämmerung more likely, it leaves open the more optimistic possibility, with which this book concludes: that a decadent era could give way instead to a recovery of growth and creativity and purpose.

But my first goal in these pages will be to convince you that our society is, indeed, decadent; that my definition actually applies to the contemporary West over the last two generations and may apply soon to all the societies that are currently catching up to Europe and North America and East Asia. To many readers, this argument will seem counterintuitive: a definition of decadence that dealt only with excess and luxury and various forms of political sclerosis might fit our era, but the idea of an overall stagnation or repetition—of late-modern civilization as a treadmill rather than a headlong charge—doesn't fit particularly well with many readings of the age in which we live. It seems in tension with the sense of constant acceleration, of vertiginous change, that permeated so much of early-twenty-first-century life even before the shock of the pandemic. And it sits uneasily with the jargon of our time—both the breathless utopianism of TED Talks and the pop apocalypticism of prestige magazines, which differ wildly in their moods but share an assumption that the world is changing, for good or ill, at an unprecedented pace.

The question, though, is whether that jargon corresponds with reality anymore, or whether our sense of continued acceleration is now to some extent an illusion created by the Internet—the one area of clear technological progress in our era, but also a distorting filter on the world beyond your screen. The online age speeds up communication in ways that make events seem to happen faster than in the past, make social changes seem to be constantly cascading, and make the whole world seem like it exists next door to you—so that current history feels like a multicar pileup every time you check your Facebook feed or fire up Twitter. That pileup encourages a mood of constant anxiety about terrorism, ecocatastrophe, and war, and it compounds the experience of an actual disaster like the coronavirus, which is experienced both directly and vicariously, as a real-life disease and also a permanent theater of apocalypse on social media. And at the same time the digital theater provides a perfect stage for all manner of techno-boosterism: the promise that artificial intelligence or large-scale genetic engineering or even immortality is just around the corner feels more compelling when it's showing up in a news alert or embedded video on your sleekly futuristic phone.

But when you look at the data rather than just the impression, there is a strong case that while the speed with which we experience events has quickened, the speed of actual change has not. Or at least not when it comes to the sort of change that really counts: growth and innovation, reform and revolution, aesthetic reinvention or religious ferment. These have not ceased, in developing countries especially: the Middle East's recent convulsions do not fit my definition of decadence, nor does China's explosive post-1980s growth. But in the developed world, pending the consequences of the pandemic, they have slowed to a pace that looks more like stagnation the further you get from your iPhone, and the closer to reality.

This claim is counterintuitive, but it is not original. My diagnosis of our condition is a journalist's, and, as such, it owes debts to many more expert thinkers who will be quoted amply in the pages to come. After the 2008 financial crisis and the Great Recession exposed almost a decade's worth of Western growth as an illusion, a diverse cast of economists and political scientists and other figures on both the left and the right began to talk about stagnation and repetition and complacency and sclerosis as defining features of this Western age: Tyler Cowen and Robert Gordon, Thomas Piketty and Francis Fukuyama, David Graeber and Peter Thiel, and many others.

This book is, in part, an attempt to synthesize their various perspectives into a compelling account of our situation. But it also weaves the social sciences together with observations on our intellectual climate, our popular culture, our religious moment, our technological pastimes, in the hopes of painting a fuller portrait of our decadence than you can get just looking at political science papers on institutional decay or an economic analysis of the declining rate of growth. And then it also looks ahead and tries to assess the stability and sustainability of our decadence, what it will mean for our society if it should continue, and how it might ultimately end.

This means that the writing (and now, rewriting) of the book has inevitably been shadowed by two dramatic phenomena: First, the strange presidency of Donald Trump, and second, the global pandemic that began just as the hardcover edition appeared.

As a leader for a decadent age, Trump contained multitudes. He was both an embodiment of our society's distinctive vices and a would-be rebel against our torpor and repetition and disappointment; a figure who rose to power by attacking the system for its sclerosis while exploiting that same decadence to the very hilt. "Make America Great Again" was a precisely calibrated statement of what you might call reactionary futurism, a howl against a present that wasn't what was promised, the kind of mixture of nostalgia and ambition that you would expect a decadent era to conjure up.

The question is whether in conjuring him up our politics also revealed the underlying instability of our decadence; the possibility that rather than being stagnant but sustainable our system could decay much more swiftly into authoritarianism or collapse into simple chaos—or whether Trump was instead fundamentally more farcical than threatening; too decadent himself to be a real threat to the system; an example of Barzun's "futility and the absurd" brought to particularly vivid life.

Likewise with the larger populist moment in the West, the anxieties of the center, the appeal of the illiberal fringes, the activism of the left. Does all this action represent a real ideological crisis, a genuinely revolutionary moment? Or is it just a kind of digital-age playacting in which young people dissatisfied with decadence pretend to be fascists and Marxists on the Internet, with a small cohort reenacting the 1930s and 1960s in the streets of Portland or Seattle, which the vast majority still experiences as a social-media simulation, a street fight only on the screen.

Similar questions hang over the pandemic, which hit fast-forward on various socioeconomic trends and pushed Western society in multiple directions at once—deeper into simulated life for some but into the streets in protest for others; back into the domestic sphere for parents but away from romance and childbearing for the young; out of our mega-cities for many individuals but deeper into consolidated bigness for our institutions. Could COVID-19 represent the return of history, the hinge out of an age of torpor, the spur to long-postponed reform and innovations? Or like the plagues that punctuated the later centuries of the Roman world, will it be remembered as a crisis that ultimately deepened decadence, a revelation of problems that are beyond our capacity to solve, a shock to a sclerotic system that only made the system more itself?

A great deal depends upon the answer. No decadent period lasts forever; no decadent society leaves decadence behind in exactly the same way. But if we are to escape our own form without catastrophe, to have a renaissance without an intervening dark age, we need clarity about our basic situation; an end to both optimistic pretense and hysteria.

The core truth of America and the West in the first decades of the twenty-first century, a truth that shaped both the shambolic Trump presidency and the stumbling response to the pandemic on both sides of the Atlantic, is that we have not been hurtling anywhere—except maybe in a circle. Instead, we are aging, comfortable and stuck, cut off from the past and no longer optimistic about the future, spurning both memory and ambition while we await some saving innovation or revelation, burrowing into cocoons from which no chrysalis is likely to emerge, growing old unhappily together in the glowing light of tiny screens.

"What fascinates and terrifies us about the Roman Empire is not that it finally went smash," wrote W. H. Auden of the last world empire in its endless autumn, but rather that "it managed to last for four centuries without creativity, warmth, or hope."

"There was nothing left that could conquer Rome," G. K. Chesterton wrote on the same theme, "but there was also nothing left that could improve it. . . . It was the end of the world, and the worst of it was that it need never end."

Whether we are waiting for Christians or barbarians, a renaissance or the Singularity, the dilemma that Auden and Chesterton described is now not Rome's but ours.

PART 1

The Four Horsemen

1

Stagnation

"Do people on your coast think all this is real?"

The tech executive sounded curious, proud, a little insecure. We were talking in the San Franciscan office of a venture capital firm, a vaulted space washed in late-afternoon Californian sun. His gesture encompassed all of Silicon Valley, the whole gilded world around the Bay, the entire Internet economy.

That was in 2015. Here are three stories from the five years since.

A young man comes to New York City. He's a striver, a hustler, working the borderlands between entrepreneurship and con artistry, drumming up investments for his projects without being completely honest about his financial prospects. His first effort, a special credit card for affluent millennials, gets attention disproportionate to its profitability and yanks him into the celebrity economy, where he meets an ambitious rapper-businessman. Together they plan a new company: a kind of Internet brokerage where celebrities can sell their mere presence to the highest bidder. As a brand-enhancing advertisement for the company, they decide to leverage their connections to host a major music festival—an exclusive, expensive affair on a Caribbean island that will be the must-get ticket for influencers, festival obsessives, and the youthful rich.

The festival's online rollout is a great success. There is a viral video of supermodels and Instagram celebrities frolicking on a deserted beach, a sleek website for customers and the curious, and soon people are dropping down substantial, even obscene, amounts on luxurious festival packages—the kind that promise not just backstage access but also a private cabana on the beach. In the end, about eight thousand people buy tickets, at an average cost of $2,500 to $4,000. Tens of millions of dollars, the superfluity of a rich society, yours for the right sales pitch.

But the festival as pitched does not exist. Instead, our entrepreneur's big plans collapse one by one. The private island can't hold the crowds. The local government doesn't cooperate. Even after all the ticket sales, the money isn't there and the time definitely isn't there, and he has to keep talking new investors into bailing out the old ones and inventing new amenities to sell to ticket buyers to pay for the ones they've already purchased. He does have a team, exhausted and impressively driven, working around the clock to ready . . . *something* for the paying customers, but what they actually offer in the end is a sea of FEMA tents vaguely near a beach, a soundstage that doesn't work, a catering concern that supplies slimy sandwiches, and a lot of cheap tequila. Amazingly, the people actually come—bright young things Instagraming their way to the experience of a lifetime, only to have their photo streams and video feeds become a hilarious chronicle of dashed expectations, the tent city ruined by an unexpected rainstorm, the spoiled life giving way to drunken anarchy, and the failed entrepreneur trying to keep order with a bullhorn before absconding to New York, where he finds disgrace, arrest, prison, and the inevitable Netflix documentary.

That's the story of Billy McFarland and the Fyre Festival. It's a small-time story; the next one is bigger.

A girl grows up in Texas, she gets accepted to Stanford, she wants to be Steve Jobs. She has an idea for a revolutionary technology, one that will change an industry that hasn't changed in years: the boring but essential world of blood testing, which is dominated by lumbering monopolies, feared and avoided by potential paying customers who don't like having their arms stabbed by strangers, and yet intimately linked to public health—to the prevention and cure of almost every possible disease. Like Jobs building the Mac, she envisions a machine, dubbed the Edison after the paradigmatic American inventor, that will test for diseases just as well as the existing technologies despite using just a single prick of blood. And like Jobs she drops out of college to figure out how to build it.

Ten years later, she is the Internet era's leading female billionaire, a constant magazine cover girl, with a sprawling campus and a $4 billion valuation for her company, a lucrative deal with Walgreens to use her machines in every store, and a stream of venture capital that seems unlikely to run dry. Her story is a counterpoint to every criticism you ever hear about Silicon Valley—that it's just a callow boys' club, that its apps and virtual realities don't make the world of flesh and blood a better place, that it solves problems of convenience but doesn't cure the sick. And she is the toast of an elite, in tech and politics alike, that wants to believe the Edisonian spirit lives on in the digital age.

But the Edison box—despite long hours, endless effort, the best tech team that all that venture capital can buy—simply doesn't work. And over time, as the company keeps expanding, it ceases to be an innovator and becomes instead a fraud, passing off tests from normal draws as results from a single prick, sweeping bad results from single-prick testing under the rug, and using all its money and influence and big-time backers to reassure skeptics and discredit whistleblowers. Which succeeds until it doesn't, at which point the company simply evaporates—a $4 billion valuation and all the venture capital that sustained it gone like that, leaving a fraud prosecution, a bestselling exposé, and the inevitable podcast and HBO documentary to sustain its founder's fame.

That's the story of Elizabeth Holmes and Theranos. It's a big story, definitely. But our third story is bigger still, and it isn't finished yet.

An Internet company decides to revolutionize an industry—personal transportation, the taxi and limousine market—that defines old-school business-government cooperation, with all the attendant bureaucracy and incompetence and unsatisfying service. It sells itself to investors with the promise that it can buy its way to market dominance in this sclerotic field and use its cutting-edge tech to slash through red tape and find unglimpsed efficiencies. On the basis of that promise, it raises billions upon billions of dollars across its ten-year rise, during which time it becomes as big as promised in Western markets, a byword for Internet-era success, cited by boosters and competitors alike as the model for how to disrupt an industry, how to "move fast and break things" as the Silicon Valley mantra has it. By the time it goes public in 2019, it has $11 billion in annual revenue—real money, exchanged for real services, nothing fraudulent about it.

Yet this amazing success story isn't actually making any sort of profit, even at such scale; instead, it's losing billions upon billions of dollars, including $5 billion in one particuarly costly quarter. After ten years of growth, it has smashed the old business model of its industry, weakened legacy competitors, created a great deal of value for consumers—but it has done all this without any discipline from market forces, using the awesome power of free money to build a company that would collapse into bankruptcy if that money were withdrawn. And in that time, it has solved exactly none of the problems that would have prevented a company that needed to make a profit from building such a large user base: it has no obvious competitive advantages besides the huge investor subsidy; the technology it uses is hardly proprietary or complex; its rival in disruption controls 30 percent of the market, even as the legacy players are still very much alive; and all of its paths to reduce its losses—charging higher prices, paying its workers less—would destroy the advantages that it has built.

So it sits there, widely regarded as one of the defining success stories of the Internet era, a unicorn unlike any other, with billions in losses and a plan to become profitable that involves vague promises to somehow monetize all its user data and a specific promise that its investment in a *different* new technology—the self-driving car, much ballyhooed but as yet not exactly real—will square the circle and make the math add up.

That's the story of Uber—so far. It isn't a pure Instagram fantasy like the Fyre Festival or a naked fraud like Theranos; it managed to go public and maintain its outsize valuation, unlike its fellow money-losing unicorn WeWork, whose recent attempt at an IPO hurled it into crisis. But like them, it is, for now, an example of a major twenty-first-century company invented entirely out of surplus, less economically efficient so far than the rivals it is supposed to leapfrog, sustained by investors who believe its promises in defiance of the existing evidence, floated by the hope that with enough money and market share, you can will a profitable company into existence, and goldwashed by an "Internet company" identity that obscures the weakness of its real-world fundamentals.

Maybe it won't crash like the others; maybe the tens of billions in investor capital won't be wasted; maybe we won't be watching a documentary on its hubris five or ten years hence. But Uber's trajectory to this point, the strange unreality of its extraordinary success, makes it a good place to begin a discussion of economic decadence—as a case study in what it looks like when an extraordinarily rich society can't find enough new ideas that justify investing all its stockpiled wealth, and ends up choosing between hoarding cash in mattresses or playing a kind of let's-pretend instead. In a decadent economy, the supposed cutting edge of capitalism is increasingly defined by let's-pretendism—by technologies that have *almost* arrived, business models that are *on their way* to profitability, by runways that go on and go on without ever achieving liftoff.

Do people on your coast think all this is real? When the tech executive asked me that, I told him that we did—that the promise of Silicon Valley was as much an article of faith for those of us watching from the outside as for its insiders; that we both envied the world of digital and hoped that it would remain the great exception to economic disappointment, the place where even in the long, sluggish recovery from the crash of 2008, the promise of American innovation was still alive.

And I would probably say the same thing now, despite the stories I've just told—because notwithstanding Billy McFarland and Elizabeth Holmes, notwithstanding the peculiar trajectory of Uber, many Silicon Valley institutions deserve their success, many tech companies have real customers and real revenue and a solid structure underneath, many of their products more than proved their worth in the time of the coronavirus, and overall the Internet economy is as real as twenty-first-century growth and innovation gets.

But what this tells us, unfortunately, is that twenty-first-century growth and innovation are not at all what we were promised they would be.

The Age of Deceleration

In 2017, the year after a socialist challenged for the Democratic nomination and a populist Republican was elected president, the US economy passed a notable milestone. For the first time, as measured in dollars adjusted for inflation, the median American family—the typical household; the modern equivalent of the nineteenth-century small farmer or the 1950s suburbanite—was earning more than $60,000 a year.

To have an election roiled by populism amid such apparent plenty might seem unusual. But some context is clarifying. The peak income year of 2017 wasn't the top of a long climb but just a return to a previous high: that $60,000 median income barely exceeded the median income in the previous peak year of 2007, which in turn barely exceeded the peak of 1999. In other words, in sixteen out of the eighteen years between the turn of the millennium and the Trump presidency, the average American family earned less market income—a lot less, in the bad years—than in the last year of the Clinton presidency. And one layer down from household income, in the household wealth that income is supposed to build, the stagnation was also striking. In 2017, ten years after the wealth piled up by the housing boom turned out to be illusory, the median American household was worth about $97,000, slightly below late 1990s levels.

In 2017 the unemployment rate passed a notable milestone as well, dropping to 4 percent, defying post–Great Recession pessimists who had feared that it would remain permanently elevated. But like the household-income trend, that milestone was less impressive in context: it had taken seventeen years to return to the unemployment rate of 1999, neither wage growth nor productivity growth had returned to the 1990s pace, and the workforce participation rate, which counts the millions of American adults who are no longer even searching for work, was almost 4 percentage points lower than it had been at the turn of the millennium—a jobs gap, relative to the Clinton era, that represented almost ten million additional nonworking Americans. Among men, the gap was particularly stark: the 11 percent of prime-age men who weren't working in 2018 was the highest rate since the Great Depression.

All economic indicators are vulnerable to some critique, every grim data point can be caveated and qualified, and the ones I've just cited are no exception. Some of the decline in workforce participation reflects a growing number of adults who are in some sort of school. The decline in two-parent households explains part of why family income has stagnated; treat people as singletons rather than households, and the picture looks better. And the stagnant median-income numbers don't include the topping-off provided by various transfer programs and welfare benefits; throw in the benefits supplied by our ample deficit spending, and household income has clearly risen since 1999.

These complexities mean that you should be wary of anyone who comes to you bearing a catastrophic story about the American economy; a tale of immiseration and collapse. In fact, the United States is still an extraordinarily wealthy country, its middle class still prosperous beyond the dreams of centuries past, its welfare state still effective at easing the pain of recessions and buoying the poor.

But if narratives of stark decline are false, it's entirely reasonable to look at the last fifty years of developed-world economic history, the entire late-modern era, and see an era of *deceleration followed by stagnation*.

The deceleration began around the time of the moon landing. In the United States, hourly wages peaked in the early 1970s and dipped thereafter, household income growth began to slow, the larger economy experienced so-called stagflation and three sharp recessions under Richard Nixon, Jimmy Carter, and Ronald Reagan. Though perhaps the inflection point had really arrived slightly earlier. One of the striking patterns of the modern era was logarithmic economic growth, in which the time it took for the global economy to double in size grew shorter and shorter and shorter every century after 1492, pushing us, in theory, toward the infinite growth that utopians dub the Singularity. But that pattern had broken around the time that John F. Kennedy was promising to put a man on the moon, and the doubling time for the global economy has been slowing ever since. In this sense, 1960, to borrow a quip from Scott Alexander, was "the year the singularity was cancelled."

In response to these post-JFK economic disappointments, policy makers of both political parties embraced the policy mix that now gets labeled "neoliberalism": lower taxes and deregulation, free trade and anti-inflationary monetary policy. By the late 1990s, this response seemed to have been somewhat effective: household wealth was growing, workforce participation climbed as more and more women entered the labor force, overall growth rates were pushing back up toward 4 percent, wages and productivity were rising. But then the dotcom bubble burst, and thereafter straightforward stagnation became the order of the day, with weak recoveries, weak household income growth, declining productivity and household wealth, and far more workforce dropouts than before.

This disappointing fifty-year experience is not America's alone. Just as the long postwar boom in the United States was matched by the *trentes glorieuses*—the glorious thirty years—in France and many of its European neighbors, the downshift toward stagnation since the 1970s has been shared across the developed world, albeit with regional differences in the details. On the Continent, median income growth has been slightly better and workforce participation somewhat higher than in the United States, but overall growth has been even more disappointing: the "Eurosclerosis" in the 1970s and 1980s, an even slower recovery than America from the 2017 financial crisis, and a steady decline in productivity growth, which has averaged just 0.5 percent in the eurozone over the last decade—half the United States's already unimpressive rate. In Japan, growth was more impressive during the 1970s and 1980s, leading to the brief post–Cold War panic over looming Japanese hegemony. But thereafter the deceleration was more sudden, as after the early 1990s Asia's most developed economy entered its own lost decades, from which the loose monetary policy and labor market reforms of Prime Minister Shinzo Abe have only partially enabled an escape.

The differences between Europe, America, and East Asia are real, but what's more striking are the basic similarities between the world's three most developed regions. Twenty years ago, it was common for Americans (especially American conservatives) to regard stagnation as much more of a European problem than an American one, and to believe that the United States's free-market policies and commercial culture were preserving a vigor increasingly absent in dirigiste France and corporatist Japan. But America looks less unique today—less dynamic, less exceptional—and the distinctions between the economies of the developed world look more like the narcissism of small differences.

To be clear, there is still more economic dynamism in the United States than in, say, Italy or Greece. But not as much as the clichés of American exceptionalism would suggest. American entrepreneurship has been declining fairly steadily since the 1970s: during the Carter presidency, hardly an ideal time for the American economy, 15 percent of all US businesses had been founded in the previous year; today that rate is about 8 percent. It's become harder to survive as a non-incumbent, with the share of start-ups *failing* in the first year having risen from around 20 percent in the mid-1980s to closer to 30 percent today. In 1990, 65 percent of US companies were less than ten years old; today it's about 52 percent. The total "firm formation rate," as a percentage of the number of firms overall, has dropped by a third over the last thirty years. And those firms increasingly sit on cash or pass it back to shareholders rather than invest it in new enterprises. According to a report from Senator Marco Rubio's office, private domestic investment averaged 8 percent of GDP between 1947 and 1990; in 2019, despite a long recovery and a corporate tax cut intended to get money off the sidelines, the investment-to-GDP ratio was just 4 percent.

This suggests that the people with the most experience starting businesses and getting rich look around at the available investment opportunities and see many more start-ups that resemble Theranos and the Fyre Festival than resemble Amazon or Apple—let alone the behemoths of the pre-Internet economy. And the dearth of corporate investment and innovation also means that the steady climb of the stock market has boosted the wealth of a rentier class—basically, already-rich investors getting richer off dividends—rather than reflecting or driving a general increase in prosperity. A 2019 paper by three economists titled "How the Wealth Was Won" found that 54 percent of the growth of US companies' stock market value reflected "a reallocation of rents to shareholders in a decelerating economy," while actual economic growth accounted for just 24 percent. "From 1952 to 1988, less than half as much wealth was created" in the stock market, the authors note, "but economic growth accounted for 92 percent of it."

The decline of investment and the rise of the shareholder-as-rentier is also happening amid a new age of corporate consolidation, with wave upon wave of mergers and acquisitions in traditional industries and a swift consolidation even in the supposed frontier economy of the Internet, where a small group of giants now rule the typical user's every click. And those online giants are unlike the big businesses of yore: the Internet age's major companies, from Facebook to Twitter, have huge reach but limited profits, and an even more limited need for labor to keep them humming. Unlike the old factory towns of Ford Motor Company and General Motors, with their huge workforces, the geography of Silicon Valley is dominated by a mix of elite-college graduates and service workers, with little mass employment for the middle class.

Also in decline, perhaps because the new behemoths aren't hiring the way the old ones did, is that supposedly most American of qualities: wanderlust. Americans no longer "go West" (or east or north or south) in search of opportunity the way they did fifty years ago; the rate at which people move between states has fallen from 3.5 percent in the early 1970s to 1.4 percent in 2010. Nor do Americans change jobs as often as they once did. For all the boosterish talk about retraining and self-employment, all the fears of an increasingly precarious employment system, Americans are less likely to switch employers than they were a generation ago, and the supposed rise of an Internet-enabled "gig economy" is something of a myth. (Between 2005 and 2018, a Bureau of Labor Statistics study found, the increase in solo work driven by companies such as Uber was exceeded by declines in other kinds of freelancing.) Nor do they invest in the future in the most literal of ways: the US birthrate was long an outlier among Western countries—considerably higher than both Europe's and Japan's—but since the Great Recession, it has descended rapidly, converging with the wealthy world's general below-replacement norm, and hitting historic lows amid the pandemic.

In this sense, it's not surprising that America and western Europe have experienced similar political crises over the last few years: the same populist surges, the same right-wing revolts against elites and immigrants, the same reemergence of socialism on the left. For all the many transatlantic differences, our basic economic experience is the same: persistent stagnation, chronic disappointment, and a growing conflict between the promise of progress and a reality where everything seems—surprisingly, depressingly—to stay the same.

The Limits of Neoliberalism

There is no shortage of theories to explain this "great stagnation" (to borrow a phrase from one of the theorizers, the George Mason University economist Tyler Cowen), and there is also no need to simply choose between them. Like most broad trends, the economic decadence of the developed world is overdetermined, and almost every serious attempt at explanation will contain some element of truth.

The most politically appealing theories—the ones animating our populist and socialist insurgencies—tend to blame neoliberalism itself, claiming that the medicine for 1970s stagflation has proven to be poison in large doses. The push for ever-freer trade has hollowed out Western economies, the argument goes, offshoring productive industries and killing decent jobs, making financiers and "knowledge workers" rich while the middle class shrinks steadily. Meanwhile, low tax rates, intended to spur investment, have enabled the rich to keep more of their gains while starving the programs required to protect the poor and boost the working class. Antitrust policy has become so fixated on the supposed benefits of consolidation—lower prices for consumers—that it has ignored all the ways that market-dominant corporations can warp policies and strangle innovation. And anti-inflationary policies, forged to counteract a crisis that's now generations behind us, have been adopted as a dogma by the West's financial and political elite, which demands fiscal austerity under every circumstance and deprives struggling economies of the cash they need to grow.

You don't have to accept every aspect of this argument (and, indeed, the populists of the left and right disagree about which aspects to stress) to see that it describes a real phenomenon: perhaps not the outright failure of neoliberalism, but diminishing returns from some of its preferred policies, and an overconfidence among the Western leadership class that solutions from the 1970s are permanently applicable.

On trade, for instance, the general principle that open markets have more winners than losers led policy makers to assume that this would necessarily happen, and to overestimate how quickly communities affected by outsourcing would recover and how swiftly other sectors of the economy would compensate. In particular, the Massachusetts Institute of Technology economist David Autor has argued persuasively that the "China shock"—the dramatic offshoring that followed Beijing's entrance into the World Trade Organization in 2001—inflicted more economic damage on working-class communities in the United States than many experts anticipated, without generating the compensating growth and job creation expected elsewhere.

This is not a knockdown case against free trade, just a case against overconfidence in its incautious application. And the same argument applies to other features of the neoliberal program. It's quite possible that lower tax rates spur growth and innovation when rates are cut from 70 percent highs, but also that a program of permanent upper-bracket tax cutting, as practiced by America's Republican Party, won't produce the hoped-for spillover effects among the bottom 95 percent. It's possible that the initial economic insight that some corporate consolidation could be good for consumers was useful for antitrust decision-making in the 1970s and 1980s but needs to be corrected as monopolies regather. It's possible that a program of deficit reduction and tight money that makes sense when inflation is galloping doesn't make sense when we're closer to deflation, that countries sometimes need a loose monetary policy to fight stagnation, and having a financial overclass too fixated on the perils of a for-now imaginary inflation is a recipe for permanently lower growth.

Then alongside this brief against an overextended neoliberalism, there's the more subtle argument, pushed by the more serious sort of libertarian, that the neoliberal program hasn't so much been pushed too far as pushed in the wrong direction. In this argument, we don't need less deregulation but a different kind than what we have, because incumbents and insiders in the West have captured the sprawling regulatory state and used it to freeze out potential competition.

The age of stagnation, in this theory, is the fruit of what Brink Lindsey of the Niskanen Institute and Steven Teles of Johns Hopkins University describe as a "captured economy," in which everything from land-use rules, to exclusionary zoning, to occupational licensing, to ever-expanding intellectual-property protections, to corporate subsidies and tax breaks all converge to create a system that's basically the worst of socialism and the worst of capitalism conjoined—plutocratic and sclerotic, overregulated and undertaxed, with an upper class enriching itself off rents rather than innovation and a service class that can't advance beyond its station.

The overlap between this more libertarian argument and the left-wing critique of neoliberalism is apparent in one of the ur-texts of the post–financial crisis left: French economist Thomas Piketty's 2013 tome *Capital in the Twenty-First Century*, which mined centuries' worth of statistics to argue that capitalism inherently makes the rich richer (because returns on capital will always be higher than simple economic growth) unless some powerful force intervenes. The forces that intervened in the twentieth century were the Great Depression and two world wars, which not only provided the impetus for massive government interventions in the economy but also destroyed outright a great deal of capitalist wealth, leading to a temporary golden age for the Western middle classes. But now, according to Piketty, we are returning to historical norms—to a slower rate of growth than what the booming mid-twentieth century conditioned us to expect and to a "patrimonial capitalism" in which a class of rentiers gets rich passively via investment and inheritance while everyone else falls further and further behind.

Piketty's theory about the inevitable drift of capitalism was extremely controversial, and a complicated, highly technical debate sprang up around that aspect of his book. But for our purposes, it's enough to say that Piketty's villains, the *grands rentiers* (the global superrich) and *petit rentiers* (the mass upper class forged by meritocracy), are both instantly recognizable types, and his description of how the modern upper class has consolidated its position would be at home in Lindsey and Teles's more libertarian analysis as well.

The Pikettian left and the libertarian center right differ in which kind of rentier they are most eager to indict: Piketty and his admirers are hardest on the superrich, blaming their political influence and essential selfishness for foiling necessary large-scale redistribution, while libertarian antirentiers are more likely to argue that the richest of the rich still generally rise on their own merits (think Jeff Bezos or Warren Buffett), while it's the mass upper class that's really guilty of what the Brookings Institution's Richard Reeves calls "dream hoarding": the combined effects of inherited wealth, educational requirements, real estate prices, and tax breaks that essentially reproduce privilege from one generation to the next.

But there is a basic common ground here, a shared left-and-libertarian critique of consolidation and self-dealing that clearly describes some essential features of our long deceleration. From New York to London, Paris to San Francisco, our upper class is not only richer and bigger but also more self-segregated and well defended than fifty years ago—flocking to the same unchanging list of grade-inflated elite schools, planting themselves in the same small group of "global" cities, concentrating their privileged families in exclusive neighborhoods protected by stringent zoning rules, defending their turf by pricing out everyone except the necessary service class, which is largely composed of immigrants welcomed because they'll work harder for less money than the upper class's fellow countrymen. Small wonder that mobility and entrepreneurship are declining: if you're an outsider to, say, Silicon Valley, you can't "go West" to pursue the opportunities it offers if you can't afford to live and work there.

Meanwhile, the fact that this new elite is officially more merito-cratic (however debatable the reality) than past ruling classes seems at times to justify its grab-what-you-can spirit, its fearful accumulation of advantage—lest a bad SAT score undo your children's hard-won priv-ilege. If the old patrimonial capitalism at least featured some noblesse oblige and even generated its share of trust-busting class traitors, the newer sort feels more justified in its self-dealing, more self-righteous in its selfishness. And the cost of its privilege, it appears, is economic disappointment for everyone else.

The Limits on Growth

This story is depressing but also, in a sense, modestly encouraging, since it implies solutions to stagnation, however politically difficult they might be. Bust or weaken the new monopolies; roll back vari-ous elite privileges; tax wealth; tax Harvard; deregulate but differently; cut welfare, but this time for the rich; protect and boost the middle class; try to make the Covid-era dispersal of talent away from meg-acities a permanent change—do all of this and more, and the devel-oped world's economies might once more fulfill their old promise of broadly shared, accelerating growth.

But such solutionism may be insufficient to the problem's scale. A glance at the historical record suggests that something more than just inequality and austerity and outsourcing is contributing to deceleration and stagnation. If an unequal society and an entrenched ruling class were sufficient to choke off growth, the industrial revolution would have never gotten off the ground in the first place. If soaring fortunes necessarily came at the expense of middle-class incomes, then the 1990s, the last decade of solid growth, would have been the worst recent era for middle-class prosperity rather than the best. If correcting neoliberalism with pro-tectionist policies were the path back to another *trentes glorieuses*, France would be the strongest economy in Europe. If correcting neoliberalism with socialism were the golden ticket, Venezuela would be the tiger of Latin America rather than a basket case. And if austerity has weakened Western economies, it's often the sort of "austerity" that would have been considered wildly profligate fifty years ago—with far more welfare spending and far higher deficits and borrowed-against-the-future costs than in the booming 1950s and 1960s, which, even if such deficits are necessary, suggests that something dramatic and unfortunate has changed between that era and this one.

What has changed, according to the less solutionist and more pessimistic analysis, is that we've entered an age of economic limits—an era of "secular stagnation," as the chastened neoliberal Larry Summers wrote in 2013, in which "the presumption that normal economic and policy conditions will return at some point cannot be maintained." For the pessimists, the unusual features of the post-2007 landscape—the persistently low interest rates, the low rate of inflation, the disappointing rate of growth, the great fortunes parked in rent-seeking rather than risk-taking—are actually inevitabilities in a developed world where there just aren't enough impressive enterprises to invest *in*; a developed world that inflates bubbles and then pops them (or invests in Theranos and then repents) because that's all there is for capital to do; a developed world slowly growing accustomed to unexpected limits on its future possibilities.

The most convincing theorists of limits include Cowen, in his 2011 book *The Great Stagnation: How America Ate All the Low-Hanging Fruit of Modern History, Got Sick, and Will (Eventually) Feel Better*, and his fellow economist Robert Gordon, in his magisterial 2016 work, *The Rise and Fall of American Growth: The U.S. Standard of Living Since the Civil War*. Both authors would agree with portions of the arguments I've just sketched about neoliberalism pushed too far or misapplied, and an economy stalled by inequality or captured by a self-dealing upper class. But both offer a wider lens on the developed world's stagnation and a longer list of forces slowing growth. The two favor different metaphors: Cowen talks about the three forms of "low-hanging fruit" that the West and especially America spent its long economic expansion plucking, only to find the lower branches bare and the potential sources of new growth hanging out of reach; Gordon prefers to talk about the six "headwinds" holding down economic progress. But their arguments can be effectively combined into a list of five major structural forces that make a return to pre-1970s growth rates unlikely.

First is *the weight of demographics*—the aging of rich societies and the collapse in Western and East Asian birthrates, which combine to make existing welfare programs more expensive, future GDP growth more limited, and the culture of the developed world more cautious, complacent, and risk averse. (The causes and consequences of this trend will be discussed in more detail in chapter 2.)

Second is *the overhang of debt*, which will get much worse as the baby boomers age and their expected health care bills come due. Debt and deficits aren't necessarily the short-term constraint imagined by Tea Party Republicans and fiscal scolds; the evidence from the last decade suggests that a Greece-style debt crisis or inflationary spiral is unlikely for the major Western economies. But the deficit is still a long-term constraint, both on public investment in good times and countercyclical spending in bad ones, that did not exist in the world of 1955. Likewise, the fact that today's slower-than-the-1950s growth rate depends on historically high deficits and historically low interest rates doesn't mean that today's growth is illusory and destined to evaporate, as some hard-money pessimists assume. But it does suggest that we are, in effect, using our extraordinary wealth to permanently prop up a weak private-sector economy rather than enjoying a strong private-sector economy that increases our extraordinary wealth.

Third are *the constraints on education*, which likewise didn't exist a hundred years ago when (as Cowen notes) "only 6.4 percent of Americans of the appropriate age group graduated from high school." Going from that 6 percent to a 70 percent graduation rate three generations later had a dramatic effect on economic productivity, as did the similar surge in college attendance and completion. But this kind of change, from an unschooled population to an educated one, can really happen only once. Further improvements in educational attainment are certainly possible (the stagnation in educational attainment is somewhat worse in the United States than in Europe), but not on anything like that twentieth-century scale. Any future improvement is likely to be a grinding process, constrained not only by policy failures and socioeconomic stratification but also by innate human capacities. And even as credentialism advances, there is some evidence that the Western world is slipping backward on more fundamental measures such as literacy rates and IQ. The famous Flynn effect, in which IQ scores increase generation after generation, has stalled out in parts of northern Europe. In the United States, literacy rates for white students peaked in the 1970s and have slipped since.

Fourth are *the constraints imposed by the environment*. The growth that America achieved in the eighteenth and nineteenth centuries by taming a wilderness and putting fallow land to use is never going to be repeated. All growth henceforth is constrained by the need to adapt to climate change—an adaptation, Gordon notes, whose costs represent a twenty-first-century "payback" for the growth rates the West achieved in the industrial revolution, when "the environment was not a priority and the symbol of a prosperous city was a drawing of a factory spewing pure black smoke out of its chimneys."

In theory, these costs might be mitigated by renewable-energy innovations that make fossil-fuel regulations and carbon taxes unnecessary and obsolete. But even then, Cowen points out, the innovations involved would be generally "defensive," pursued in order to sustain present habits, present expectations, the present standard of living. A world of electric cars might be a good thing for the earth, a good thing for our civilization's sustainability—but the electric car is not a world-altering innovation in the style of the steamship or the airplane or the gas-powered automobile that it aspires to replace. The same goes for many green projects: unlike the innovations of the nineteenth and early twentieth centuries, their goal is to find new technologies that mostly allow our society to stay essentially the same.

And even these efforts are hampered by the fifth major force preventing a return to past growth rates: the fact that since the 1970s, our technology-mad, innovation-obsessed society has slipped, without quite realizing it, into *a period of technological stagnation*.

Where Have You Gone, Thomas Edison?

If many trends I've just discussed mostly seem recognizable or painfully obvious, the claim that ours is an age of technological stagnation is more controversial, cutting against so much public propaganda. Which is why it's best introduced through impressions and thought experiments first, because they're more likely to break the spell of tech-era boosterism.

Start with an idea that belongs to two important American historians, Perry Miller and David Nye: the concept of the "technological sublime." This refers to shared cultural moments in which some feat of technical mastery elicits the same kind of spiritualized reaction as the majesty of nature or the glory of France's Chartres Cathedral. From the early nineteenth century onward, the recurrence of such moments in America and the West became almost liturgical, with each new technological breakthrough offering a kind of pilgrimage or festival in which (in Miller's words) the "technological majesty" of the new achievement—the steamship, the railroad, Henry Adams's dynamo, the Fordian assembly line, the Hoover Dam, the Golden Gate Bridge, the skyscrapered urban skyline, the jet airplane, the atomic bomb, and the moon landing—was united to the "starry heavens above and the moral law within to form a peculiarly American trinity of the Sublime."

But has anything that fits this description happened since the moon mission? There have been shared moments, like the sinking of the *Titanic* and the Hindenburg disaster in the past, in which some great wonder failed or was destroyed: the *Challenger* and *Columbia* space shuttle explosions, and the fall of the Twin Towers, which was a kind of black mass of the technological sublime. There have been sublime simulations, conjured up on movie screens and soon in the depths of virtual reality. There has been a growth in what Nye calls "the consumer's sublime" of Disneyland and Las Vegas. There have been sublime technological objets, like the iPhone, whose original release was the closest my own generation possesses to a shared experience of techno-wonder. There have certainly been men and women who get famous selling the *promise* of the sublime—Elon Musk's hyperloops being the most famous examples. And there have been moments of a nostalgic sublime—such as the final flight of the space shuttle *Discovery*, carried into history on a special Boeing 747 airliner, which had people craning their necks to watch as the retired spacecraft was ferried from Florida to the Smithsonian in Washington, DC.

But the hyperloop is a blueprint, Las Vegas is a simulacrum, virtual reality is not—and as the science-fiction writer Neal Stephenson wrote after watching *Discovery* pass overhead, the nostalgic sublime of its final flight mostly accentuated the possibilities we've given up:

"My lifespan encompasses the era when the United States of America was capable of launching human beings into space. Some of my earliest memories are of sitting on a braided rug before a hulking black-and-white television, watching the early Gemini missions. This summer, at the age of fifty-one—not even old—I watched on a flat-screen as the last Space Shuttle lifted off the pad."

That image—a sci-fi writer using the small marvel of a flat-screen TV to watch a larger marvel recede into the past—is a compelling one for our era, which for all its digital wonders has lost the experience of awe-inspiring technological progress that prior modern generations came to take for granted. The technological sublime, unlike the natural or religious sort, does not renew itself in every generation. And though we are habituated to that reality, as Stephenson's lament suggests, it is not at all what was expected fifty years ago.

Here is David Graeber, writing in the very left-wing *Baffler* several years ago, making a version of this point:

> As someone who was eight years old at the time of the Apollo moon landing, I remember calculating that I would be thirty-nine in the magic year 2000 and wondering what the world would be like. . . . It seemed unlikely that I'd live to see all the things I was reading about in science fiction, but it never occurred to me that I wouldn't see any of them.
>
> . . . The common way of dealing with the uneasy sense . . . is to brush it aside. . . . "Oh, you mean all that *Jetsons* stuff?" I'm asked—as if to say, but that was just for children! [But] even in the seventies and eighties . . . sober sources such as *National Geographic* and the Smithsonian were informing children of imminent space stations and expeditions to Mars. In 1968 Stanley Kubrick felt that a moviegoing audience would find it perfectly natural to assume that only thirty-three years later, in 2001, we would have commercial moon flights, city-like space stations, and computers with human personalities maintaining astronauts in suspended animation while traveling to Jupiter. . . . The *Star Trek* mythos was set in the sixties, too, but the show kept getting revived, leaving audiences for *Star Trek: Voyager* . . . to try to figure out what to make of the fact that according to the logic of the program, the world was supposed to be recovering from fighting off the rule of genetically engineered supermen in the Eugenics Wars of the nineties.

Now, of course, the absence of supermen and flying cars and Martian colonies does not mean that progress has halted; perhaps it is just happening on a more human scale. But having considered the sublime, let's step down to the level of the ordinary, and borrow from Mark Steyn, a conservative writer whose politics are roughly the opposite of Graeber's:

Stagnation

Imagine . . . a man of the late nineteenth century, perhaps your own great-grandfather, sitting in an ordinary American home of 1890. And now pitch him forward in an H. G. Wells machine . . . to that same ordinary American home, circa 1950. Why, the poor gentleman of 1890 would be astonished. . . . There is a huge machine in the corner of the kitchen, full of food and keeping the milk fresh and cold! There is another shiny device whirring away and seemingly washing milady's bloomers with no human assistance whatsoever! Even more amazingly, there is a full orchestra . . . coming from a tiny box on the countertop! The music is briefly disturbed by a low rumble from the front yard . . . a metal conveyance is coming up the street at an incredible speed—with not a horse in sight . . . there is snow on the ground, and yet the house is toasty warm, even though no fire is lit and there appears to be no stove. A bell jingles from a small black instrument on the hall table. Good heavens! Is this a "telephone"? . . . He picks up the speaking tube. A voice at the other end says there is a call from across the country—and immediately there she is, a lady from California talking as if she were standing next to him, without having to shout, or even raise her voice! And she says she'll see him tomorrow! Oh, very funny. They've got horseless carriages in the sky now, have they? What marvels! In a mere sixty years!

. . . But then he espies his Victorian time machine sitting invitingly in the corner of the parlor. . . . So on he gets, and sets the dial for our own time. And when he dismounts, he wonders if he's made a mistake. Because, aside from a few design adjustments, everything looks pretty much as it did in 1950: the layout of the kitchen, the washer, the telephone. . . . Oh, wait. It's got buttons instead of a dial. And the station wagon in the front yard has dropped the woody look and seems boxier than it did. And the folks getting out seem . . . larger, and dressed like overgrown children . . .

But other than that . . . he might as well have stayed in 1950.

Let's pause and acknowledge the one exception to the above scenario. . . . Instead of having to watch Milton Berle on that commode-like thing in the corner . . . you can now watch Uncle Miltie on YouTube clips from your iPhone. But be honest, aside from that, what's new?

Now, it's fair to say that Steyn is underrating the marvels of the Internet somewhat. Just as you could take Graeber's examples and point out that the science fiction of the sixties was often too pessimistic about how fast certain aspects of computer technology would advance, imagining data engines as huge, lumbering, boxy things rather than the pocket companions that we now take for granted, you could rewrite Steyn's story and make the Internet sound far more marvelous than he does: An encyclopedia in your pocket! Instant access to every song, movie, television show, and novel! Virtual worlds that you can enter via headset! A store that delivers everything you need within a day, perhaps soon via drone!

But how do all those marvels of convenience really stack up against prior innovations? How much have they actually changed our world and lives? Consider Gordon's way of contrasting our recent digital-age progress to the major inventions of the nineteenth century:

A thought experiment. . . . You are required to make a choice between option A and option B. With option A, you are allowed to keep 2002 electronic technology, including your Windows 98 laptop accessing Amazon, and you can keep running water and indoor toilets; but you can't use anything invented since 2002. Option B is that you get everything invented in the past decade right up to Facebook, Twitter, and the iPad, but you have to give up running water and indoor toilets. You have to haul the water into your dwelling and carry out the waste. Even at 3:00 a.m. on a rainy night, your only toilet option is a wet and perhaps muddy walk to the outhouse. Which option do you choose?

I have posed this imaginary choice to several audiences in speeches, and the usual reaction is a guffaw, a chuckle, because the preference for option A is so obvious. The audience realizes that it has been trapped into recognition that just one of the many late-nineteenth-century inventions is more important than the portable electronic devices of the past decade on which they have become so dependent.

Again, this doesn't make the Internet unimportant. Indeed, in Gordon's view, it's the most important thing that's happened across the last fifty years, the source of our only major post-1960s productivity surge. (Theranos was a pleasant fiction, but the Amazon effect is real.) But that surge, and its effect on our everyday lives, is still a blip compared with the cascade of changes between 1870 and 1970, and a letdown compared with what we dreamed about not so very long ago.

The Silicon Valley tycoon Peter Thiel, another prominent stagnationist, likes to snark that "we were promised flying cars. We got 140 characters." And even the people who will explain to you, in high seriousness, that nobody would really *want* a flying car can't get around the basic points that he and Graeber, Steyn and Gordon are making. Lots of inventions that were confidently expected fifty years ago are, indeed, now dismissed as fantasies or "*Jetsons* stuff." Everyday life was, indeed, more radically transformed by earlier technological breakthroughs. And over the last two generations, the only truly radical change has taken place in the devices that we use for communication and entertainment, so that a single one of the nineteenth century's great inventions still looms larger in our everyday existence than most of what we think of as technological breakthroughs nowadays.

When you consider just how much the world changed between 1850 and 1970, or between 1900 and 1950, or even between splitting the atom and landing on the moon, you can understand why so many observers in the early and middle years of the twentieth century expected developments that now seem to us implausibly utopian: John

Maynard Keynes's fifteen-hour workweek, which the British economist assumed would be sufficient for the "old Adam" in us once the New Jerusalem of plenty had arrived; or the vision of the French economist Jean-Jacques Servan-Schreiber, whose 1967 bestseller *The American Challenge* Thiel likes to quote because it predicted American growth would be so extraordinary that "the year will be comprised of 39 workweeks and 13 weeks of vacation. . . . All this within a single generation."

As Thiel points out, this sounds ridiculous today. Yet it didn't seem that way to people living fifty, sixty, seventy years ago, because of the pace of change they themselves had seen. And not just the pace but also the scope: as Gordon argues, in past eras, the West saw dramatic growth and innovation across multiple arenas—energy and transportation and medicine and agriculture and communication and the built environment. Whereas the story of the last two developed-world generations is of a society where progress has become increasingly monodimensional, all tech and nothing else. Indeed, it's telling that even within the Silicon Valley landscape, the most stable success stories are often the purest computer-and-Internet enterprises—social media companies, device manufacturers, software companies—while the frauds and failures and big money-losers and possible catastrophes tend to involve efforts to use tech to transform some other industry, from music festivals to office-space rentals to food delivery to blood tests.

So the basic stagnationist case, caveats and all, seems to capture a real change. We used to travel faster, build bigger, live longer; now we communicate faster, chatter more, snap more selfies. We used to go to the moon; now we make movies about space—amazing movies with completely convincing special effects—in which small fortunes are spent to make it *seem* like we've left earth behind. And we hype the revolutionary character of our communications devices in order to persuade ourselves that our earlier, wider-ranging expectations were always unreasonable—that this progress is the only progress we could reasonably expect.

Meanwhile, we also hype the changes that are supposedly just around the corner: the alternative energy revolution that's always poised for takeoff; the genetic engineering breakthrough that will deliver designer babies any day now; the dramatic artificial intelligence leap forward that will either usher in utopia or end with our extermination at the hands of some misanthropic Skynet; the radical life-extension hack that will either add fifty years to our lifespans or enable us to upload ourselves into virtual immortality; the "new study" that offers hope for curing Alzheimer's or Parkinson's or cancer; the robots that are supposedly about to take over all our jobs. Even the stars are making a comeback: I'm writing this paragraph with a copy of *Bloomberg BusinessWeek* beside me that hypes the new Silicon Valley–funded space race.

Decadence is not universal; these promises do, at times, reflect real breakthroughs, interesting research, genuinely promising developments. Whatever else he may be, Elon Musk is not decadent, and in 2020 SpaceX really did put astronauts back in space for the first time since the retirement of the Space Shuttle program.

But the broader gee-whiz spirit is still consistently at odds with the general decelerative pattern of the last few generations. Yes, there have been strides made in solar, wind, and other renewables. But real energy prices are as high as they were in the crisis atmosphere of the 1970s, and the "alternative" share of the energy pie is barely higher than it was back then. Yes, the Green Revolution of the 1970s made the doom-and-gloom scenarios of Paul Ehrlich, author of *The Population Bomb*, and likeminded alarmists look ridiculous, and enabled the econoptomist Julian Simon to win a 1980s-era famous bet with Ehrlich over whether commodity prices would rise or fall. But those same prices have risen since the 1990s, while the agricultural-yield returns to the Green Revolution have declined. Meanwhile, travel speeds have dropped and transportation innovations have been delayed and delayed, and while we may get driverless cars in some form eventually (albeit perhaps a form that can't drive in the rain or snow), the harder limits on machine intelligence have not yet been overcome.

Indeed, beneath the hype and scaremongering about artificial intelligence, there is just as much evidence that we're actually headed for an "AI winter"—in which research funding and public interest both dry up—as there is that we'll all be in thrall to a superintelligence soon enough. Robots have obviously taken some jobs, with particularly disruptive consequences in some industries, and no doubt they will take more. But a society being fundamentally transformed by automation would have sharp productivity growth, of the kind we used to have and briefly enjoyed in the Internet's first flower, rather than the productivity stagnation afflicting both the United States and Europe.

For all the talk about radical life extension, too, prior to the successful push for a coronavirus vaccine, most recent medical progress involved rare conditions that affect small populations, rather than big killers such as cancer, heart disease, and Alzheimer's. Obviously, if you're a parent of a child with cystic fibrosis, for which a long-awaited treatment just arrived, or a mother whose baby was just saved from a congenital defect by surgery in the womb, or an Iraq War veteran with a miraculous-seeming prosthetic, the progress that we have experienced is amazing, and the fields that generate them are obviously not decadent. But the miracles are happening for extreme and marginal cases more often than the masses. No major new type of antibiotic has been developed since the 1980s, and the age of blockbuster drugs seems to be over: pharmaceutical companies across the 1990s and 2000s spent more money on research but approved fewer and fewer new medicines, with the predictable result that research and development spending has been declining throughout the 2010s. In most developed countries, life expectancy is increasing more slowly than it did fifty years ago; in Germany and France it has flatlined; in the United States and the United Kingdom, it has lately gone into reverse. And even once surmounted, the coronavirus challenge might be a harbinger of public-health threats to come, from emergent pathogens and growing antibiotic-resistance in the familiar ones.

The pattern in the pharmaceutical industry—more researchers

yielding fewer breakthroughs—is reproduced elsewhere on a larger scale. The title of a 2017 paper from a group of Stanford University economists asked, "Are Ideas Getting Harder to Find?" The answer was a clear yes: "We present a wide range of evidence from various industries, products, and firms showing that research effort is rising substantially while research productivity is declining sharply." In *The Great Stagnation*, similarly, Cowen cites an analysis of innovation history from the Pentagon researcher Jonathan Huebner, whose model of an innovations-to-population ratio for the last six hundred years of Western history shows a long rise and a swifter fall—a slowly ascending arc through the late nineteenth century, when major inventions were rather easy to conceive and to adopt, and a steepening decline ever since, as rich countries spend more and more on research to diminishing returns.

To Huebner, this rise-and-fall pattern implies that we are reaching some inherent limit on possible innovation; indeed, he suggests boldly that we are around 85 percent of that limit, that we'll hit 95 percent by the late 2030s, and then approach 100 percent thereafter.

That seems overconfident in its pessimism. There is no reason to assume that an innovation decline proves some law of inevitable exhaustion, and plenty of reasons to believe that a period of stagnation can be followed by a sudden age of discovery when the right spark comes along. Indeed, the sparks might already be swirling. It could be that there are eras when the pace of innovation isn't fully reflected in measures such as productivity and life expectancy. It could be that some of the major innovations of today, from the specialty surgeries I mentioned earlier to non-GDP-enhancing breakthroughs like the mapping of ancient DNA, will have future implications for everyday human life that are far more dramatic than we realize now. The pandemic itself could be a key accelerant, since in the vaccine push it has already forced innovations through bureaucracies, cleared away regulatory hurdles, and summoned up the equivalent of the wartime urgency that the developed world has long conspicuously lacked.

Or to use Cowen's favored metaphor, if we have plucked most of the low-hanging fruit that the industrial revolution made possible to reach, there might still be a ladder that someone could invent that would make the higher branches suddenly easier to reach, and for all we know, that ladder might be being extended even now. In which case, we will look back on our present decadence as simply a lull—a period when innovation slowed temporarily before self-driving cars and CRISPR and nanotech and private spaceflight sent it surging forward once again.

That possibility will be considered in more detail later. But the lull is still a multigenerational reality right now, and human history offers no reassurance that it will necessarily end. As Gordon and Cowen note, it's the great surge of innovation in recent Western history that's the historical anomaly, not the disappointing years since our great leap moonward. At some point, every advanced-for-its-time society has ceased advancing; there is no reason to assume that the modern world is inherently immune from the torpor that claimed the Ottomans and imperial China in the not-so-distant past.

Especially since there is a strong entanglement between all the trends discussed in this chapter. Slow innovation and slow growth create feedback loops where there is less money for research and then fewer breakthroughs to boost productivity and wealth. An economy dominated by near monopolies is more likely to resist or squash innovation; an economy of rentiers is more likely to want to freeze the existing order and resist the destruction that dynamism inevitably brings; an economy floated on deficit spending and committed to vast old-age entitlements will have less money for research in the long run; an economy at a high stage of development will find it hard to refit its basic infrastructure to accommodate new inventions or give them political space to be adopted.

And this entanglement extends into the effects of the most striking *social* trend in the late modern world, which the next chapter will take up: the extent to which, for complicated and mysterious reasons, the richest societies in human history have collectively decided not to reproduce.

2

Sterility

The two most powerful literary dystopias of this age in Western history are both the work of women: one a Canadian, Margaret Atwood; the other an Englishwoman, P. D. James. Their novels, Atwood's *The Handmaid's Tale* and James's *Children of Men*, are not always considered together because the authors' reputations are quite different. Despite a number of forays into science fiction, Atwood is firmly defined as a "literary" novelist and, despite her occasional disavowal of the label, as a feminist author as well. James, meanwhile, mostly wrote a very English sort of detective story, with more grit and gore and writerliness than Agatha Christie but the same essentially Anglican sensibility. As a consequence, their dystopias were received differently: Atwood's book as a major literary figure's attempt to craft a feminist answer to *1984*; James's novel as a genre writer's interesting departure, with a political-cultural message that tilted toward Christianity and conservatism.

And the books are indeed quite different. In Atwood's novel, written amid the Reagan-era resurgence of religious conservatism, a near-future United States is taken over by a ruthless theocratic movement that begins rolling back not just third-wave feminism but also women's rights to property, free movement, literacy—even to a Christian name. The novel's totalitarian Republic of Gilead is like a feminist fever dream of what religious-right grandees like Pat Robertson and

Jerry Falwell desired: a society of not just male privilege but also total male domination, with women confined to servile roles or (in the case of the narrator) living as slaves in the households of the regime's no-menklatura, bearing children for powerful men whose wives are barren, and taking on names ("Offred," meaning "of Fred") that make their status as property explicit.

In James's dystopia, meanwhile, instead of female subjugation, there is a kind of horrifying and undesired emancipation, imposed by nature or by nature's God, from the demands and possibilities of reproduction. In *Children of Men*, the entire human race—or, rather, the *male* half of the human race—turns sterile overnight, so that from 1995 onward, not a single baby is born anywhere on earth. Governments race one another to find a cure, but what seems temporary turns out to be permanent and incurable, and a kind of torpor settles over the world as it reconciles itself to extinction. The narrator's England becomes a senescent police state, rife with suicide, exploiting the labor of immigrants from younger (if still foredoomed) societies, with cats in prams, cults on every corner, and armed gangs of "Omegas" (kids born in the last fertile year, like millennials but *way* more entitled) rampaging in the countryside. Until, of course, there is an unexpected pregnancy . . .

The James dystopia, then, reads fairly naturally as a culturally conservative critique of Western decadence, with Christian themes and motifs cropping up as the possibility of new fertility arises. Whereas Atwood's novel, while not necessarily anti-Christian (the Republic of Gilead executes Baptists and Catholics along with gays and secular subversives), reads primarily as a warning about the dangers of religious reaction and the need to defend the modern liberal order, flaws and all, against those whose thirst for meaning leads them into totalitarian temptations. Not surprisingly, many of the biggest fans of *Children of Men* the novel (the movie adaptation is a slightly different matter) have been cultural traditionalists, religious and otherwise. Meanwhile, the fact that Donald Trump is not precisely Christian has not prevented *The Handmaid's Tale*—and its award-winning Trump-era television adaptation—from being invoked by liberals as a story for our times, a candle lit against the rise of a misogynist authoritarianism.

But if the books are different, they also have an underappreciated unity, because the plot engine of *Children of Men*, the stark absence of children, is also crucial to *The Handmaid's Tale*—not as the dystopic scenario itself, or not precisely, but as the reason for Gilead's invention, the development that drives its harsh Deuteronomic logic. Atwood, being a subtle and cunning social critic, does not envision a theocracy leaping fully formed from the right-wing brain of 1985. Instead, she imagines a cabal of right-wing Christian revolutionaries *turning* theocratic in response to a less absolute version of James's doomsday scenario: a massive fertility crisis, apparently linked to pollution and sexually transmitted diseases, that leaves most American women unable to conceive. The handmaid's role is central to the Gileadean order not just because it serves the patriarchy but also because something terrible has happened to make childbearing a rare gift; to make the political control of female reproduction seem so essential as to justify totalitarianism.

In this sense, Atwood and James actually invented cracked-mirror dystopias, with their major and minor themes reversed. In both stories, there is a fertility crisis; in both, its consequences include a turn to dictatorship in the West. The difference is that James is most interested in the crisis itself, while Atwood is more interested in imagining a terrifying totalitarian response. But both novels draw their power from the same deep source and start their extrapolation from the same distinctive fact about the Western world in modern times: the fact that amid all of our society's material plenty, one resource is conspicuously scarce.

That resource is babies.

The Empty Cradle

Of course, our society does not face the kind of apocalyptic or near-apocalyptic fertility crisis depicted in James and Atwood's novels. Male sperm counts have fallen at a somewhat eerie pace, but the disaster in *Children of Men* is not upon us (yet); women delaying childbearing is nothing like the total crash in female fertility envisioned in *The Handmaid's Tale*. But both novelists treat their catastrophes as, in part, extensions of the cultural renunciation of procreative sex that followed the sexual revolutions of the 1960s and 1970s—and that renunciation has continued and spread since their books first appeared. There is variation from country to country, culture to culture, but below-replacement fertility is the fundamental fact of civilized life in the early twenty-first century.

To replace itself from generation to generation, a society needs to average 2.1 births per woman. Across the European Union in 2016, the average was 1.6 children per woman. In Japan, it was 1.41; South Korea, 1.25; China, 1.6; Singapore, 0.82. In Canada, it was 1.6; in Australia, 1.77. The American fertility rate was, by these standards, relatively robust: 1.87. But it was still too low to sustain the present population on its own, and it was falling faster, despite economic growth, than most demographers had expected. By 2019, it was down to 1.7, the lowest ever recorded, and most evidence suggests that there will no post-lockdown baby boom in 2021 or 2022; instead, the fears and isolation and economic hardship induced by the pandemic will drive the birthrate lower still.

These are, note well, overall fertility rates. Recent immigrants to developed countries tend to have higher-than-average fertility (although the offspring's fertility converges fairly quickly with the native born), so the fertility rates for native-born women are almost without exception lower than these figures. Aside from Israel, there is no rich country in the world whose population would not, absent immigration, be on track to shrink.

Why is this happening? In broad terms, the downward trend is old and overdetermined. Plunging infant mortality rates meant that more children survived to adulthood, reducing the incentive to have the largest family possible. The shifts from an agrarian to an industrial and then to an information economy made children less valuable as extra household laborers and made an intense educational investment in each child make far more economic sense—which in turn raised the costs of childrearing for the ambitious and successful. The birth control pill made accidental pregnancy less likely and delayed parenting more plausible. The feminist revolution created strong economic incentives for women to delay childbirth as long as possible. The divorce revolution and the decline of marriage meant that fewer people than in the past were spending the childbearing years in a stable, monogamous partnership. Secularization meant that fewer people felt a moral obligation to be fruitful and multiply. The welfare state provided an old-age guarantee that lessened the need for kids as sources of financial support when you yourself cannot work any longer. And the blessings of a rich consumer society provided a plethora of goods, services, and experiences that an under-forty-five-year-old might wish to spend time and energy and money consuming—even as the day-after-day, hour-after-hour burdens of childrearing remained substantial, mitigated modestly (at best) by technological progress and alleged labor-saving devices.

Some kind of large-scale fertility decline, then, looks like an inevitable corollary of liberal capitalist modernity. But at the same time, there's a great deal we don't understand about the phenomenon, and various explanations and variables that seem to conflict with one another. For instance, the fact that birthrates plunge during recessions—as they did in an extreme way during the Great Recession—suggests that personal finances play a major role in fertility decisions; hence the possibility that the economic stagnation discussed in the last chapter, and especially stagnation in working-class incomes, explains some of the recent birthrate drop. But the stagnation hypothesis seems to cut against the broader historical experience of the modern West, since people used to have large families while living in what seems to modern people like the most squalid and impossible conditions, and decades and centuries of economic growth—including the recent recovery in the United States—have been accompanied by general fertility declines. In other words, our great wealth relative to the human past discourages fertility, but then setbacks and disappointment within that wealthy context discourages it further still.

It's also not clear exactly how welfare states and public spending interact with birthrates. A number of studies have suggested that Europe's more generous safety net modestly discourages people from having large families, because larger welfare states require higher taxes on potential parents and reduce the incentive to have multiple kids to take care of you in your old age. Fifteen or twenty years ago, this evidence was cited to explain why the United States still had higher birthrates than France or Germany, the argument being that our lighter tax burden and relatively less generous welfare state must spur procreation. But then more recently, without a dramatic change in our tax burden and the scale of public spending, American birthrates have converged with those of many northern European countries—and some of those countries have *higher* birthrates than European countries with weaker welfare states.

The fact that often those northern European welfare states have strong pronatalist components—France and Sweden and Ireland, in particular—suggests a possible way to reconcile the conflicting evidence: perhaps an old-age safety net reduces birthrates, but a profamily welfare state can raise them. But then again, there are a number of case studies, particularly in East Asia, where pronatalist policies do not seem to have a clear effect on birthrates; countries like South Korea and Singapore have used both policy and propaganda to little avail as their fertility rates have dropped toward half or less than half replacement level. And even in France and Sweden, the high birthrate is partially an artifact of those countries' relative openness to immigration; in social democratic Finland, by contrast, a vigorous program to support families, complete with the famous "baby box" that doubles as a cradle, sent to every expecting mother, has done little to prevent the number of Finnish babies from scraping a depth not seen since a dreadful famine in the 1860s.

The role of religiosity and social conservatism presents a similar uncertainty. Religious practice correlates with higher fertility within most societies, and conservative religious practice correlates especially: Mormons and Orthodox Jews have way more kids than their secular counterparts; evangelical Christians have more kids than both atheists and the more liberal sort of Protestants; recent Muslim immigrants to the West have a lot of children, and then their fertility declines with both assimilation and diminishing devotion; and the most child-free cities in the West are generally places associated with a maximalist social liberalism—San Francisco, Stockholm, Seattle.

But this pattern does not always hold across societies. Sweden is much more secular than Poland, but the Swedes overall have more kids than the Poles. Northern Europe is more secular than southern Europe, but birthrates in Spain and Greece are lower than in Great Britain or much of Scandinavia. This divergence has led some to suggest that "feminism is the new natalism," which is overstated; again, the more liberal societies' openness to immigration explains some of the differences here, and the plunging birthrate in gender-egalitarian Finland is a clear counterexample to any feminism-as-natalism claim. But there may be kind of a trap for societies, like Italy and Japan, that maintain certain traditionalist gender norms while welcoming (or hustling) women into the workforce—almost as if when women are expected to play traditional homemaker roles and also work full-time, they go on a kind of reproductive strike.

The biggest question of all, meanwhile, is: Why has fertility settled *this* low? It made sense that it would fall dramatically from its premodern heights, but why has it ended up subreplacement? Projections in the 1960s suggested that developed-world fertility would settle around 2.2 children per woman. Instead it appears to be settling around 1.7, and even that may be optimistic. Yet the desired family size in the Western world is still closer to 2.5 children, so it's not that everybody suddenly wants to have just one kid. Women want as many children as men, so it's not just a question of female preferences dictating things now that feminism has enabled them to be expressed. There have been periods—the baby boom above all—when the general trend was suddenly suspended; when society modernized rapidly, and birthrates boomed nonetheless. The United States, the largest and richest Western country, sustained near-replacement-level fertility for a long time—several decades—after dipping below in the 1970s; long enough that many of us took it for granted that American birthrates were somehow exceptional. But now we've fallen back into the subreplacement crowd with everyone else. Why?

If exceptions might help explain the rule, then the example of Israel is interesting: it's the only rich, highly educated country where birthrates leveled off well above replacement instead of just below it, and then actually rose again. The Israeli fertility rate in 1985 was 2.7 births per woman; today, in a still-richer country, the rate stands at 3.1. Some of this can be explained as a case study in how religiosity drives fertility, given both the strength of the ultraorthodox community in Israel and the fact that from the 1970s onward, Israel has welcomed a more devout and conservative type of immigrant than have most Western countries. But the Israeli birthrate has remained high, and even climbed higher, among secular Israelis as well. So instead of relying on religion alone to explain the Jewish state's exceptionalism, it may be more reasonable to speculate that fecundity increases with the felt stakes of ordinary life, and that Israel's distinctive identity, history, and geopolitical position—perpetually threatened, perpetually mobilized—creates very different attitudes toward the self-sacrifice involved in parenthood than the less existentially shadowed culture of other rich societies.

This argument could be extended back to another major and

much larger exception to the modern fertility decline: the world of the postwar baby boom, which was shaped not only by the temporary religious revival of the late 1940s but also by the solidarity forged in wartime, the need (in Europe) to rebuild a shattered civilization, and the apocalyptic threat of nuclear war. But the end of that period of exceptionalism, and the fertility collapse of the late 1960s and 1970s that followed, also points to another plausible explanation for the depths that Western fertility is scraping: the fact that since the sexual revolution, men and women seem to be having more and more trouble successfully and permanently pairing off.

This relationship trouble has "liberal" and "conservative" explanations, with liberals emphasizing how the toxic legacy of patriarchy makes it hard for men to adapt to female empowerment and the role changes it requires, and conservatives emphasizing how a sexually permissive culture divorces sex from love and tears up the social scripts that might bring the sexes happily together. But the facts themselves are indisputable: people reacted to the social revolutions of the 1960s first by marrying less and divorcing more and having fewer children, more of whom were born outside of wedlock, and then eventually by marrying much less, having many fewer children, and even—in trends from the last two decades—having less sex, period. This last, perhaps most startling trend shows up in studies all across the developed world, from Britain and Germany, to East Asia, to the United States, where the decline correlates with the rise of the Internet, the iPhone, and all the virtual alternatives to old-fashioned copulation. In low-fertility Japan, a recent study from the Family Planning Agency found that 45 percent of women ages sixteen to twenty-four and a quarter of men "were not interested in or despised sexual contact." In low-birthrate Finland, a 2015 study compiled evidence of "increasing lack of sexual desire, decreasing frequency of sexual intercourse," and a decline in the frequency of female orgasms since the 1970s and 1990s.

Maybe the decline of sex and baby-making as well as marriage, the substitution of masturbation for intercourse and asexuality for both, just reflects the free choices of a free people, to be celebrated rather than deplored. But that blithe assessment ignores the widening gap between what most people still say they want—relationships, marriage, children—and their growing inability to find those partners and conceive those children. A developed world in which those preferences were met still could have lower birthrates and fewer marriages than in the past, but it would still have more sex, more marriages, and more children than the world as it exists—a world that has been sterilized and atomized, somehow, against its inhabitants' professed desires.

Welcome to Twilight City

Beyond the unhappiness that comes with unfulfilled hopes and expectations, this sterility has important economic consequences. Low birthrates swiftly turn rich societies into aging societies, with fewer workers and more retirees, which in a very direct way first slows the growth of GDP and then (as in Japan, already, and perhaps eventually parts of Europe as well) makes it start to shrink. But the indirect effect is just as important: aging societies, societies with fewer young people coming up for every citizen aging into senescence, are simply less likely to be dynamic, less interested in risk taking, than societies with younger demographic profiles.

Here's Megan McArdle, in an *Atlantic* essay from the last decade on Europe's difficult economic future, explaining how this works:

> ... picture two neighboring towns, sharing all the same infrastructure and economic opportunities, with one key difference: their median age. In the first town, which I'll call Morningburg, the average resident is 28. In the second, which I'll call Twilight City, the average householder is 58.
>
> Research indicates that even with all the same resources at their disposal, these two places look very different. . . . In Morn-

ingburg, young workers are rapid, plastic learners, eager to try out new ways of doing things. Since they're still hoping to make a name for themselves and maybe get rich, they take a lot of risks. They push their managers to expand into new markets, propose iffy but innovative product lines, maybe start their own firm if the boss won't let them advance fast enough. For the right opportunity, they'll put in 18-hour days for a year or more.

In Twilight City, time horizons are shorter—people aren't looking for projects that will make them rich or famous 20 years from now. They are interested in conserving what they have. That's mostly rational, given Twilighters' life stage; but studies show that older people worry more than younger ones about losses and are therefore especially averse to risk. Twilighters also tire more easily and need more time off for illness, so hours worked decline slowly each year. Wages stay steady, however; Twilighters, like most people, get very angry if you try to cut their salary . . .

This is not a recipe for growth, job creation, and innovation on the scale that a society tilted more to young people once produced. The weight of demographics explains a lot of the economic stagnation discussed in an earlier chapter—it's a big factor in why wages have been stagnant for a generation, why economic growth has been slow across so much of the West, and perhaps even why technological progress has disappointed since the 1960s. Economists reckoning with demographic decline keep finding stark effects. A 2016 analysis of US states found that a 10 percent increase in the fraction of the population over sixty decreased the growth rate of per capita GDP by 5.5 percent. A 2017 paper found that companies in younger labor markets are more innovative; a 2018 report found that the aging of society helped explain the growth of monopolies and the declining rate of start-ups. Another paper in the same year found "a clear relationship between an older workforce and lower productivity," suggesting a demographic explanation for the persistent decline of productivity growth.

The empty cradle helps explain the growth of inequality as well. In Piketty's *Capital in the Twenty-First Century*, his vision of the permanent triumph of the one percent depends heavily on the assumption that slow population growth will inevitably lead to slower growth overall—and, more subtly, on the fact that fewer children means fewer heirs to divide up family wealth. The narrowing of family trees ensures that fortunes will grow ever more concentrated instead of diffusing with each successive generation, as they would in a society where more wealthy people had more than just two kids.

Almost inevitably, then, society with fewer babies will be less dynamic and more stratified, which makes population decline a case study in how decadence overtakes a civilization, because it's an example of how growth and development can create the necessary preconditions for cultural trends (in this case, toward sexual individualism, postfamilialism, childbearing delayed that becomes childbearing foregone) that in turn make further development less likely by undercutting the very forces (youth, risk taking, dynamism) necessary for continued growth.

It's a sign of civilization's development, almost by definition, when adults have a wider range of potential identities than "mother" and "father" available to them, and the gradual downward trajectory of birthrates in the modern era has often reflected gains to human welfare: victories over infant mortality, over constant childbearing as an absolute requirement of the marital state, over backbreaking agrarian economies. But when that trajectory crosses over into below-replacement territory, the individual's horizons can only really widen further at the future's eventual expense. Which means that as much as individualism is the fruit of growth, wealth, prosperity, and achievement, in our own era it also seems to be the seedbed of stagnation.

The Thinning Family Tree

It's also a potential seedbed of pessimism and despair. The personal disappointments that come with unfulfilled childbearing aspirations are probably an underappreciated aspect of late-middle-aged unhappiness today. But there's also a more general sociological and psychological consequence of low birthrates, a general impact of smaller family size on how people experience everyday life, their families, friendships, and communities, and—perhaps above all—on the way they think about the future of their society.

Start with my own family as an illustration: the Douthats on my father's side and the Snows on my mother's, both examples of what you might call "old stock" Americans, white Protestants, for the most part, with a few Irish newcomers mixed in. My maternal great-grandfather, a New England academic, had five children, four of whom lived to have families of their own. His son, my grandfather, also had five children—two sons and three daughters—who grew up as part of a dense network of cousins.

On my father's side, in a line that ended up in Southern California via Arkansas, the families were a little smaller. (The Douthats have never been the most fecund group, perhaps wary of imposing our hard-to-pronounce last name upon too many heirs.) But my dad was one of three siblings—two sons and a daughter—born to a middle-class salesman in 1950s Santa Monica, meaning that I had six aunts and uncles overall.

Then the social revolutions of the 1970s arrived. There were divorces, later marriages, single parenthood, abortions. In the end, all those aunts and uncles, their various spouses, and my parents— twelve baby boomers, all told—had only seven children: me, my sister, and five cousins. So instead of widening, my family tree tapered, its branches thinned. And it may thin again, since, so far, the seven cousins in my own generation, all adults, have only five children. Four of them are mine.

This is a very normal Western family history. Everywhere across the developed world, the decline of birthrates means that families have grown more attenuated: fewer and later marriages, fewer brothers and sisters and cousins, more people living for longer and longer stretches on their own. This postfamilialism is associated with care-free singlehood—a long "adultescence." But in an aging society, its most important effects will be felt among older Americans. And we're only just now beginning to experience what postfamilialism means for people across the life cycle, as the young singles turn into middle-aged bachelors and divorcees, and then into isolated retirees.

My maternal grandfather, for instance, lived to ninety-four and managed to live at home until he died, puttering around his Maine farmhouse and maintaining as much good cheer and independence as a bent, arthritic ninetysomething could reasonably hope for. That was possible precisely because he was part of a large family: three of his children had moved to distant states, but two still lived within a ten-minute drive, the distant children came to visit frequently, his own younger brother retired up the country road from him, and all of these direct relations were part of a larger network that checked in on him, talked to him, took care of him, and generally made his independence sustainable until the very end.

Will that be true for his kids—my parents and aunts and uncles—and for the generation after them? In 2017 the *New York Times* ran a story on what old age can look like in Japan, a country further along the postfamilial curve than the United States, deeper into this particular form of demographic decadence. It made for grim reading, starting with a heat wave rippling through the "identical white buildings" of a vast retirement community where, "with no families or visitors to speak of, many older tenants spent weeks or months cocooned in their small apartments, offering little hint of their existence to the world outside their doors. And each year, some of them died without anyone knowing, only to be discovered after their neighbors caught the smell."

Other problems start much earlier, well before mortality encroaches. The children born into a low-fertility world have certain obvious advantages: delayed fertility means that their parents have more resources, smaller families mean that each kid gets more parental attention. But at the same time, when they're born to older parents (and especially older fathers, whose sperm quality decays markedly) these kids will be more likely to have developmental disorders and learning disabilities. They will have fewer intimate peers, fewer siblings and cousins, and a weaker network of natural allies and sympathizers as they navigate the trials of adolescence. Their parents will be older when they confront early-adulthood challenges, more likely to become burdens when their progeny are still trying to establish themselves, less active and helpful as grandparents (if they become grandparents at all), more likely to die before their offspring reach middle age. And since everyone passes through each of these life stages, our low-fertility society is presently conducting, as the cultural critic Judith Shulevitz puts it, "a vast empirical study upon an unthinkably large population: all the babies conceived by older parents, plus those parents, plus their grandparents, who after all have to wait a lot longer than they used to for grandchildren."

In this landscape, the end of middle age seems to be a particular crisis point—the moment when the advantages of solo living can evaporate, when the promise of independence becomes a curse, when the absence or delay of grandchildren removes a reason for optimism and purpose. The grim social indicators of the last twenty years in America, the rising suicide rates and addiction trends and "deaths of despair," are often worst among the late-middle-aged and early-elderly—especially among older and divorced men, who seem unable to confront the prospect of decades of postfamilial existence.

Human beings are relational creatures. We depend on community for everyday happiness, and we imagine and encounter the future most intensely through our own progeny, our flesh and blood. But in a world with fewer children and, as birthrates drop and marrying age rises, still-fewer grandchildren or none at all, when people look ahead into their countries' future, they inevitably see less than previous generations to recognize immediately as their own. And the alienation is heightened when the descendants they do have seem to be faring worse than they did—as in those white working-class communities where opioid addiction, worklessness, and family breakdown have advanced apace.

This combination of small families and social disarray feeds a grim vision of the future, in which, after you've passed, your few kids and fewer grandkids will be beset, isolated, and alone. Sudden crises can have a profound effect: if you have just one child or grandchild (or your neighbor or friend has just one), and he or she dies or gets wounded in a foreign war, gets knocked into bankruptcy or foreclosure by a major recession, or ends up addicted, jailed, or dead during the opioid epidemic, your perspective on the future can be altered more dramatically than someone whose social web is larger, whose ties to the future expand instead of narrow.

Another story from the *Times* in 2017 featured Roger Winemiller, a farmer who lost two adult children to opioid overdoses within nine months. The article focused on inheritance and loss, illustrated by the farmer's doubts that his remaining son, who has also struggled with addiction, can inherit the farm that Winemiller inherited from his uncle twenty years earlier.

It's a dark story. It would be darker if he had only two children; if their deaths left the older Winemillers alone.

The Politics of Low Fertility

This psychological alienation is crucial to understanding contemporary political debates. Since the baby boom evaporated, elites in both the United States and Europe have embraced mass immigration as a solution for the economic problems associated with sterility—because immigration offers new population growth, new people, new workers, and new ideas to counteract the stagnation created by falling family size. In the public rhetoric of the West's leaders, the link between immigration and dynamism is always stressed, and for understandable reasons: we who do not have enough babies to be dynamic on our own are left to hope that other people's babies can supply the labor, the creativity, the hours worked and start-ups founded and Social Security taxes paid and retirees cared for—all the stuff that keeps the whole system going and that a subreplacement fertility rate casts into doubt. And since migrating to a wealthy country can be a humanitarian and economic blessing for the migrant, the whole deal seems like a win-win—economically and morally both.

Up to a point, this makes sense. Up to a point, the economies that have welcomed immigrants have tended to grow faster than those that haven't. Up to a point, immigration (in some forms) is linked to (certain kinds) of cultural creativity and innovation.

But as a technocratic solution to the economic problems created by postfamilialism, mass immigration is a double-edged sword. It replaces some of the missing workers but exacerbates intergenerational alienation and native-immigrant friction because it heightens precisely the anxieties about inheritance and loss that below-replacement fertility is heightening already. It delivers the promise of a more dynamic future, potentially, than the future promised by low birthrates, but for natives who are aging and whose communities aren't thriving, it also suggests the benefits of that imagined future belong increasingly to people who seem culturally alien, to inheritors who aren't your natural heirs, to other people's children and grandchildren rather than the dwindling numbers of your own.

So much of the populism that's been on the march in the United States and Europe (but not so much in Japan and South Korea, which, not coincidentally, have looked more to robots than to immigrants to address their demographic problems) is rooted in the way this sentiment—a mix of racism and xenophobia and the very human, not-at-all-deplorable tendency to identify and care for one's own— intertwines with anxieties created by economic stagnation and social fragmentation. The endless argument about whether "racism" or "economic anxiety" explains the Trump vote or the Brexit vote rarely grasps the fullness of this intertwinement: the extent to which people experiencing economic disappointment, people whose natural connection to the future was fraying as social crises thinned out already attenuated family ties, have been rebelling against an elite solution to their problems that they felt involved handing over the future *even more* to somebody else, and reacting against that solution with an anger too complicated to be reduced to economics, culture, or simple bigotry alone.

Of course, it might be said that these anxious, alienated, and dispossessed voters are the victims of their own collective choices. Had older generations of the French and British and Americans simply had one more child in every family, they would today enjoy a larger economy, better growth prospects, less inequality, more of a community around them in their old age, and a stronger link to the future in old age. In that alternative dispensation, the West would need fewer immigrants but might find it easier to welcome them, since the prospect of assimilating refugees and migrants might look less like a challenge to the country's core identity, and a younger society would seem to have more dynamism and wealth to go around. No politician is likely to address Trump voters or Brexit supporters or French populists alienated from their country's future and say, "You should have had more children when you had the chance." But there is truth to that judgment nonetheless.

At the same time, *les deplorables* also have the right to question whether, even without their own backlash, the mass-immigration solution to low birthrates could ever work out as well as the technocrats responsible for it thought. Will the masses of young migrants admitted to Germany as refugees by Chancellor Angela Merkel in 2015 really thrive in the high-tech economies of the present-day West, to say nothing of a future that will be either stagnant, roboticized, or both? Are the underassimilated, half-radicalized inhabits of French *banlieue*, the grim suburbs ringing the rich and touristed urban cores, really the workers that an aging, declining, self-doubting society needs? Are immigration's economic benefits really worth the social and political risks associated with importing many people from cultures so alien to the late-modern West? Isn't it possible, instead, that the technocrats might end up winning themselves the worst of both worlds, since mass immigration hasn't actually staved off stagnation and sclerosis, but it has created a restive minority population and a reactionary backlash that between them are pushing the entire system deeper into crisis?

But if low fertility exacerbates political polarization, it might also partially defuse the crises it provokes—because even if the politics of older-white backlash seem dramatically disruptive at the moment, other aspects of sterility might tend to hold the system in a graying stasis. Here it's worth keeping in mind McArdle's key point about Twilight City: it's a place where people are older, and therefore temperamentally set in their ways and afraid of change. So it's very easy to imagine the politics of declining birthrates leading to support for a kind of soft authoritarianism, with a state that does more to protect you through the life cycle and in old age, with a more heavily regulated economy, plus a more vigorous assertion of national identity as a substitute for attenuated familial identities—but for all this to happen *without* the political upheavals and outright violence that we saw when society was younger, more active, and hormonal. Such soft authoritarianism might, in its more effective form, build on tendencies evident in Eastern European and even Scandinavian politics. In a more chaotic form, it might follow the example of the Trump administration, offering a form of cable news entertainment for its supporters, by turns cruel and incompetent but mostly performative and virtual and inspiring performative and virtual responses, while in the real world people keep doddering through the normal motions of their lives.

The dystopias discussed at the beginning of the chapter offer a range of possible scenarios for politics in a sterile, aging world. *The Handmaid's Tale* scenario is the dramatic case, where a dying society turns revolutionary, with decadence giving way to ideological conflict and then totalitarian dictatorship. For something milder but still anarchic and authoritarian all at once, there's Alfonso Cuarón's movie adaptation of *Children of Men*, in which the slowly dying Britain imports younger immigrants to fill its labor needs and then cages and mistreats them, sparking enough terrorist violence, urban riots, and chaos on the streets to evoke the 1960s.

But in James's original novel, the chaos is more minimal. It's literally the apocalypse, the end of the world, and, yet, her aging, dying society is quiescent, not revolutionary, slouching from democracy into a nonideological dictatorship, enduring spasms of violence that are random and apolitical, accepting euthanasia and suicide without complaint. There is a would-be revolutionary cell in the novel, consisting of some of the society's younger members, but it's mainly distinguished by its futility, its inability to get anyone to care. The society of *Children of Men* isn't collapsing into chaos; it's just settling into the senility of repetition, content to live despairingly but peaceably, paying down, for a last few decades, the accumulated capital of its vigorous and vanished past.

Which, politically, might be closer to what you'd expect, albeit in a less dystopian form, in a society destined to just grow steadily grayer for a long time without renewal. You would expect stalemate and sclerosis, at the very least, rather than sudden crisis or catastrophe—a 1914 or a 1968. And it's just possible, as the next chapter will argue, that below the stormy surface of our politics, a stalemate is what we really have.

3

Sclerosis

One of my rare visits to Barack Obama's White House took place on a bright spring afternoon in 2009, when Rahm Emanuel, then still regarded as a ruthlessly effective White House chief of staff, invited a bunch of newspaper columnists to sit outside his West Wing office in the not-yet-humid DC air and talk about all the things that his administration intended to accomplish. Then the president himself appeared "unexpectedly" midway through the meeting, his handsome face not yet aged by presidential burdens, tossing a football he'd just been given by the Super Bowl winners and exuding the man-of-destiny confidence that had carried him through the 2008 campaign.

He had good reasons to be confident. The nearly $1 trillion stimulus package, fattened with money for long-standing liberal priorities, had passed a few months earlier. Arlen Specter, the long-waffling moderate Republican from Pennsylvania, had recently jumped ship to join the Democrats, giving them a sixty-seat Senate supermajority, and Emanuel, without naming names, implied that other moderate Republicans might soon follow suit. Obama's approval rating was holding around 60 percent; the face of the Republican Party was a splenetic Rush Limbaugh. Conservatives were talking as though this was going to be a new liberal age; liberals took that scenario for granted.

Never such confidence again. Within six months, Scott Brown's victory in a Massachusetts special election proved that a backlash was rising; within eighteen months, the House of Representatives had been lost to the Republicans, and thereafter the Obama presidency descended into gridlock, acrimony, and disappointment. The stimulus money stopped flowing, the ambitious liberal agenda was left unfinished, the dreams of a grand bargain to reduce deficits evaporated. What survived as a monument to that early optimism was one major piece of legislation: the health care law nicknamed after the president. And that turned out to be less of a big f—ing deal than either its enemies or advocates imagined—less a revolution of the system than a jerry-rigged addition to a disliked and complicated mess that had to be defended via exactly the kind of executive unilateralism that Obama had once denounced from the hustings.

In hindsight, then, the mood in the White House that spring afternoon in 2009 was deluded. But it was an important delusion, because it reflected an understandable belief: namely, that American politics could still work the way it used to work, under presidents as different as Franklin Roosevelt and Ronald Reagan. A failed presidency (Hoover, Carter, W.) would lead to a landslide for the opposition party, which would be interpreted as a mandate for governing, which would lead to a dramatic shift in policy, which would continue until the opposition party adapted to the new political reality and produced a Dwight Eisenhower or a Bill Clinton. And in the meantime, there would be room for bipartisanship as well, when the landscape demanded it, to respond to sudden challenges or simply stabilize the public fisc.

This is an overly simplified portrait of the American past, of course. The realities of the New Deal and the Reagan Revolution were never so uncomplicated as their respective mythologies suggest, and policy making in the American republic has always been constrained—by its framers' design—by gridlock, compromise, delay. But the confident Obamanauts weren't wrong to see, in the examples of presidential predecessors, case studies in how a successful political majority could be established and then govern and endure beyond a two-year electoral window. Nor were they wrong to think that the Reagan-to-Bush Republican coalition was exhausted, corrupt, out of ideas, and bereft of strong leadership, and that in a healthy political order, something new—either their resurgent liberalism or some renewed conservatism—would rise to take its place.

In a *healthy* political order. But in this order, no such new thing has arisen, because the Obama team was wrong not only about its own capacity but also about the capacity of the broader system to allow for normal policy making and a normal kind of governing coalition. The Obama experience began with grand ambition; it ended up illustrating one of Jacques Barzun's lines about a decadent era: that "institutions function painfully" no matter who's in charge. And while the Obama administration's failures weren't extraordinary front-page disasters like the Iraq invasion or the financial crisis, it was their very ordinariness that confirmed the reality of sclerosis—proving that even without a global economic meltdown or a massive intelligence cock-up, even with a team of cool technocrats supposedly taking over for the cowboys and bringing back light and reason, a consistent ineffectuality in American governance is just the way things are.

Thus it was ordinary that the Obama White House's technocrats, elected in the aftermath of a disaster created by private interests too intertwined with the public interest to be allowed to fail, presided over a further consolidation of the public and the private, a stronger Washington–Wall Street symbiosis in which banks and corporations were protected but home owners were left to suffer, and not a single important person went to jail.

It was ordinary that the White House's pedigreed wonks failed to anticipate the depths of the recession and pivoted to health care in defiance of the public's economy-first mood; ordinary that they designed a health care bill that had to be sold with a flagrant lie about how you could keep your plan no matter what; ordinary that the bill was pushed through in such a legislatively complicated way that its provisions were vulnerable to successive challenges in the courts; ordinary that its online rollout was botched, and the losers' pain drove political backlash that made further legislating difficult.

It was ordinary that after expanding the deficit, defensibly, to fight the recession, Obama would then fail to reach a bipartisan agreement to restrain the long-term growth of debt; after all, no major deal combining spending cuts and tax increases has been reached since 1991, twenty-eight years ago and counting. It was likewise ordinary that there wouldn't even be a revenue-neutral tax reform (the last one was in 1985), that there would also be no deal on immigration reform (the last one was in 1986), and that after posturing as a critic of presidential unilateralism, Obama would end up claiming novel powers in an effort to make immigration policy on his own. It was normal that he would do the same on health care and climate policy. It was normal that the day-to-day functioning of the federal system depended on government-by-brinksmanship, with debt-ceiling showdowns and fiscal cliffs and government shutdowns necessary preconditions for even modest deals.

Then, too, it was normal that in foreign policy the Obama administration would extend the war in Afghanistan into its second decade without any strategic plan for victory and, after an attempt at withdrawal opened the door to the rise of the Islamic State, extend the American presence in Iraq as well. After all, since the 1960s, the United States military has stopped winning wars and turned to simply managing them—toward defeat in the case of our fifteen-year Vietnam disaster; to permanent stalemate in the case of our almost twenty years in Afghanistan; to perpetual occupation in the case of our nearly thirty-year involvement in Iraq. It was also normal that the war where the Obama White House officially avoided both stalemate and occupation, our splendid little intervention in Libya, was actually a bigger disaster overall, with a North African power vacuum and a Europe-shaking migration crisis as its major legacies.

And it was entirely normal that the Libyan intervention, like the post-ISIS return to Iraq and the stumblebum attempts to influence the course of the Syrian civil war, lacked any specific congressional authorization, continuing a pattern of congressional abdication in foreign policy and domestic policy alike. It was entirely normal that the White House's chief diplomatic achievements, the Iran nuclear deal and the Paris climate accords, also lacked congressional authorization, meaning that they could be rolled back (and were) with the stroke of a successor's pen. And it was, finally, entirely normal that every other Obama initiative—the reset with Russia, the predictable Israel-Palestine push, the "pivot to Asia"—was in tatters by the time he left the White House.

Late in Obama's second term, a Brookings Institution scholar set out to analyze "major failures" in recent presidential administrations (with the obvious Iraq and 9/11-related examples, and the handling of Hurricane Katrina and the VA scandal as domestic templates). He found that "government had four failures during Reagan's final two and a half years (1.6 per year), five during George H. W. Bush's four years (1.2 per year), fourteen during Clinton's eight years (1.8 per year), twenty-five during George W. Bush's eight years (3.1 per year), and sixteen during Obama's first five and a half years (2.9 per year)."

Such analysis is fundamentally impressionistic, combining large and small examples, and a different definition would yield different averages. But as impressionistic assessments go, it sounds about right—and one can assume that the pre-pandemic pace in the Trump administration (with Puerto Rico after the hurricane and the child-separation disaster at the Mexican border as conspicuous case studies) would match the Obama-era rate, with only an inevitable deficit-expanding tax cut to offer as a meaningful legislative achievement, and with Trump's Ukrainian folly leading to the third attempted impeachment in the last fifty years, compared to just one case in the entire prior history of the republic.

Then, of course, the pandemic itself arrived, and outside the vaccine push, much of the public health response was a debacle—partially because of presidential flailing, but also because of more systemic problems, from bureaucratic failure to partisan gridlock to a class of leaders who were constantly suspending the rules for favored causes, or just for themselves.

This, too, is what normalcy means in an era of governmental decadence—a world where epic disasters come along to punctuate the more everyday expectation that the government will fail more often than it once did, that presidencies will effectively collapse more frequently, and that changing parties or chief executives can affect the scale of the failures but not their predictability and pace.

Welcome to the Kludgeocracy

Describing American government in these terms is not terribly controversial, though Obama partisans might dispute some of my specific critiques. Where there's vigorous disagreement is over *why* government fails so often; why the same Washington that once won global wars and built the atom bomb and sent human beings moonward now can't pass a normal budget; why a political system that used to produce reasonably durable governing coalitions now has wave elections constantly washing parties in and out of power.

Let's start with the more conservative-friendly explanations, which tend to focus on *the problems inherent in modern government's size and scale and postconstitutional drift.*

The most sophisticated version of this explanation doesn't just emphasize the basic problems with centralization and expert control that the free-market right always tends to emphasize. It also stresses the way that time makes these problems worse, as popular programs become part of an informal social contract that makes them nearly impossible to reform; as the administrative state gets barnacled by interest groups that can buy off and bludgeon would-be reformers; and as the proliferation of regulations handcuffs administrators and deprives them of the room to respond to changing times.

These patterns explain why even government programs that seem to work well enough when they are first implemented tend over time—over say, the eighty years from FDR's heroic age of liberalism to Obama's age of liberal frustration—to devolve into what Jonathan Rauch, in his Clinton-era book *Government's End*, described as a "large, incoherent, often incomprehensible mass that is solicitous of its clients but impervious to any broad, coherent program of reform."

The Obamacare case study is useful here, not least because it's a rare example where a meaningful reform, as opposed to just a deficit-funded tax cut or spending boost, did ultimately pass—unlike Clinton's health care fiasco, or Bush's doomed Social Security reform effort, or the Trump administration's Obamacare repeal-and-replace effort, or every attempted immigration reform deal. The opposition to the Obama health care bill was obviously ideological, reflecting a clash between libertarian and social democratic principles. But most Americans aren't thoroughgoing libertarians; indeed, even most Tea Partiers weren't thoroughgoing libertarians. The real reason that Obamacare opposition became so fierce, and the debate so toxic, was that the health care system as it exists is as Rauch described government as a whole: a huge sprawl of client populations and powerful interest groups, all of which have a strong financial stake in the existing system, and all of which have spent decades building up the lobbying shops and inner-ring knowledge required to either frustrate or redirect reform.

These groups start with the corporate actors that reformers tend to describe as "special interests," such as drug manufacturers and insurance companies—which is why there was no way for the health care reform to advance without the Obama White House buying off Pfizer and appeasing Aetna. But behind Big Pharma and Big Insurance stood a longer line of more sympathetic groups that might stand to lose from health care reform: seniors who receive Medicare and doctors who accept it; the patients and doctors and (above all) hospital networks that seem to overspend on health care and would therefore bear the brunt of cost control; middle-class and not-quite-rich families that don't want their taxes going up; middle-class near-seniors who would be squeezed if they're required to buy age-rated insurance;

struggling young people who would be squeezed if they're required to subsidize those fiftysomethings; union members who like the current health insurance tax deduction exactly as it is.

This thicket of clients and stakeholders and interest groups barely existed when Franklin Roosevelt was clearing the ground for the New Deal; it grew far more sparsely when Lyndon Johnson established Medicare and Medicaid. But those presidents' achievements fertilized and thickened it, leaving future reformers little choice but to do what Obama ultimately did and rely on inefficient and overly complicated workarounds, disguised or delayed tax increases, and, of course, some simple lies. Buy off some groups, hide the costs from others, promise some losers that they wouldn't really lose, play fast and loose with parliamentary rules when the backlash comes rolling in, and you can win an unpopular policy victory—which, because the reform creates new clients and the system frustrates change, your critics may find themselves unable to reverse even when they reclaim power.

I'm being hard on Obama, so it's important to stress that this is what *success* looks like. His administration really did expand health insurance coverage, however inefficiently and at however much political cost, and if the health care law has not lived up to the administration's projections, it also hasn't had the budget-busting effects that its critics feared. But the fact that a law as messy in its design and modest in its effects as Obamacare might be the best-case scenario for reform in an advanced and complex welfare state is an illustration of the larger point. At a certain size and scale of state spending and administrative complexity, and after a sufficient period of time has elapsed from the initial founding of the system (whether you date it to the progressive era, or the New Deal era, or the Great Society), sclerosis becomes the default state, interest-group conspiracies the default mode of governance, regulatory capture the default fate of attempted reforms, and any attempt to sweep the money changers from the temple will last, at best, a year or three before they find a way to rush back in.

But meanwhile, the voting public, while complicit in this process, also expects the government to act, to *do things*, to follow through on the promises that politicians inevitably make, or to respond to crises as they arise. This means there is still necessarily action in a sclerotic system; it's just likely to be extraconstitutional, carried out either by the president via executive fiat or by the portions of government that are insulated from the risks of backlash, the judiciary and the federal bureaucracy. Thus, most modern American policy making, as certain conservative critics predicted long ago, no longer takes place in the branch supposedly charged with making laws. Instead, Congress gratefully abdicates whenever possible, off-loading risk and responsibility to the courts and the White House and the administrative state—either by simple inaction or, in cases where legislation does pass, by punting hard questions to administrative rule makers and to litigation. This leaves the United States with a government that effectively functions via negotiations and power struggles between the judiciary, the Oval Office, and what Donald Trump likes to call the deep state.

Which, of course, produces policies that are more arbitrary and opaque and unstable and subject to sudden reversals than legislation forged in democratic deliberation. The political scientist Steven Teles, borrowing from computer science, calls this tendency "kludgeocracy," meaning a system in which every solution is basically "an inelegant patch put in place to solve an unexpected problem and designed to be backward-compatible with the rest of the system." As with computer programming, the pileup of kludges creates "a very complicated program that has no clear organizing principles, is exceedingly difficult to understand, and is subject to crashes." The frequency of these crashes feeds a quite rational public distrust of government, which makes legislators even more hesitant to do anything but posture. Which congressman wants ownership of the next HealthCare.gov rollout, the next border crisis, the next Libyan war, the next COVID-19 test development?

A difficulty for conservatives and libertarians who claim all of this as vindication, though, is that political conservatism has itself succumbed to the same forces, embraced the same temptations, accepted the same postlegislative approach to policy making. There are high-minded exceptions among Republican politicians—Mike Lee of Utah comes to mind—who would like to see Congress reclaim its powers and assert itself as the Constitution envisages. But for the most part, Republican controlled Congresses have been very comfortable with abdication; happy to see courts and presidents arrogate more power to themselves when they rule and dictate as Republicans would like. Likewise, there are conservative judges who genuinely believe in judicial restraint and deference to the elected branches. But in many cases the conservative movement has become comfortable with judicial activism in reverse; with using judicial power aggressively on issues where conservative legislators have either been defeated or (more often) simply fear to tread. And the rigorous conservative critique of big government often becomes, in the hands of Republican politicians, an excuse to simply protect the party's own interest groups—promising to save Medicare from Obamacare, to protect farm subsidies or corporate welfare from liberals looking to redistribute wealth, to reject big government for *them* while protecting big government for *us*. Indeed, in the age of Trump, it sometimes felt as though this interest-group protection racket was the entire Republican agenda.

Of course, a serious conservative or libertarian would argue that political conservatism's corruption is itself further vindication of its critique of governmental sprawl. But that tends to reduce the limited-government critique to a counsel of despair, especially since every advanced country has adopted some version of the welfare state, some kind of administrative bureaucracy, to manage large populations and complex societies. It may be impossible to prevent sclerosis in such systems, but waxing nostalgic for pre–New Deal America still seems like an insufficient response.

Polarization and Its Discontents

Which is why most nonconservatives are drawn to other explanations for our situation. Among would-be centrists and self-consciously bipartisan observers, a different nostalgia holds sway, one that yearns not for an age of smaller government but for a lost age of compromise, and portrays the expedience and cynicism of both Republicans and Democrats as the poisoned fruit of *the ideological polarization of the parties,* and the disastrous effects of polarization on a constitutional system whose architects never envisioned parties in the first place.

According to this theory the whole groaning system could still work reasonably well, the problem of government-by-interest-group could still be overcome, if the parties still worked the way they did in the 1950s: as motley coalitions with soft conservative and liberal tilts but no organizing ideology, no movement-based enforcement or rigid party line, and a collection of mildly corrupt party bosses and backroom dealmakers running party nominations and managing legislative negotiations. Ultimately the American order depends not just on the parties negotiating effectively under duress—in wartime or to avert economic crisis—but on their negotiating in the everyday as well, with congressmen willing to supply votes for a president of the rival party (as Republicans did for LBJ's Civil Rights Act of 1964, or as the Democrats did for parts of Reagan's tax agenda), and presidents capable of triangulating away from their own base (as Nixon did with some Great Society programs, or Clinton with welfare reform). And what's gone wrong, what makes that kind of negotiation now impossible, is a combination of polarization, rationalization, and (paradoxically) too much democratic control *within* the parties—layered atop a constitutional system whose myriad veto points make it impossible for a majority to govern if the minority simply votes in lockstep with its base.

The culprits in this account include the Democratic Party reformers of the late 1960s and early 1970s, who broke the power of the party bosses and unwittingly made dealmaking and compromise that much harder; Newt Gingrich, who transformed the early-1990s Republican minority into something much more like a parliamentary party, ideologically zealous and centralized around his leadership; Fox News and talk radio, which ratified this shift by holding Republican politicians to impossible standards of ideological purity; the rise of similar ideological enforcers on the left, from the Bush-era netroots, to MSNBC, to the activist left of the late Obama years; and then the politicians of both parties who saw advantage in consistently breaking the informal norms that kept Washington working, beginning with the Democratic defeat of Robert Bork's nomination to the Supreme Court in 1987 and escalating through nomination battles thereafter, all the way to Mitch McConnell's pocket veto of Merrick Garland, the slow death of the filibuster, and the threats of court-packing from the left.

But the deeper problem, according to this diagnosis, is that the American Constitution, in its very design, tends to break down when ideological conflict grows too intense. All those Madisonian checks and balances and veto points require some form of cooperation, but with ideological parties cooperation becomes increasingly impossible, and no branch has the kind of buck-stops-here position that the prime minister's office occupies in many parliamentary systems. In the happier case, this leads to a situation like our own, where the branches gradually stop working normally with one another, and government depends on Teles's kludgeocracy to muddle through. In the unhappier cases—as in certain coup-ridden Latin American countries that adopted imitations of our Constitution—the failure of the system's incapacity leads to attempted secession, civil strife, and eventually calls for strongman rule.

Strikingly, just as political conservatism manifests precisely the vices that conservative intellectuals describe as characteristic of politics under big government, so too does a certain kind of centrism flirt with the strongman temptation that its critique implies we face. I'm thinking here of the kind of self-consciously moderate pundits who compare American government unfavorably to the smooth efficiency of the Beijing Politburo . . . or the kind of "No Labels" independents who imagine some hybrid of Mike Bloomberg, Elon Musk, and James Mattis emerging to lead America out of polarization . . . or the not particularly ideological voters who thrill to the idea of a businessman-president who just get things done. If Trump's ascent reflected, in part, the pathologies of political conservatism, he also traded (like Ross Perot before him) on the populist version of this centrism, the sense that both parties are so corrupt that a demagogue who says, "I alone can fix it," is the businessman-caudillo that our gridlocked republic needs.

But it's not just centrists who emphasize the fateful weakness of our constitutional order in an age of partisanship; this diagnosis is a staple of liberal and left-wing rhetoric as well. The difference is that the left is more likely to envision more small-d democracy as the solution, and also more likely to insist that the polarization of the parties has been asymmetric, that the Republican Party more than the Democrats has yanked American democracy off center, and that much of our present discontent can be laid explicitly at the feet of a deranged contemporary right.

According to this thesis, it's not just that Republicans have leaned into polarization more than Democrats—it's that beginning in the late 1960s and early 1970s, the GOP's leaders made a devil's bargain with populism and xenophobia, and, over time, the populists and bigots and intransigents have simply taken over, rendering the party itself a threat to the republican order. If this is the case, then it's too bland to say that we don't have an immigration deal "because of polarization," or a fiscal grand bargain "because of polarization," or a better health care bill "because of polarization." We don't have those things *because of the Republicans*—because before, under, and now after Trump, conservatives have literally become insane, going full throttle into revanchism and reaction and paranoia in ways that have no analogue on the Democratic side.

Some part of this is obviously true, in the sense that the party that nominates an erratic reality-television star and birther conspiracist for the presidency is probably making a special contribution to our decadence. But the left's framing is too moralistic and deterministic about the deeper past and—oddly—too kind to recent Republican leadership. The GOP did absorb a lot of populist energy in the sixties and seventies, some of it racist and malign. But that kind of absorption is a normal thing in American history and, indeed, a healthy thing: you want populist concerns to be addressed through the major-party system; you want national leaders to be at once responsive and responsible, sifting legitimate concerns from bigotry and addressing them through policy rather than pure tribalism. And between 1970 and 2000, that seemed to generally happen in the GOP: as crime rates fell and welfare was reformed, the racial dog whistles also diminished, and the party seemed to have effectively brought a lot of white voters along to the more color-blind, outreach-oriented conservatism that George W. Bush imagined himself to be pursuing.

But what happened thereafter was that the Republican Party's Bush-led establishment (*not* its populist grassroots) presided over two disasters, the Iraq War and the financial crisis, that were more extreme than the normal gridlock and failure of our recent presidencies, even as diminishing returns from the Reaganite/neoliberal prescription left the economy in a general state of torpor. Then instead of learning, adapting, and repenting, both the Republican Party establishment and the right's media-entertainment complex spent the Obama years alternately riling up and ignoring their own voters, playing the politics-as-entertainment game and then complaining when their base expected them to deliver on their over-the-top sound bites. They became, in effect, the most decadent part of a decadent system, which left them particularly incapable of legislating and deal making and particularly vulnerable to a strongman—or at least the reality-television and Twitter version thereof.

The pattern of American politics under that Twitter strongman's presidency confirmed the reality of sclerosis while also suggesting that the Democrats might be its next victims. The story of the Trump administration was one of corrupt weakness, of would-be authoritarianism undone by incompetence, of continued abdication by the legislature and continued negotiation over policy between the courts and the executive, of continued stalemate between incompetent populists and disliked but still resilient elites. Meanwhile, the story of Trump's liberal opposition was one of half-accomplished transformation—whether constrained by the Biden presidency, time will tell—into an ideological formation, woke progressivism, that mirrors the decadent phase of the conservative movement in its ideological demands and airless certainties, and promises to deepen the larger stalemate in which the left and the right are locked.

The important thing to stress here, though, is that as with our discussion of the roots of economic stagnation, we don't have to actually choose between these varying explanations for political sclerosis; we can accept versions of them all. We can say that a system that grafts a twentieth-century administrative state onto an eighteenth-century constitutional system was bound to run into difficulties eventually; that a sprawling and ineffective big government and a nihilistic skepticism about government can be dangerously symbiotic with each other; that partisan polarization has contributed to the decay of our political process, and failures unique to the GOP and its leadership have accelerated it. We can also say that this decay exhibits the characteristic features of what I'm calling decadence, in the sense that it's a story of success (the antiquity and long endurance of America's constitutional order, the popularity of the foundational programs of the welfare state) as a precondition for sclerosis; of development (the increasing ideological coherence and even the voter-targeting efficiency of parties and campaigns) leading to gridlock; of a once-effective political order becoming impervious to constructive change.

But then, finally, we can say that too much focus on the particularly American aspects of this story is probably a mistake, because as in the economic and demographic realms, you can see a similar decadence at work—albeit on a different timescale—in the nations of western Europe.

The European Stalemate

If the distinctly American features of sclerosis were the only ones that matter, the Old Continent should be in considerably better shape. Europe has parliamentary systems with fewer veto points, smaller polities with more efficient governments (at least in northern Europe), greater accountability for bureaucrats, and less danger of extraordinary public-sector sprawl. It has center-right parties that have historically stiff-armed populism rather than embracing it, and a technocratic elite that's resisted the pull of polarization. It has a strong recent history of not only transpartisan but also multinational cooperation between different political factions and coalitions, all in the service of a grand civilizational project rooted in the optimism of the postwar period—the dreams of progress after the horror of war.

But that project, the European Union, has become a case study in decadence itself. Indeed, more even than America's groaning institutions, the present condition of the EU is a perfect example of how the pursuit of development and progress can lead eventually into cul-de-sacs, how the quest for some great good can carry on far beyond what the good actually requires, and how the same political genome can produce both vigorous growth and eventual sterility.

The good served by some form of European unity is obvious: friendship and cooperation and peace on a long-warring continent, free commerce among neighbors, easy travel across national borders for tourists, students, and pensioners. But the assumption of the men and women running Europe for the last two generations has been that if some unity is good, then more unity must always be better. If free trade works, then open borders would work better. If cooperation between nations was effective, then supranational government was the natural next step. If the Continent could have a common market, then it should naturally have a common currency as well. And at a certain point, that optimism ceased to be justified, and the Eurocrats found themselves building the infrastructure of sclerosis.

The centralization of authority alone—the rise of the Brussels bureaucracy and the clever-dick way that Eurocrats worked around inconvenient national referenda in order to push along political unification—would have been unwise enough. As Fukuyama points out, the process of EU centralization effectively sacrificed Europe's advantages in efficiency over the United States (the lack of veto points in its parliamentary systems; the greater accountability available in smaller polities) for the sake of a dream—a United States of Europe—that was never likely to actually take flesh. "With the shift of policy making away from national capitals to Brussels," he writes, "the European system as a whole is beginning to resemble that of the United States in depressing ways," with ever-greater influence for lobbyists and entrenched interests, a greater judicialization of politics, and a weakening of governmental legitimacy in the eyes of the (mis)governed. In effect, the centralizers of the modern EU created a regime in Brussels that imitated the worst flaws of Washington, DC, but with less democratic accountability and zero historical legitimacy.

Then to that basic unwisdom, the Eurocrats decided to add the common currency, which transformed their union from a merely unpopular and annoying bureaucratic superstructure into something more destructive, especially for the Continent's poorer nations—a Hotel California that offered immediate pleasures upon entry but imposed destructive terms when bad times hit and yet simultaneously made it nearly impossible to leave.

This peril should have been apparent from the start: the fact that a monetary union without a fiscal union didn't make sense, because the richer countries (the Germans, above all) wouldn't have any incentive to let the poorer countries weaken the currency and inflate away debts during downturns, was something that economists of every school could see. But in political terms, the only major opposition to the euro came from cranks and nationalists, whose resistance was dismissed as retrograde and failed almost everywhere save crankish, nationalistic England. Elsewhere, the momentum of the European project carried all before it . . .

. . . until the financial crisis hit, the easy money dried up, and the nations on Europe's periphery found themselves with crashing economies and soaring debts and no way to increase the money supply (as the United States did under Federal Reserve chairman Ben Bernanke). At this point, the answer from the Eurocrats was to simply use the disaster to push their project further: to concentrate more power in the barely democratic institutions at the center; to impose German fiscal terms on Greece, Spain, Italy, and Ireland; and to double down on a kind of no-choice politics that vitiated national sovereignty in the name of a central authority that lacked legitimacy to begin with.

This doubling down was not an accident. In his devastating history of the euro, *Euro Tragedy: A Drama in Nine Acts*, the Princeton University economist Ashoka Mody treats part of his entire story as a mystery: "Why," he asks, "did Europeans attempt such a venture that carried no obvious benefits but came with huge risks?" One answer, as the conservative writer Christopher Caldwell and others have suggested, is that the risks were seen as opportunities. Only in crisis, it was assumed, could the people of Europe be prodded and pushed toward ever-closer union. Only in an atmosphere of panic would nation-states cede the necessary sovereignty. Only a crisis in the monetary system would produce the incentives required to get, perhaps, to fiscal unity as well.

But in the event, this "disaster euro-ism" didn't produce the desired results. The German economy weathered the financial crisis well enough, so there were no political incentives for Angela Merkel's government to accept the kind of transfers to weaker European economies that are normal in a real federal system such as the United States—where rich states subsidize poor states with their federal tax dollars. In those weaker economies, and elsewhere on the Continent as well, the postcrisis push for centralized austerity helped produce a nationalist backlash; a revival of further-right and further-left alternatives. This backlash was also a response to the European elite's insouciance about mass immigration—an insouciance enabled by the Continent's democratic deficit—which peaked with Merkel's open-door response to the Syrian refugee crisis. The consequences were swift: Brexit in Britain, a populist government in Italy, a boost for preexisting nationalist governments in eastern Europe, a far right party gaining ground in Germany, the respectable center left collapsing everywhere from Scandinavia to Spain.

All of this turbulence, however, has not produced dramatic policy change. Instead, it's delivered European politics to a stalemate different from the American one, but equally enervating. Instead of two polarized parties, Europe has a center-right and center-left that are no longer powerful enough to really govern, challenged by a populism (right-wing in most cases, left-wing in a few) that's potent enough to disrupt but not sufficiently popular to rule. It has a central elite that's too unpopular to impose its will on the periphery, even as the periphery's leaders, however populist they may be, flinch from taking any step that might actually unravel the whole disastrous system. On the Continent, everyone wants to attack the EU, but nobody—not Viktor Orban in Hungary, not Matteo Salvini in Italy, not the radical left-wing party Syriza in Greece, not the nationalist Poles—is actually willing to swallow hard and accept the costs of an exit. And the place that actually has exited, Great Britain, became almost ungovernable in the process; a synecdoche for the entire European battle between weak and hapless centrists and too-zealous-to-rule populists.

Europe as a whole, then, has "progressed" in its unification to a point where it can neither go forward nor go back, and its nations have generally seen consensus break down to a point where the center is too hated but its populist rivals are still too feared for either group to govern. And this dynamic contributed to Europe's own struggle to contain the coronavirus—the fumbles of both technocratic and populist governments, the absence of an effective centralized EU response, and the strange echo of the Euro crisis in the way that the Germans managed relatively effective containment while their neighbors conspicuously failed. It was a different sort of political decadence than the kind manifested in Trump's incompetence, but the effects—and the number of dead—were very much the same.

The Abe Alternative

In East Asia, on the other hand, the successful suppression of the virus suggests that political decadence isn't evenly distributed across the developed world. So does the recent political experience of Japan, which is an exhibit for the argument that any effective response to political sclerosis would need to incorporate some elements of the populism and nationalism roiling Europe and America, rather than simply retreating to shibbolethic defenses of "norms" and "liberal values" that seem more like expressions of the ruling class's self-interest than solutions to stagnation and decay.

During the 1990s and early 2000s, the Japanese political system exemplified all the dysfunctions discussed in this chapter. The convergence of economic stagnation with legislative stalemate that's defined the developed world's experience arguably arrived in Japan first. In the twenty-three years from 1990 through 2012, Japan had fourteen prime ministers, and the job's essential impossibility seemed as permanent a fact as the island nation's anemic growth.

But between 2012 and 2020, Japan has had only one prime minister, Shinzo Abe, and he was arguably the developed world's most politically successful leader during that period, retiring for health reasons without any of the defeats suffered by other paladins of the technocratic center. Abe's tenure was defined by two approaches that are seemingly in tension but actually reinforcing. He was more culturally conservative and nationalistic relative to the late-twentieth-century Japanese norm, with a touch of Make Japan Great Again to his gestures, rhetoric, and historical claims. At the same time, he was willing to pursue bold and persistent social and economic experimentation to break the grip of stagnation, from unconventional monetary policy and fiscal stimulus, to a strong campaign to expand Japan's workforce (more women, more immigrants) and raise its subreplacement birthrate, which has indeed inched up relative to other East Asian nations. His "Abenomics" is possibly the most comprehensive attempt to fight stagnation in any major developed country; it's certainly the most prominent case where a sustained program has been carried out by a single elected political leader who has been generally rewarded for his experiments rather than undone by a backlash.

Yet if Abe shows that a certain political effectiveness is still possible under decadent conditions—that a populist-nationalist leader can be a policy innovator rather than just feckless or authoritarian or both—the experience of Abenomics to date also shows the limits of a single leader's energy. The structural reforms that are supposed to supplement his aggressive monetary and fiscal stimulus have stalled, the push to expand Japan's workforce has been halting, and the birthrate is higher than in South Korea or Singapore but still stuck around 1.5. Although the unemployment rate is low and the growth rate has been better under Abe than under his predecessors, that "better" is only relative, and the Japanese economy still keeps flirting with both deflation and contraction. Even a big program and a popular leader, it seems, only makes a difference on the margins: the dramatic acceleration that Abenomics aims for, the return to the pre-1990s growth, remains persistently out of reach.

If Japan shows some signs that decadence in politics and policy can be resisted, then, it also shows the limits that decadence imposes even on the most vigorous of statesmen. The Japanese case is also interesting because it went earlier than many other nations into the low-fertility trap, the apparent alienation of the sexes from each other, and the strange asexuality noted in the last chapter. And over the same period, Japan has also gone deeper into the virtual entertainments, video games, and pornography, which increasingly dominate cultural production in our age. Clearly, cultural practice, the state of a society's imagination, and the horizons of its creativity have a role to play in decadence—and it's to the state of culture under decadence that we will turn our attention next.

4

Repetition

In the autumn of 2015, when Star Wars fans were cheering trailers for *The Force Awakens* and political pundits like myself were still predicting confidently that Donald Trump would never be the Republican presidential nominee, there was a brief Internet-enabled celebration of "Back to the Future" Day—marking both the thirtieth anniversary of the original movie and the arrival of the precise date, 10/21/2015, to which Michael J. Fox's Marty McFly leaps forward from the Reagan 1980s in *Back to the Future Part II*.

The slightly daft commemoration encouraged conversations about which aspects of twenty-first-century life the *Back to the Future* sequel anticipated correctly: the Chicago Cubs finally winning the World Series; the national prominence of Marty's nemesis, Biff Tannen, whom the screenwriters had modeled on a certain orange-haired billionaire—and the disappointing absence of hoverboards and flying DeLoreans. But few of the online celebrants came to grips with the most striking thing about *Back to the Future*'s thirtieth anniversary: that we are now as far from the Reagan 1980s as the teenage Marty was from his parents' 1950s, and yet the gulf of years separating us from 1985 feels far narrower than the distance from the Eisenhower era the original film used to such great effect.

The power of the original *Back to the Future* depended not just on having its hero leap backward across some arbitrary thirty-year period, but on the radical cultural gulf between Marty's youth and his parents' postwar adolescent courtship. The past and future of the Robert Zemeckis film lay on opposite sides of (among many other things) rock 'n' roll, civil rights, Vietnam, the sexual revolution, drug culture, the moon landing, feminism, the apocalyptic 1970s, and, finally, the Reagan Revolution. The movie worked because its two settings were not just different times; they were completely different worlds, separated by just over a generation's worth of history.

Whereas if you had remade *Back to the Future* in 2015 and sent a Martina McFly back to '85, you would have a lot of quips about the shock of life without the iPhone, some amazing shoulder pads, and probably some sort of critique of Reagan-era unenlightenment on same-sex marriage and sexual harassment. But there wouldn't be the sense of visiting a past that's actually another country, because compared to the gulf separating the Eisenhower-era and Reagan-era versions of the fictional Hill Valley, California, the 1980s and the 2010s just don't feel that far apart.

A small case study: in the original *Back to the Future*, Marty McFly invaded his father's sleep dressed as "Darth Vader from the planet Vulcan." The joke was that the pop culture of the 1960s and 1970s could be passed off as a genuine alien visitation because it would seem so strange to the ears of a 1950s teen. But thirty years after 1985, the year's biggest blockbuster was a Star Wars movie about Darth Vader's grandkid . . . which was directed by a filmmaker, J. J. Abrams, who was coming off rebooting *Star Trek* . . . which was part of a wider cinematic landscape dominated by "presold" comic-book properties developed when the baby boomers were young. A Martina McFly visiting the Reagan-era past from the late 2010s wouldn't have a Vader/Vulcan prank to play, because her pop culture and her parents' pop culture are strikingly the same.

And not only at the movies: from the academic heights to popular bestsellers, from Christian theology to secular fashion, from political theory to pop music, a range of cultural forms and intellectual pursuits have been stuck for decades in a pattern of recurrence—of Barzun's "repetition and frustration" and "boredom and fatigue."

The Repetition Will Be Televised

Like the claim that technological change has slowed rather than accelerated, this claim may not be immediately intuitive, and a debate over cultural repetition is even more inherently subjective than the debate over technological stagnation. Though not completely so: you can measure, for instance, the share of major motion pictures based on so-called presold IP—meaning stories based on intellectual properties that have strong brand recognition—and see the decline of originality play out starkly at the box office over the last few decades. Similarly, you can tabulate the declining sales of literary fiction and calculate the increasing dependence of the publishing industry on recursive franchises and young-adult blockbusters. You can even quantify a striking turn toward repetition in pop music. One recent study found a sharp decline in the diversity of chords in hit songs, the number of novel transitions between the chords, and even the different timbres produced by the instruments involved. Another found that pop lyrics in Top 40 songs have grown steadily more repetitive since the 1960s. Yet another revealed that of the top thirty most-played Christmas songs, twenty-two were written in the youth of the baby boomers, between 1940 and 1970.

Still, these attempts at rigor are the exceptions; in the end, you have to accept a certain subjectivism in analyzing cultural forms. The best such analysis comes from a 2011 essay by Kurt Anderson in *Vanity Fair*, which I'll quote here at length:

> Rewind any other 20-year chunk of 20th-century time. There's no chance you would mistake a photograph or movie of Americans or an American city from 1972—giant sideburns, collars,

and bell-bottoms, leisure suits and cigarettes, AMC Javelins and Matadors and Gremlins alongside Dodge Demons, Swingers, Plymouth Dusters, and Scamps—with images from 1992. Time-travel back another 20 years, before rock 'n' roll and the Pill and Vietnam, when both sexes wore hats, and cars were *big* and bulbous with late-moderne fenders and fins—again, unmistakably different, 1952 from 1972. You can keep doing it and see that the characteristic surfaces and sounds of each historical moment are absolutely distinct from those of 20 years earlier or later: the clothes, the hair, the cars, the advertising—all of it . . .

Go deeper, and you see that just 20 years also made all the difference in serious cultural output. New York's amazing new buildings of the 1930s (the Chrysler, the Empire State) look nothing like the amazing new buildings of the 1910s (Grand Central, Woolworth) or of the 1950s (the Seagram, UN headquarters). Anyone can instantly identify a '50s movie (*On the Waterfront, The Bridge on the River Kwai*) versus one from 20 years before (*Grand Hotel, It Happened One Night*) or 20 years after (*Klute, A Clockwork Orange*), or tell the difference between hit songs from 1992 (Sir Mix-a-Lot) and 1972 (Neil Young) and 1952 (Patti Page) and 1932 (Duke Ellington). When high-end literature was being redefined by James Joyce and Virginia Woolf, F. Scott Fitzgerald and Ernest Hemingway, great novels from just 20 years earlier—Henry James's *The Ambassadors,* Edith Wharton's *The House of Mirth*—seemed like relics of another age. And twenty years after Hemingway published his war novel *For Whom the Bell Tolls*, a new war novel, *Catch-22*, made it seem preposterously antique.

Now try to spot the big, obvious, defining differences between 2012 and 1992. Movies and literature and music have never changed less over a twenty-year period. Lady Gaga has replaced Madonna, Adele has replaced Mariah Carey—both distinctions without a real difference—and Jay-Z and Wilco are still Jay-Z and Wilco. Except for certain details (no Google searches, no e-mail, no cell phones), ambitious fiction from 20 years ago (Doug Coupland's *Generation X,* Neal Stephenson's *Snow Crash,* Martin Amis's *Time's Arrow*) is in no way dated, and the sensibility and style of Joan Didion's books from even twenty years before that seem plausibly circa 2012.

. . . Not long ago in the newspaper, I came across an archival photograph of Ian Schrager and Steve Rubell with a dozen of their young staff at Morgans, the ur-boutique hotel, in 1985. It was an epiphany. Schrager's dress shirt had no collar, and some of the hair on his male employees was a bit unfashionably fluffy, but no one in the picture looks obviously, laughably dated by today's standards. . . . Yet if, in 1990 or 1980 or 1970, you'd examined a comparable picture from 27 years earlier—from 1963 and 1953 and 1943, respectively—it would be a glimpse back into an unmistakably different world.

As a part-time movie critic, I can attest that this pattern is at its most extreme in the film industry, where the economics of the business depend increasingly on the constant recycling of famous properties that originated as mass-market entertainments between the 1930s and the 1970s. Unoriginality is, of course, hardly new in Hollywood, but there has been a meaningful trend away from novelty and creativity over the last generation. Genre forms have always trumped pure innovation, but the range of genres has recently constricted: the romantic comedy has essentially disappeared; the teenage farce, likewise; and there hasn't been a hugely successful original comedy in the American market since *The Hangover* in 2009. We have reached a point where comic-book and sci-fi franchises "are not a big part of the movie business," as Mark Harris wrote for the online magazine *Grantland* in an era-defining essay in 2017:

They are not the biggest part of the movie business. They *are* the movie business. Period. . . . Almost everything else that comes out of Hollywood is either an accident, a penance (people who run the studios do like to have a reason to go to the Oscars), a modestly budgeted bone thrown to an audience perceived as niche (black people, women, adults), an appeasement (movie stars are still important, and they must occasionally be placated with something interesting to do so they'll be cooperative about doing the big stuff), or a necessity (sometimes, unfortunately, it is required that a studio take a chance on something new in order to initiate a franchise). A successful franchise is no longer used to finance the rest of a studio's lineup; a studio's lineup is brands and franchises, and that's it.

Even the exceptions to this rule, the still-creative portions of pop cinema, are often tethered to the boomer era. When big-screen science fiction isn't just a straight-up eighties-vintage franchise movie—a *Star Wars* or *Star Trek* or *Alien* or *Predator*—it's usually a strange multilayered exercise in recursion, like Denis Villeneuve's *Blade Runner: 2049*, which trades on a peculiar nostalgia for an eighties dystopia that's tellingly more technologically proficient than our own, or Steven Spielberg's *Ready Player One*, in which the hero's journey of the future takes place inside a virtual world built from the pop culture that the youthful Spielberg helped create. And then there are still-stranger cases, like the *succes de scandale* of 2019, Todd Phillips's *Joker*, which both its fans and detractors treated as something novel and radical—an upending of superhero clichés in the service of a politically engaged or politically dangerous message of despair or revolution. In reality, the movie was just a competent, handsome imitation of Scorsese's harsh depictions of 1970s New York, embedded in the endlessly rebooting DC Extended Universe to make it marketable, linked to the problems of 2019 primarily by wishful thinking.

In other realms, the pace of repetition is sometimes slower and the quality of the material more impressive, but you can still see the same cultural recursions. There is often more creativity in today's television than at the movies, as a thousand think pieces attest. But mass-audience TV still keeps trying to resuscitate shows such as *Roseanne* and *Murphy Brown*, while it keeps *The Simpsons* and *South Park* on life support and recycles endless variations on *Law & Order*. Meanwhile, the golden age of television that played out recently on cable, with its antiheroes and gritty takes on classic American genres (the Western in *Deadwood*, the gangster movie in *The Sopranos* and its imitators, the detective story/police procedural in *The Wire*, the office drama in *Mad Men*) is essentially a small-screen version of the 1970s-era golden age of the Hollywood auteur—the age of Scorsese and Francis Ford Coppola and Robert Altman, their work impressively imitated but not necessarily reinvented by the smaller screen's auteurs. The fantasy worlds and dystopias of *Battlestar Galactica* and *Game of Thrones* and *The Handmaid's Tale* offer the same "gritty-reboot" treatment to genres that came into vogue forty years ago, when dystopia and nostalgia first conquered the more gee-whiz, optimistic forms of sci-fi. Even at its most creative, television struggles to escape the shadow of the boomer era, the patterns set two generations back.

None of this is meant to diminish the originality of writer-directors such as David Chase, David Simon, and Lena Dunham, who really did pioneer a richer and more daring approach to televised storytelling than what had heretofore existed; nor is it to deny the rarer possibility of cinematic greatness even in the Marvel Age. (Even in a decadent society, it is possible to produce a pop masterpiece.) But it's telling that even the great shows of the early 2000s often felt vital and relevant precisely because they were so good at *holding up a mirror* to frustration, futility, repetition, decay, corruption—in a word, to decadence. Think of Tony Soprano's famous lament: "It's good to be in something from the ground floor. I came too late for that, and I know. But lately, I'm getting the feeling that I came in at the end. The best is over." That could serve as the epigraph not only for the portrait of the American upper-middle class (mobbed up and otherwise) in that show but also for the portraits of the modern American city's politics and culture in *The*

Wire; the portrait of Washington, DC, in shows such as *House of Cards* and (rather less self-seriously) *Veep*; and other decadence-infused productions, from *Breaking Bad*, to *True Detective*, to *Girls*. The stagnationist, tech-skeptical view of Silicon Valley as a lot of money and ego and talent chasing a lot of essentially small ideas is also the view served up by Mike Judge's *Silicon Valley* on HBO. Nowhere is Barzun's image of a "falling-off" in Western life more vividly embodied than by Walter White and his frustrated ambitions, or Hannah Horvath and her drifting urban pals. (Something similar is true in literary fiction: its cultural currency has declined with its sales, and the breakout exceptions are often fictions—the work of Michel Houellebecq, the bad-hookup *New Yorker* short story "Cat Person," the novels of Sally Rooney—that replace the old nineteenth-century marriage plot with stories about how the sexes struggle to relate to one another anymore.)

And TV's golden age may have been a temporary thing, succeeded quickly by the rather different age of "peak TV," in which the flood of content is overwhelming but also often algorithmically optimized, tending inevitably toward its own forms of repetition, mediocrity, the safe imitation of more daring forms. This transition to decadence can even happen midshow, as it did in the concluding seasons of *Game of Thrones*, whose showrunners rushed to the finish line because they hoped to helm (what else?) another *Star Wars* sequel, and whose source material dried up because George R. R. Martin became too rich and famous and in demand to do the hard work of invention—leaving his attempted revision of J. R. R. Tolkien's great original to languish, a victim of its author's overwhelming, creativity-swallowing success.

The Eternal Return to 1975

The Anderson account of repetition and stagnation applies to intellectual and ideological realms as well. Famous 1970s-era texts such as Christopher Lasch's *The Culture of Narcissism*, Tom Wolfe's essay

"The 'Me' Decade and the Third Great Awakening," and Robert Bellah and his coauthors' sociology of American religion, *Habits of the Heart* seem entirely relevant to American culture today, whereas their equivalents from the 1950s—*The Lonely Crowd*, say, or *The Man in the Gray Flannel Suit*—feel like dispatches from a lost world. A book like Ta-Nehisi Coates's *Between the World and Me* earned frequent comparisons to James Baldwin's *The Fire Next Time* because its indictment of American racism could have been written in 1975 as easily as in 2015. A popular problems-of-feminism *Atlantic* cover story such as Anne-Marie Slaughter's "Why Women Still Can't Have It All" essay from 2012 could have its cultural references tweaked and be dropped into 1978 or 1994 without anyone noticing.

The same goes on on the right, where Jordan Peterson's popular tracts against the dangers of postmodernism are fresh and shocking only if you don't remember the 1980s; if you do, they're mostly a reminder that it's been almost forty years since postmodernism was actually radical and new. More generally, the conservative critique of academic liberalism was distilled in the three decades between William F. Buckley's *God and Man at Yale* in 1955 and Allan Bloom's *The Closing of the American Mind* in 1987, and everything in the three decades since Bloom just recycles or reiterates their points.

This is somewhat defensible because the academic politics that conservatives are critiquing keep cycling through the same recurring patterns, too, with the campus battles of the 1960s giving way to the PC wars of the 1980s giving way to our own social justice struggle sessions. Admittedly the progressive fervor that crested in the pandemic summer of 2020 carried academic ideology into new territory, colonizing newsrooms and Hollywood and corporate America, bringing wokeness closer to the status of a reigning ideology. Yet even so, as Musa al-Gharbi noted in a 2019 essay for the website Heterodox Academy, many of the ideological frameworks and buzzwords of the "awokened" activists—the special emphasis on victimhood and trauma, concepts of language-as-violence, the rhetoric of "safe spaces" and "microaggressions" and more—date to the Vietnam and post–civil rights era, the coming-of-age of the baby boom. Likewise with other supposedly novel forms of radicalism: Police and prison abolition are activist causes from the 1960s, before the crime wave soured Americans on that particular style of utopianism; the vogue for polyamory brings the open marriages and "key parties" of the 1970s around again.

Meanwhile, the academic precincts from which these ideas have emerged, or reemerged, are on the same elite campuses, the same Very Important Schools as held sway over American higher education and high culture sixty years ago. There is no list more decadent in its stagnation and repetition than the *U.S. News & World Report* college rankings.

The reality of recurrence may be slightly harder for progressives to acknowledge than conservatives, because progressivism is more invested in its supposed position at the vanguard of cultural change, pressing boldly on to new frontiers. This makes it difficult for the left to recognize the generational recycling of its ambitions and anxieties: the fact that many progressive "breakthroughs" are just the culture cycling back to something that we did not that long ago—up to and including kick-ass female action heroes such as Wonder Woman (who followed a path blazed by Sigourney Weaver's Ripley in the *Alien* movies, or the robot-wrangling Sarah Connor in the *Terminator* movies, or even the blaster-wielding Princess Leia in *Star Wars* forty years ago) or the African American heroes in *Black Panther*. (In truth, individual black stars were arguably more important in the years of Eddie Murphy and Richard Pryor and *The Cosby Show* and early Oprah and Denzel than in our officially representation-obsessed age—though in our age the proliferation of channels and streaming services certainly creates more roles and opportunities for minority actors and directors overall.)

But if conservatives are a little more comfortable discerning cyclical patterns in history, on the conservative side there is a temptation toward apocalyptic thinking. The hour is always late, the demon of postmodernism or cultural Marxism is taking full possession, and *this* is the era that will bring about the final dissolution of traditional values/Christianity/America; *this* is the moment when the left's commissars succeed in shutting down right-wing and religious speech and criminalizing political incorrectness and finishing conservatism's long defeat.

A little more perspective, though, would suggest that many of our culture war debates, though they burn hotter and colder at different moments (and have different partisan valences depending on cynicism and self-interest), reflect the same recurring cycle of hard-to-resolve arguments created by the genuine revolutions of fifty or sixty years ago. Social change has not ceased, certainly, but many of today's changes are aftershocks from those revolutions rather than new earthquakes. Many of our left-wing social movements, no less than Trumpian populism, are rooted in disappointment rather than optimism, emphasizing unmet promises and changes that were supposed to come and didn't. And on many fronts a defining feature of the culture war is still stalemate, today as much as thirty years ago.

Gay rights is the great exception, where a genuinely dramatic and rapid change in public attitudes convinced progressives that it was possible to simply settle culture war debates. And then, when that conviction was tested by the election of Donald Trump, the progressive mood somewhat understandably swung from triumphalism to hysteria—from the arc of history bending toward justice to the dark night of fascism descending.

But other examples point more toward an age of déjà vu. The corporate-sponsored Pride parades and Caitlyn Jenner magazine cover stories are new and striking; for the 5 percent of the population that's gay or transgender, the last forty years have indeed brought about a revolution. But in the larger arenas of race and sex and religion, the rapid sociological changes that followed the 1960s have given way to stasis. The white-black wage gap narrowed dramatically from the 1940s through the 1970s; it has neither narrowed dramatically nor widened dramatically since. So too with residential and educational segregation: when you control for the decline of the white population, they have neither worsened nor improved. The male-female wage gap narrowed dramatically across the 1970s, then the narrowing slowed, and despite Lean In and #MeToo, it has flattened out (and even, among younger workers, slightly widened) since the early 2000s. Both Black Lives Matter and #MeToo feminism are reacting against this stagnation, this sense of a revolution left unfinished. Like more overtly nostalgic movements on the right, they are reaching back to what was promised decades ago, trying to recover lost possibilities, trying to shake free of stasis.

Meanwhile, the country is clearly more libertarian on sexual issues than two generations ago, but public opinion on abortion, the crucial issue for culture war divisions, has been remarkably stable since the 1980s, with thermostatic moves toward "pro-life" under Democratic presidents and "pro-choice" under Republicans. The rise of the "nones," people with no religious affiliation, is an important post-1990s shift in the United States. (Less so in Europe, where the broad trend toward secularization was mostly accomplished by the 1980s.) But most of that disaffiliation has been among Americans who were already basically nonchurchgoers. Church attendance rates declined dramatically across the 1960s, mostly driven by Catholicism's crisis after the Second Vatican Council; they have declined at most marginally since the 1980s, and Protestant churchgoing has not declined at all.

Against these backdrops, the similarities between the Clarence Thomas Supreme Court confirmation fight in 1991 and the 2018 Brett Kavanaugh confirmation fight, between the current Black Lives Matter moment and the O. J. Simpson– and Rodney King–era debates about police brutality in the mid-1990s, between abortion debates in 1990 and the abortion debate today—even between the sexual scandals of Donald Trump and the sexual scandals of Bill Clinton (albeit with the parties supporting the priapist reversed)—are not coincidental. They reflect what Barzun calls the constant "deadlocks of our time": the persistent controversies that await some new dispensation to be transcended or resolved.

That pattern extends beyond culture wars to other ideological debates in American politics, where the left-wing and right-wing coalitions have generally been locked in place since the Reagan Revolution, stalemated not only politically but also intellectually, cycling through the same domestic arguments, the same basic range of issues and ideas. The reason that American conservatives are so persistently nostalgic for the Reagan presidency, now more than thirty years gone, and the reason that liberals remain fascinated with their 1960s-era icons is that so little has changed politically since the upheavals that took place between Jack Kennedy's assassination in '63 and Reagan's '80 victory. Or to borrow Mark Steyn's time-travel conceit from an earlier chapter: most of today's policy arguments, rhetorical frames, constituencies, and interests groups would all be more recognizable to a time traveler from the early 1980s than the debates of the late 1970s would have been to a voyager from the Depression era arriving in the age of Carter. The overall battle lines have shifted, mostly in the more individualistic direction: the right won some economic victories in the 1980s and 1990s, the left won some cultural victories in the 1990s and 2000s. But many, many arguments (over race, abortion, taxes, welfare) look very much as they did two generations ago. And even conscious attempts to break this deadlock end up, at least provisionally, reaffirming it: Donald Trump's victory in 2016 was built on a real break with his party's Reaganite orthodoxies, but much of his populism evaporated upon contact with the unpopular-but-entrenched Republican agenda in Washington, DC.

Likewise in religion, where the conflict between traditionalists and progressives within Christianity and Judaism has been stalemated for forty years, with seemingly new developments—the election and liberalizing efforts of Pope Francis, the repeated stirrings of a progressive evangelicalism—swiftly bringing the same exact moral and theological debates to the surface, with the same predictable results. And outside those warring camps, the big story in Western religion is often the absence of interesting stories. The religious center today is the same vague spiritual individualism, the "moralistic therapeutic deism" blending New Age and Christian elements, that writers such as Lasch and Bellah first described in the 1970s. What's missing is ferment and experimentation of the kind that yields religious renewal within existing institutions (as has happened often within Catholicism and established Protestantisms) and yields competitors as well: Mormonism, Christian Science, the Jehovah's Witnesses, the Seventh-day Adventists, Pentecostalism, and even, God help us, Jim Jones, David Koresh, and Scientology.

As with other features of decadence, there are advantages in religious mediocrity; just ask the late inhabitants of Jonestown. But the dangers and excesses of cults may be the price a religious culture pays for innovation, renewal, spiritual genius. When Netflix recently aired a documentary called *Wild Wild Country*, a portrait of an Indian guru and his American devotees who tried to build a utopian commune in the high desert of Oregon forty years ago, the lunacy of the effort was obvious—but so was the boldness, the yearning for transcendence, the willingness to believe in a life-changing message and a holy man.

There is less of that spiritual ambition in the Western world today. The decline in "the number and scale of controversial fringe sects" since the 1980s, historian of religion Philip Jenkins argued recently, is both "genuine and epochal," and a bad sign for the vitality of the religious center—since such mad experiments on the fringes often indicate that more mainstream religions have a "a solid core of spiritual activism and inquiry." (The cults we do have, like the NXIUM "sex slave" operation that was the subject of multiple recent documentaries, are distinguished by their lack of metaphysical ambition, their banal corporate-life-coach spirit.) And the religious torpor betokened by the decline of cults can be linked to intellectual torpor generally—the religious element in the culturewide feeling, to borrow from the pessimistic Peter Thiel, that there are fewer and fewer "secrets left to be discovered."

This torpor extends to skeptics and atheists as well. For all the excitement and debate in the mid-2000s around the so-called "new atheism," their school was just about the least new thing under the sun, recycling arguments that were new and controversial in the eighteenth century, as though nothing had been written—including by atheists!—in the interim, and as though nothing had happened in the intervening years to make anyone doubt the idea that abolishing belief would lead us into a radiant tomorrow. The genuine tensions in postreligious thought—above all, the difficulty reconciling a hard neo-Darwinian materialism with a liberalism that still tacitly depends on Christian metaphysical concepts and moral absolutes—shadow the contemporary atheist manifestos, obvious and yet entirely unresolved. The alternatives to Christianity that might make a post-Christian liberalism cohere, from deism to pantheism, fire a few imaginations, but much of the secular intelligentsia seems content with a basic incoherence in its worldview, content with an agnosticism that treats the essential questions about the nature of the universe and the destiny of man with a weary "Who's to say?" sort of shrug.

This shrug limits the possibilities for vigorous anticlericalism, a Jacobin or Marxist anti-Christianity. It means that the pressure on traditional religion from secular elites is real but soft; a matter of social pressure and legal harassment that falls far short of persecution. But the soft push meets a soft pushback, an exhausted and incoherent secularism wrestles weakly with an exhausted-seeming and internally divided Christianity—and neither exercise much real influence over the spiritual but only somewhat religious territory in between. Meanwhile, the voices that have confidently predicted a new Great Awakening at various moments since the seventies, a sudden spiritual revolution or Christian revival—which was supposed to follow Communism's collapse, or be associated with the turn of the millennium, or happen in response to the shock of 9/11—look like the voices predicting radical technological transformation over the same period; the last two generations have not produced the changes that they prophecied.

Their prophecies may eventually be vindicated, of course. Just as technological stagnation need not last forever, a cultural revolution powerful enough to escape the gravitational pull of decadence may even now be taking shape. Maybe Trump is the last gasp of white male conservatism, and woke progressivism will carry all before it in a way that the seventies-era New Left failed to do. Maybe wokeness is it self the awakening that we've been waiting for—an essentially spiritual movement that will fill the space left by the decline of Mainline Protestantism, and create a new era of religious reform and moral purpose. Maybe the current recycling of New Age impulses from the 1970s—the renewed interest in astrology, the dabbling in woke and alt-right forms of neo-paganism—will be more than just a repetition of the Age of Aquarius; maybe it will join with the implicit theology of progressivism to deliver the West to a fully post-Christian religious synthesis. Or maybe Pope Francis's attempted liberalization of Catholicism will succeed in rescuing liberal Christianity from irrelevance; maybe religious traditionalism will ride the populist moment back to influence.

Or maybe all these trends give an illusion of forward movement and momentum, when they're actually bearing us ceaselessly back, back toward 1975.

Is Google Making Us Boring?

But surely it can't still be the 1970s in an arena that had barely been imagined in the Ford era! What about the exception to the technological stagnation: the Internet, with all its wonders. Surely that is generating some cultural innovation? Doesn't Kurt Anderson brush away too much by reducing the Internet to "certain details," because surely the digital age has led to the *invention* of cultural forms, invisible in meatspace but immersive when you dive into the pools within your screen? Photos of our era may look strangely like photos of 2000 or 1990, but that's because we don't see YouTube or Wikipedia or Facebook or Instagram in photographs; we don't see blogs or tweets or podcasts; we don't see the fantastic gaming realms; we don't see the fashions and identities that people assume and take off and play with on the Internet; we don't see all the engineering that goes into building these virtual worlds, these digital cathedrals of our time.

Some of this is true: as the digital is the exception to technological stagnation, so digital culture is a partial exception to cultural repetition. But just as we should hesitate to oversell the Internet and recognize that some of the boosterism around tech is a response to the absence of technological progress elsewhere, we should hesitate over the claim that Internet culture represents what it initially claimed to offer: a small-d democratic renaissance, a revolt of eccentricity against conformity, a place where the individual talent could find an audience without having to climb up the usual ladders or compromise with the machine.

That story was more plausible fifteen years ago, when online was fresh and new and strange. But just as tech as a business has consolidated rapidly, with the Amazons and Facebooks dominating and start-ups competing to be bought, so too has tech-era culture become consolidated as well, with more homogenization than diversification in many sectors. The economics of the Internet turn out to favor a culture of conformity; as Miles Klee wrote recently in *MEL* magazine, "The Internet promised exponential divergence but congealed into another monoculture." When Napster and then iTunes wrecked the record industry, or Amazon "disrupted" the book business, the new landscape did sometimes allow for more amateurs to break through. But it mostly favored name brands and superstars because their brands became *more* important in the absence of the old middlemen.

So the publishing industry now runs more than ever on star power, and it's harder to make a living as a midlist author than before; likewise, the music stars who can dictate terms online and make a fortune touring are still flush, but the medium-power acts—which are also, in many cases, the most artistically interesting—have lost market share and money. The anticreative trends in the movie business are only likely to be heightened if the Internet finally collapses the old theatrical-release business model, leaving a few Netflix/Amazon/Disney content behemoths and their algorithms in charge of which movies get made and delivered to your media device, which classic films get streamed or promoted (hint: not many), which Marvel character gets a movie or which extremely recent animated classic gets a live-action reboot next. The same goes for the competition among art forms for patronage, attention, dollars: movies, music, and television have weathered the transition to the Internet era far better than classical music or ballet or art museums, which have all seen similar superstar effects (New York museums still attract huge crowds; not so much elsewhere) while their audiences generally decline. And the pandemic has clearly accelerated all these trends: crippling movie-theater chains, driving an ever-large audience to algorithmic content and tiny-screen experience, and devastating every art form that depends on live performance.

Or take the culture industry where I make my living: the world of journalism. When I started my career in the early 2000s, there was a lot of bright talk about how blogging and other Internet-specific forms were going to revolutionize a hidebound business—bringing outsider creativity and intellectual diversity and a global perspective to the stuffy pages of newspapers and magazines. In some parts of the Internet, this happened: there are talents in journalism today that never would have been nurtured without the World Wide Web, richer debates in some quarters than took place on traditional op-ed pages, and an access to expertise and an exposure to intellectual subcultures that wasn't possible in print.

But this is the minor theme of the last twenty years of journalism. The major theme is, again, cultural consolidation—a landscape in which the big players (like my current employer) flourish or at least

survive, and the middle tier of institutions, the local and regional players especially, are eviscerated, with the coronavirus offering a more-
sudden-than-expected coup de grace. A democratized, low-dollar
landscape of content production turns out to favor the mob, not the
eccentric talent, as anyone who has spent time on social media can attest. The various critiques of the old mainstream media, from the right
and the far left and weirdos everywhere, had real teeth, but the blog-
gers of the early 2000s didn't overthrow the mainstream media; the
best of them were absorbed by mainstream institutions, and the rest
became Twitter cops and Facebook ranters, joining the conformist
horde that now determines—with an assist from friendly algorithms—
what exactly people read and share and hate-click. Just as online video
mostly spreads smut rather than nurturing auteurs, in overthrowing
the centrist staleness of the old media, the Internet has mostly given us
a bumper crop of hackish crap, of political pornography for the partisan mind, of news coverage whose problem isn't its fakeness so much
as its crushing mediocrity.

Even the true marvels of Internet culture have this problem. Nothing like Wikipedia would have been possible in 1910 or 1950. Its
crowdsourced capaciousness is a miracle, and I delve into its pages
for some reason or another practically every day. But it is still a consolidated product, a cultural monopoly, the only online reference of
its scale and reach. There were three different old encyclopedias kick-
ing around my parents' home, and a bookshelf full of history books
whose information was harder to "access" than Wikipedia entries but
far more detailed and diverse in the perspectives it presented. On the
Internet, unless you're a true specialist, anyone who sets out to research the art of the fifteenth century or the music of Mozart or the
antiquity of China will start in the same place, find the same deposit
of information, encounter the same hive mind—a hive mind that is
larger than the team that wrote the 1910 *Encyclopædia Britannica* but
hardly immune to bias and groupthink, and skewed in its own strange
ways toward the obsessions of the male, the tech oriented, and the

Very Online. And a hive mind that, unlike the authors of the old *Britannica* and its competitors, can't produce a single perfect sentence, a single memorable turn of phrase, save by accident in the back matter of some obscure entry that the teams of homogenizing editors might forget to touch.

Which, again, raises the problem of mediocrity. To the extent that the medium of online determines the cultural messages it carries, it pressures creators to make things clickable, browsable, capable of holding attention briefly, but always with the understanding that the reader or watcher will swiftly move on to the next hyperlink, the next video, the next tweet or status update or Instagram pic. It is not impossible for genius to flourish under such constraints, but depth becomes a near impossibility; not for nothing did Nicholas Carr title his powerful critique of Internet culture *The Shallows*. If the hit single has survived Napster and then iTunes, the old-fashioned album emphatically has not, and there's an argument—infuriating to novelists, but possibly true—that the novel ceased to matter to mass culture on June 29, 2007, the day Steve Jobs introduced the iPhone. The philosophical treatise, the hard poem—to the extent that form follows function, these belong to print rather than to screens, and it's not remotely surprising that the decline of the fine arts has accelerated under the dominion of the Internet.

Nor is it surprising that the two genres that currently dominate online are political polemic and pornography—because both are ideally suited for a click-here-then-there medium, in which the important thing is to be titillated, stimulated, get your spasm of pleasure, and move on.

The Endless Autumn of the Baby Boom

But maybe blaming our machines for cultural mediocrity is too easy, when the real problem, hinted at throughout this chapter, is that we're all cultural prisoners of the baby boomers. This is not, I promise, a preamble to a rant about how the boomers were simply the destructive and solipsistic force depicted in conservative polemic and resentful millennial and Gen-X backward glances. They *were* destructive and solipsistic, but the same is true for many individual geniuses, and like many an impossible-to-deal-with artist, the '68 generation's inflated self-image is somewhat justified by the real creativity and ferment of its youth.

Boomers can't claim direct credit for all of that ferment, since many of the men and women who made the 1960s *the Sixties* had been born before (slightly before, for the musicians and novelists; well before, for the intellectuals and theologians) the technical beginning of the baby boom. But the boomers were young during the last great burst of creativity in Western history; the last great surge of mass cultural invention. And the genius of sixties rock and seventies cinema, the importance of feminism, libertarianism, and environmentalism to subsequent events, the stamp left by protoboomers like the Beatles and Bob Dylan and full boomers such as Steven Spielberg and Steve Jobs, is all real, no matter what kind of moral judgment one passes on the era as a whole.

But if one gives this kind of cultural credit to the 1960s and the 1970s, why the subsequent stagnation as the boomers passed from youth into influence and power? Shouldn't a truly fertile period yield more fertility thereafter, instead of just repeating itself endlessly in reenactments of the 1960s campus protests, plus reboots of *Star Trek* and *Roseanne*?

Not necessarily. In an essay on "Golden Ages" in his book *Prejudices: A Philosophical Dictionary*, the late sociologist Robert Nisbet suggested that an age of great aesthetic or intellectual achievement is usually defined by what he calls a "dialectical antinomy." By this, he meant that for the "blaze of creativity" to leap up often requires strong ideas and trends and forces that are in clear tension with one another—for instance, a strong communitarianism and a strong individualism, strong secularizing trends and a powerful understanding of the sacred, revolutionary moral ideas and a powerful moral consensus.

One doesn't have to call the 1960s and 1970s a "golden age" in full—the seventies were obviously more glitz and tinsel and depravity—to see that this description fits the era well. The boomers were the last rebellious generation to come of age not only with various traditional edifices still standing but also with a sense, in the Eisenhower fifties, that those edifices had actually been *strengthened* by the experiences of the Depression and World War II. This gave the rebel culture of the sixties a real adversary to struggle against: the old bourgeois norms refreshed by suburbanization and prosperity; a Christianity that had just experienced a sustained revival; a patriotic narrative of history that had been burnished by victory in the Second World War; a common culture that had become more binding through the influence of radio, television, mass-market periodicals, and movies. The old men of that world, the father figures to be wrestled with and overcome, were war heroes and giants—literally so in the cases of Lyndon Johnson and Charles de Gaulle. The old forms were still powerful and vital, and so to subvert or overthrow or replace them, the new forms had to be powerful as well.

And they were, for a time. The boomer utopianism that now feels rote, dated, and commercialized was a genuine revolution when it first emerged, and it *had* to feel like a revolution because it was attacking something that still felt confident, rooted, possibly enduring. Sit down with the first season of *Mad Men* or an equivalent primary source and then watch the 1970 Woodstock documentary and marvel at the antinomy. Read a sheaf of *New Yorker*s from the heyday of William Shawn, E. B. White, and James Thurber, and then read your way through the New Journalism—starting with Tom Wolfe's savaging of Shawn, and then on through Garry Wills, Joan Didion, and Hunter S. Thompson—and you'll see a conflict between two potencies, two strong cultural approaches, with the younger one not just tearing at weak points but also feeding off the older order's strength. Pick up a novel or a memoir whose characters inhabit the pre–Vatican II Catholicism of the 1940s and then read the liberalizing theologians whose work defined the Catholic 1960s and 1970s, and you'll see one generation's confidence clashing with another's, a liberal certainty blazing up to overthrow a religious culture that felt timeless just a few short years before.

In each case, the important thing is the tension; the way a multitudinous younger generation's utopianism, libertinism, mysticism, and skepticism drew on the older generation's traditions and attachments, on the education it had received in the older culture, while rejecting or reworking the older culture's core commitments. Thus Wolfe draws vitality from Shawn even as he knifes him; *The Wild Bunch* and *McCabe and Mrs. Miller* exist in fruitful tension with John Ford; Karl Rahner embeds a revolutionary theology in the older frameworks of the neo-Thomists; Bob Dylan tells people "The Times They Are A-Changin'," but his Nobel years later depend on all his literary antecedents. In each case, there is an easy confidence that there is still a common culture undergirding everything; that a critique or revision will be understood not only on its own terms but also in relation to what went before; that people will appreciate the new thing because they recognize what's being challenged or remade.

But Nisbet writes in the same essay that this kind of antinomy doesn't last forever, and when the older order crumbles too quickly and dramatically, golden ages give way to ages of iron easily. "If there is no community," then "there is nothing to challenge, nothing to fuel the dynamism" required for a golden age, and if there is nothing *but* transgression, there is nothing to give acts of transgression the "purpose, substance, and meaning" that make them something more than just self-indulgence.

Both problems haunt our age. Everyone still fancies themself a rebel, and corporate titans posture as countercultural and revolutionaries. But the traditional forms and structures that once gave rebellion purpose and clarity persist only as inertial holdovers that nobody explicitly defends—or else as shadows of themselves in the unfashionable hinterland, their remaining strength a purely negative force that exists mostly to persuade the cultural elite that they haven't won yet; that they're still the same rebels they were in 1968.

They aren't, but neither have they built up a new culture strong enough to generate its own antinomies. This is why the iconoclasts of 2020 mostly went after statuary from the pre-boomer era, seeking the same frisson as the sixties generation by attacking antique monuments that nobody in the current elite particularly cares to defend: Nothing the boomers built offers so exhilarating a target. And it's also part of why you get so much recursion and repetition and recycling: it's the desire to relive the heroic age of counterculture in a world where the counterculture mostly won, and it's the attempt to make pastiches and remixes out of a new culture that's still too shallow and superficial, too weakly rooted, to lend the remix makers what they need.

Think of it, once more, as a problem encapsulated by *Star Wars*. The original movie was a brilliant boomer director's pop pastiche that referred to classical cinema in a hundred different ways; its genius was heavily dependent on the cinematic past, on Akira Kurosawa and Leni Riefenstahl as well as *Flash Gordon* serials and Joseph Campbell's theory of myth. That pastiche ushered in a new model of filmmaking, the special-effects blockbuster, that George Lucas then tried—admirably, in a way—to bring to its own inherent perfection in the prequel trilogy twenty years later. But without the classical referents, his own creativity was wildly insufficient, and he made movies that play like an alien culture's attempt to re-create a human drama based on earthling stories sent back and forth through a translator sixteen times. Which in turn led the makers of the next round of Star Wars movies—the round currently ongoing, and going, and going—to give up on originality entirely and just make not a pastiche of classic films but *pastiches of the original pastiche.*

The distinction between decadence and cultural vitality, between our own era and the years of the baby boomers' youth, is laid bare in that dispiriting progression. The vital culture critiques its own tradition; the decadent culture just repeats the critique more loudly or crudely or tediously. The vital culture makes a bricolage of classic stories; the decadent culture remakes the bricolage with a slightly different cast and a few plot beats swapped around. The vital culture creates fans de novo; the decadent culture performs "fan service." The vital culture is a workshop; the decadent culture is a museum.

Can the End of History End?

One important prophet of this museum culture was Francis Fukuyama, whose end-of-the-Cold-War magnum opus, *The End of History and the Last Man*, anticipated some of the tedium and repetition I've described. The "end" that Fukuyama discerned, contrary to many subsequent smug dismissals of his thesis, was not an ending of *events*—an end to wars or calamities or economic setbacks. Rather, it was the end of a particular dialectic of ideas, the "common ideological heritage of mankind," which had led from the feudal and hierarchical past to the egalitarian present, and which Fukuyama suggested had ended, with the mid-twentieth-century defeat of fascism and then the final crashing fall of the Communist alternative, in a victory for liberal democracy that left no other serious ideological possibilities standing.

There could still be dictatorships and autocracies and would-be revolutionaries in Fukuyama's world, there could still be reactionaries and radicals who rejected the liberal democratic settlement, and there could still be limits to liberalism's global rule. But in the realm of ideas, these alternatives were just atavisms, capable of making trouble for the liberal consensus and capable of wounding liberal civilization, but unable to fire the human imagination in a way that would make it possible to overthrow the liberal order and put something equally capacious in its place.

Fukuyama was often accused of being a liberal triumphalist, but the conclusion of his original essay was somewhat mournful about the scenario he described. "The end of history will be a very sad time," he wrote. "The struggle for recognition, the willingness to risk one's life for a purely abstract goal, the worldwide ideological struggle that called forth daring, courage, imagination, and idealism, will be replaced by economic calculation, the endless solving of technical problems, environmental concerns, and the satisfaction of sophisticated consumer demands. In the posthistorical period, there will be neither art nor philosophy, just the perpetual caretaking of the museum of human history." And then: "Perhaps this very prospect of centuries of boredom at the end of history will serve to get history started once again."

So even Fukuyama didn't imagine that his "end" would be eternal—and as a provisional description of the post-1989 world, the landscape that I'm calling decadent, his "end of history" label is a reasonable fit. Certainly much of the intellectual repetition and frustration described in this chapter feels like frustration at being unable to imagine something new, to discern "clear lines of advance," in Barzun's phrase, to escape the political and moral and even theological limits imposed by late-modern liberalism, to reclaim some lost arcadia or reach boldly for heaven or utopia.

This end-of-history frustration has stalked even—or especially—our radicals and reactionaries, from the antiglobalization movements of the 1990s, to Occupy Wall Street, to Antifa; from Al Qaeda to ISIS. Protests can shut down cities, and terrorists can blow up buildings, but there has been no program that Islamists or anarchists or Marxists can offer that actually threatens the dominion of late-modern liberalism. The best movie about radical politics under decadence remains 1999's *Fight Club*, which dramatized a distinctively male discontent with the end of history, with mediocre commercial culture and physical pampering and the nightmare of Ikea, by sending its protagonists hurtling through anarchist and fascist phases toward a climax in which they blow up skyscrapers and achieve—well, most likely, absolutely nothing.

Two years later, this happened in reality. September 11 killed thousands and spurred America into various foreign policy disasters, but Al Qaeda did not *win* anything from it, history in the Fukuyaman sense did not actually resume in 2001, and all the neoconservative and liberal-hawkish intellectuals who seemed to *want* it to resume almost as much as their Islamist enemies—the intellectual figures such as Norman Podhoretz and Paul Berman, who clearly wanted to find in Islamism the grand rival that would give the Western consensus a real fight, who would restore purpose and vigor amid decadence—ended up sending thousands of young Americans to die for a "clash of civilizations" that had only tinpot dictators and sectarian guerrillas and cave-dwelling terrorists fighting on the other side.

The same sense of futility attended the ideological responses to the Great Recession. Here was a shock to the system of the kind that Marxists had long predicted, here was a crisis that was also an opportunity for something novel to be born—and yet for a time, the main result was elite consolidation, German bankers bestriding Europe, Barack Obama and Mitt Romney tilting for the presidency in the emptiest possible campaign. "Never since the end of World War II, and perhaps since the Russian Revolution," Mark Lilla wrote in the *New Republic* in 2014, "has political thinking in the West been so shallow and clueless." By this, he meant not only that no new worldview had risen from the ashes of Communism to challenge the liberal democratic/ capitalist consensus, but also that people increasingly didn't even understand why anyone searched for alternatives to that consensus in the first place: "Try to convey the grand drama of political and intellectual life from 1789 to 1989 to young students today—American, European, even Chinese students—and you are left feeling like a blind poet singing of lost Atlantis."

That was seven years ago; the question of our moment is whether his analysis still holds. Lilla wrote those words before Trump, before Brexit, before China's slide toward digital totalitarianism under Xi Jinping's presidency-for-life, before it became commonplace to argue that the liberal order had entered into crisis, and before the pandemic delivered an undeniable crisis on a scale unseen in a century. The consensus now is that this time may really be different—that unlike 2001 or 2008, in 2020 the end of history might genuinely be over, that ideological alternatives are finally returning and events are accelerating again, that sterility and repetition is giving way to something at once more dangerous and more interesting, as the end of decadence would inevitably be. Even Fukuyama himself has joined the chorus: in his latest book, *Identity: The Demand for Dignity and the Politics of Resentment*, he argues that identity politics, the desire for recognition from groups and tribes and nation-states, might end up destroying the liberal democratic order from within.

The next two sections of this book will consider whether this sense of an ending and a new historical beginning is justified. Certainly it might be: because all things end, decadence must end, and ours may indeed be ending even as you read this book describing it.

But it is to the other possibility—the potential resilience of decadence, its possible sustainability across decades yet to come—that our attention will turn next.

PART 2

Sustainable Decadence

5

Comfortably Numb

In 1989, facing the electric chair, the prolific serial killer, rapist, and necrophile Ted Bundy granted an interview to the evangelical Christian activist James Dobson. Bundy wanted to explain the real reason he had become a mass murderer: it was, he told Dobson, the influence of hard-core pornography.

"I was essentially a normal person, I had good friends, I lived a normal life except for this one small but very potent, very destructive segment of it that I kept very secret and close to myself, and didn't let anybody know about." Porn was the "indispensable link in the chain of behavior" that led to rape and mass murder, Bundy claimed. "Like an addiction, you keep craving something harder . . . until you reach a point where the pornography only goes so far."

Bundy was a sociopath who delighted in spin and manipulation and fashioning self-exculpatory narratives, and Dobson was probably just his final mark. But if the serial killer was lying or at least exaggerating, he chose a lie that played into widespread 1980s-era fears. The social revolutions of the 1960s and 1970s had made porn more readily available, more explicit, and often more gleefully degrading; those same revolutions had been accompanied by a crime wave that included rising rates of rape and sexual assault. It wasn't only evangelicals like Dobson and other social conservatives who discerned a link between the 1972 porn film *Deep Throat* and sexual violence, between *Hus-*

tler magazine publisher Larry Flynt and male predation. The most provocative figures in 1980s feminism, Catherine MacKinnon and Andrea Dworkin, took the link for granted, offering arguments that Bundy either illustrated or appropriated—that porn validates rape fantasies and desensitizes its male users to violence, forcing them to first seek out more extreme scenarios and material and, finally, to attempt to create such scenarios in real life; to impose on female bodies the pain they first thrilled to in a magazine or on a screen.

Since Ted Bundy met his maker, we have conducted an extended social experiment that puts this thesis to the test. The age of *Hustler* has been succeeded by the age of Pornhub, of websites that make pornography more available by far than it was even at the peak of Flynt's notoriety—available immediately, available constantly, available at more impressionable ages, and in more extreme and varied forms. Hard-core pornography now passes for sex education for so many American teenagers that there are programs for disadvantaged youth that try to reeducate teens out of their porn-fixed assumptions about what the opposite sex expects. The power of big data is increasingly used to push porn users toward exactly the extremities that 1980s antiporn activists feared—making them desensitized to the vanilla and the tame and the boringly consensual, encouraging sadism and masochism and the union thereof, cultivating kinks and fetishes that, absent the Internet, most people wouldn't know they had.

If the unlikely Reagan-era alliance of Dobson and Dworkin, Christian moralists and feminist puritans, had been correct in the causal line they drew between pornography and rape, you would have expected the Internet era to make the crisis of sexual violence that much worse. There would be more Bundys and many, many more of the less Grand Guignol sort of predator, since under the tutelage of the Internet, male rapists would be trained and nurtured from their early teens and sent forth in adulthood primed to seek the most violent sort of pleasure, the darkest sort of thrill.

But that hasn't happened. Despite the rule of online porn, and de-

spite the Internet's obvious role as a vector for grooming and predation, the data we have on sexual assault suggest that rates of sexual
assault fell as the Internet was introduced and spread, as porn went
from a magazine-and-video product to an instantly-available-for-free
commodity, as more and more young Americans were sexually initi-
ated and trained by online hard-core smut.

Every data source has its problems, and the crime statistics that
show falling rates of rape miss many unreported assaults. There may
also be a concentration of victimhood, in which Internet-abetted sex
trafficking and grooming makes it easier for predators to identify and
exploit a pool of the most vulnerable women instead of stalking and
assaulting a larger group. But even allowing for increases in sex trafficking and underreported rapes from hookup culture, there is no
good reason to assume that rape reporting has become dramatically
worse over the last twenty-five years, which is what you would need to
believe to hold that the Internet has made the overall problem of male
sexual violence worse.

This means that if ubiquitous hard-core porn turns men into predators, some other countervailing force—the influence of feminist ideas,
better policing, stricter punishment, the general crime decline—has
been counteracting that effect. But it's also possible that the effect
actually runs the other way: that for many men, the fantasy worlds
of pornography are a substitute for every kind of real-world in-the-
flesh sexual behavior rather than a spur to sexual aggression. And, indeed, there is some evidence for precisely this contention. When the
economist Todd Kendall examined rates of sexual assault in US states
where the Internet spread fastest or slowest, he found a clear correlation between Internet access and declining rates of rape. Changes to
antipornography laws in European countries offered similar natural
experiments and similar results: the sudden availability of porn coincided with fewer sexual assaults. In the United States, a team of UCLA
researchers surveyed a large population of sex criminals and found
that they recalled using less porn than the average male. The desensi-

tizing effect that MacKinnon and many others had predicted showed up in the research too: constant porn use did seem to make normal arousal more challenging for many users; normal sex less immediately attractive. But the effect of that deadening was to send many users ever deeper into fantasy, ever deeper into virtual playgrounds, rather than out into the real world in search of victims.

The Safety of the Virtual

There's no social science experiment that can prove the "more porn, less rape" theory definitively. But the correlation offers a possible example of a definite pattern in late-modern life, in which the spread of immersive virtual entertainments has coincided with safer social behavior among the generations immersed in its pleasures—even pleasures that would be obviously antisocial or wicked if indulged outside the friendly confines of a screen. The same coalition of would-be censors that rallied against porn in the eighties also rallied against violent video games, which evolved swiftly from crude alien-shooting arcade games to simulacra in which any young person with a console could be an assassin or soldier or gangbanger for an hour or a day. But the *Grand Theft Auto* era was not an age of rising violence or "superpredators" or any other extrapolation from the crime wave that began in the 1960s; instead, as first-person shooters were honed and perfected, general teenage and twentysomething violence fell and fell and fell.

As went violence, so went other social indicators among the young. Teen sex and teen pregnancy dropped with the spread of the Internet; so did teen smoking, teen binge drinking, and teen drunk driving. In 1992, 42 percent of American teenagers had been in a fight; by 2015, that figure was 22 percent. In the era of the teen TV soap *Beverly Hills, 90210*, which premiered in 1990, 10 percent of adolescents had lost their virginity before age thirteen; only 4 percent enjoyed that dubious distinction in the age of Snapchat. "Today's teens are better than you, and we can prove it," ran a 2016 data-journalism headline—and the data, indeed, proved that teenage life in the 2010s was physically safer than at any point in the recent American past.

Well before the coronavirus forced everyone into full-time online existence, there was a large-scale substitution of electronic entertainment and virtual communication for the real-life behaviors that once led teenagers into peril and temptation. Whether via video games or pornography or just the buzz of online social life, the virtual makes it possible to spend a social (or at least "social") teenage life much more indoors and at home than in the past, which in turn reduces the risks that come with driving too far, partying too late, drinking too much, hooking up incautiously, and generally behaving in the ways that traditionally made adolescence dangerous. This commonsensical observation, that an indoor childhood is safer than an outdoor one, has been confirmed by the heightened virtuality of life in 2020: death rates have risen for all adult Americans, because of the coronavirus itself and some of its attendant costs, but for kids and teenagers they have fallen sharply.

Notably, all this safety and good real-world behavior is not making young people happier. Not surprisingly the Covid experience has made many of them particularly miserable, but even pre-pandemic there was a fair amount of evidence that teenagers in the Internet age are more stressed out, more anxiety ridden, more prone to depression than teenagers in the more dangerous past. But their unhappiness is a form of anomie, not a spur to acting out; the only violence such misery seems to be definitively encouraging is suicide attempts, the one form of old-fashioned teenage folly that's increasing in the age of the iPhone.

Every trend has outliers, and, for a tiny subset of the population, the virtual world might be encouraging acts of extreme violence or depravity. The school shootings that dominate our news and social media feeds, especially, may have escalated in a mimetic effect that's mediated by the Internet. But mass killing is an empty, nihilistic form of protest, terrorism without a cause, an act of megalomania that by its nature refuses solidarity with anyone except fellow pathological narcissists. And it terrorizes the *rest* of the teenage population into greater caution, greater care, with armed guards at schools and a lower tolerance for the kind of common teenage misbehavior that doesn't end in killing. So the mass shooting isn't just a gory, awful, still-extremely-rare counterpoint to the major teenage trend in the Internet age. It might also be encouraging the general tranquilization of teenage life; offering an occasional spasm of terror that ratifies the broader trend toward safety, caution, peace, and sometimes, in the most unhappy, quietus.

Nor is this tranquilizing effect confined to adolescence and its perils; it also extends to young adulthood and its responsibilities. When male workforce participation rates remained stubbornly low after the Great Recession, a group of labor economists noticed that young men especially were working less and seeking work less eagerly than older men—a trend that defied the normal recessionary pattern. These same men, the researchers found, were distinguished from their elders by the fact that they were playing *a lot* of video games—and drawing on survey data, they argued that the men were actually substituting video games for working and job seeking, placing a higher value on entertainment and leisure and a lower value on employment than a similar cohort had back when video games were less immersive. Overall, at least 20 percent of the 2005–2015 decline in workforce participation, the researchers estimated, was explained by the appeal of *Call of Duty* and *Red Dead Redemption*.

The immediate policy problem here, how to get these men back into the workforce, could be solved to some extent by higher wages. In the years following 2015, at least some of the gaming men were coaxed back into employment by a stronger economy, which led to Twitter japes about how the video games must have gotten worse. But even if gaming as a substitute for work only really becomes more appealing during recessions, the timing of that appeal makes it a cultural version of what economists call "automatic stabilizers." That term normally refers to welfare-state programs, unemployment insurance, and the like that kick in during recessions to help keep households and the wider economy afloat. But the same idea could be applied to social life. An unemployed young man is a natural troublemaker, a potential radical, tempted by criminality, open to religious appeals, drawn to ideological extremes. Whereas an unemployed young man with a gaming console is more occupied, more entertained, more at peace with his situation—and less likely to create trouble for the stagnant society that can't offer him a remunerative job. Which in turn makes stagnation itself more sustainable, because disappointment doesn't burn as hot, and rebellious urges are diverted into shoot-'em-ups with aliens.

One of the societies that has advanced furthest along this path, as I noted earlier, is Japan, which as it entered into economic stagnation and demographic decline also became one of the world's leading producers and consumers of video games and outré forms of porn. (The sex-robot future is being pioneered there as well.) Japanese society now has a rich taxonomy of terms to describe the young people, and especially young men, who have embraced virtual pleasures instead of real ones: *soushoku danshi* ("grass-eating boys"), *parasaito shinguru* ("parasite singles"), *sekkusu shinai shokogun* ("celibacy syndrome"), and more. It also has maintained an impressive social stability—low crime rates, safe streets, the traditional Japanese emphasis on honor and decorum—throughout its lost decades and political stalemates and despite the decline of its traditional familial culture. The specifics of this combination are particular to Japan, but the general pattern has obvious relevance to other rich societies. Years of "Isn't Japan weird?" coverage in the Western press have given way to a recognition that the Japanese may be just a little bit ahead of the rest of us; that their combination of virtual extremes and a peaceful, sexless descent into societal old age may be a template rather than an outlier.

For all that it relies on stimulation, then—on the allure of virtual sex and the thrill of virtual violence—virtual reality in this sense also bears a certain resemblance to the lotus plant encountered by Odysseus in his famous travels. A society in thrall to digital entertainment offers its inhabitants the opportunity to experience savage and orgiastic pleasures on a scale far beyond what the real world could ever provide. Yet it also appears in some respects to be a realm of peace and order and care and good behavior and somewhat sleepy pleasures, because the kind of people the young and discontent above all—who once threatened real turbulence and disruption and even revolution are inside texting or sexting, masturbating or playing a first-person shooter, as contented and harmless as the lotus-eaters.

Listening to Soma

Then, too, our age also offers more literal varieties of the lotus plant. Those well-behaved young people are the most medicated generation in history, from the drugs prescribed to ADHD-diagnosed boys to the antidepressants prescribed to anxious teens. Most of the medications are designed to be calming, relaxing, offering a smoothed-out experience rather than a spiky high. The increasingly legal drug of choice for adults is marijuana, which its advocates argue doesn't inspire as much dangerous behavior as alcohol and hard drugs, making the prototypical stoner a far more harmless figure than the prototypical drunk. This argument is contested, as is the evidence to date on legal pot's effect on crime and mental illness. Even the evidence that it sometimes encourages aggression, though, might mean that the drug resembles the Internet in making a small minority more violent but tranquilizing the majority—so that for most people, a stoned society is more likely to be a dreamily contented society than an unstable or angry one, and the spread of pot will make an age of stagnation seem mostly like a chill good time.

Then there is the opioid epidemic, which swept across the unhappiest parts of white America without anyone noticing because the drug itself quiets rather than inflames, supplying a gentle euphoria that lets its users simply slip away, day by day and bit by bit, without causing anyone any trouble. It's not that there aren't bursts of violence associated with the opioid trade, or addicts willing to commit murder for a fix. But, generally, Americans have ended up dying in record numbers from opioids *without* the kind of crime wave or murder spike, without the turbulence and chaos, that accompanied the crack epidemic. As the essayist Andrew Sullivan wrote for *New York* magazine in 2018, "The drugs now conquering America are downers: they are not the means to engage in life more vividly but to seek a respite from its ordeals." And unlike pot, opioids are antisocial drugs, offering bliss that's best experienced in solitude. Instead of the munchies, they make you indifferent to food; instead of supercharging the libido, they make you indifferent to sex. "Once the high hits," writes Sullivan, "your head begins to nod and your eyelids close." The best book on the epidemic, by the journalist Sam Quinones, is called *Dreamland* for a reason.

None of the commercial marijuana products or illegal fentanyls can yet match the qualities of Aldous Huxley's "soma" in *Brave New World*—the "perfect drug," one of his dystopia's boosters says cheerfully, offering "all the advantages of Christianity and alcohol" without religious guilt or hangovers. Soma is manufactured and distributed precisely in order to maintain social stability, but our own somas aren't so consciously designed; they're more dangerous, more unevenly distributed, and less universally desired. But they have some clear Huxleyan effects, insofar as they offer a temporary exit from ordinary discontents for precisely the kind of people who might otherwise be inclined to rebel or smash things up, to join a cult or start a revolution, or to opt out like the early Christians in some radical, society-altering way. They wreck lives, but they may also stabilize society; they cull unhappy people, via suicide or overdose or just a numb unhealthiness, but it's all a personal choice (or, at least, a "choice") rather than the kind of imposed-from-above social Darwinism that might provoke resistance. They don't solve social problems; indeed, they worsen them—just ask the babies born to opioid addicts, the small towns ravaged by drug overdoses—but at the same time, they prevent those problems from having the broader consequences that a society without so many drugs and distractions would expect to experience.

And the drugs pair with the virtual entertainments in the same way that soma pairs naturally with other features of the *Brave New World* World State. Huxley's perfectly stabilized society had the "feelies"— essentially VR sex. We are not so far away from something similar, at the place where sex robots and Oculus Rift converge. Our society doesn't repress youthful lust and aggression so much as it stimulates them safely through video games and smut; his dystopia had the mandatory Violent Passion Surrogate, administered "regularly once a month. We flood the whole system with adrenin. It's the complete physiological equivalent of fear and rage. All the tonic effects of murdering Desdemona and being murdered by Othello, without any of the inconveniences."

Our own versions are not so far advanced and our society is not, of course, so stable. But under decadence, the Western social order has taken a decidedly Huxleyan turn, with social trends that simultaneously vindicate one cultural-conservative premise—that choice alone doesn't make people happy, that the unbound individual is likely to become a slave to entertainments and a refugee in his own mind, that pot and circuses inevitably succeed family and religion— while proving a different conservative expectation wrong. From the 1960s onward, conservative critics of a triumphant boomer liberalism predicted that rampant individualism would make society itself dissolve; that fewer fathers and weaker churches and a general hedonistic ethos would mean more crime, more violence, more overt social breakdown. And Western trends from about 1965 through about 1990 seemed to vindicate that premise. But then something changed, and without the social fabric obviously reknitting—without the revival of civic or religious life or the strengthening of community attachments and family bonds that people on both sides of the culture war earnestly desired—crime rates fell, and teenage delinquency diminished, and the pattern of everyday life became more stable and law abiding and simply safe.

The social revolutions of fifty years ago led to a certain kind of chaos, in other words. But thanks to virtual escapism, the one great technological achievement of an otherwise stagnant age, the decadence that came in afterward looks surprisingly sustainable.

First as Tragedy, Then as Playacting

By now, the reader will probably have an obvious objection: What about politics? If the main effect of porn and video games and iPhones and pharmaceuticals is to keep people indoors and uncoupled and somewhat unhappily well behaved, to substitute entertainments for reality, to tranquilize the young as well as the old and middle-aged, then surely there is an exception in the deranging effect that social media seems to have on people's relationship with politics. Would a tranquilized society really reproduce Weimar Germany or the 1969 Days of Rage protests on social media, with online mobs swarming and death threats flying and the old extremes back in action once again? Would a society of lotus-eaters produce a populist surge and a socialist revival, a domestic civil war so intense and polarizing that people on both sides could mistake the work of a Russian hacker for the sincere convictions of their fellow citizens? Would a tranquilized society elect Donald Trump as president?

Strangely, the answer might be "yes." The populist surge, the madness of online crowds, the way the Internet has allowed the return of certain forms of political extremism, the bizarre ascent of a reality-television president, the proliferation of conspiracy theories and weird political subcultures among the most extremely online Westerners, the spread of fake news in all its varied forms—yes, if our decadence is to end in the return of history, ideological combat, street-brawl politics, and utopianism, then this *might* be how that ending starts. But it might also represent the way that virtual reality manages the political passions, not by fomenting real revolution but by encouraging people to playact extremism, to reenact the 1930s or 1968 on social media or a Reddit thread or a YouTube video channel, to approach radical politics the way they approach a first-person shooter game—as a kind of sport, a kick to the body chemistry, that doesn't actually put anything in their relatively comfortable late-modern lives at risk. A good Facebook brawl or Twitter mobbing might be the political equivalent of Huxley's Violent Passion Surrogate, delivering all the tonic effects of joining the Weathermen or the Black Panthers or Benito Mussolini's March on Rome with none of the physical inconveniences. The Internet might be bringing back the dramas and tragedies of history, only as a stage production, a costumed farce.

Likewise with Trump himself: Where was his abnormality, his incipient authoritarianism, most manifest? Where else but on his Twitter feed. As the actual, real-life president, he was weak, not strong, hemmed in, not unbound, overwhelmed by the job rather than bending its powers to his will. In the real world, the world of legislation and policy making, Trump-era politics were the same politics of gridlock and stalemate as before, with lots of lying and more corruption and occasional forays into cruelty from the man at the top but nothing resembling the ascent of *real* authoritarians in the *real* 1930s. There was a virtual Trump presidency whose depredations terrified liberals, and a virtual presidency that aired on Fox and on his phone in which he goes from strength to strength. But the real thing was often still closer to the genre the president knows best—reality television—than to the return of pre-1989 history.

Up to a point, of course. Trump's virtual presidency eventually met the challenge of the coronavirus, which was unmoved by partisan narratives and reality-show posturing alike, and once it did the consequences were disastrous. And the surprising real-world peace that characterized the first few years of his administration—the striking absence of the campus marches and the urban unrest that many people, myself included, had expected his election to engender—broke down as his presidency failed: in 2020 the country's virtual conflicts finally spilled over fully into the world of flesh and blood, with street protests and riots on a scale unseen in thirty years.

But it remains to be seen whether that spilling-over, the George Floyd protests and the battles in Portland and Kenosha, represented a decisive shift in American life, an end to virtual politics and the return of real-world action, or whether it was a temporary spasm in response to the suspension of some of decadence's automatic stabilizers—the sudden disappearance of sports and movies and other entertainments, the closure of schools and workplaces—that's likely to be supressed as the pandemic ebbs and normalcy returns.

Some of the ideological rearrangements at the top of American life in 2020 were notable, but perhaps less revolutionary than they seemed (more on that in subsequent chapters). Meanwhile the socialist candidacy of Bernie Sanders failed once the coronavirus arrived, the fate of the George Floyd marchers' more radical demands is uncertain, and it's quite possible that the crime wave that accompanied the protests will make 2020 and its aftermath a condensed reenactment of the 1960s and 1970s—radical ambition giving way to disorder giving way to backlash giving way to stalemate, but over a year or two rather than a decade.

In the same way, the political violence associated with the riots, the clashes between protestors and cops and between left-wing and right-wing agitators, was more than serious than the pre-2020 norm—but the question of *how* serious remains. Some of the action still felt more analogous to school shootings than to the political clashes of the 1930s or the 1960s, in the sense that it involved disturbed people appointing themselves as knights-errant and going forth to slaughter, rather than organized movements with any kind of strategy or concrete goal. Other violence, especially the fights between anarchists and militia types, Antifa and Proud Boys, has had more of a 1930s feel, but they were still confined to a few cities and indeed to a few sections of those cities, like a stage set with most of the country as its YouTube audience. Even the summer of 2020 did not establish a pattern that looks anything like the year of our Lord 1969, when there were more than *three thousand bombings* across the continental United States.

Now, maybe the events of the Trump era are the forerunners of something worse. That often happens; in periods before true political upheaval, the rebel, the rioter, the street fighter, even the terrorist is more tuned in to what's really going on—or what's really coming— than the law-abiding citizen. You could understand the future of Germany better in 1930 by watching Brownshirts and Reds fight in the streets than by hanging out with middle-class shopkeepers; you could see the American future more clearly in the abolitionist John Brown's wild career than anywhere else in the 1850s. Joan Didion's famous essay "Slouching Towards Bethlehem" was published "in the cold late spring of 1967," and she argued that even though the economy was strong and the country seemed superficially stable, you could tell that America's "center was not holding" by visiting Haight-Ashbury and communing with the hippies. A year later, Martin Luther King Jr. and Robert F. Kennedy were dead, the Democratic National Convention was in chaos, and the terrorist wave mentioned earlier had begun.

But our terrorists and radicals don't necessarily feel like prophets or forerunners; they often just feel more like marks. The terrorist in twenty-first-century America isn't the guy who sees more deeply than the rest or grasps the new world coming; he's the guy (almost always a guy) *who doesn't get it*, the guy who takes all the stuff he reads on the Internet literally in a way that most of the people posting don't, the guy who confuses virtual entertainment with reality, the guy who goes through the same Violent Passion Surrogate as everyone else but unlike everyone else imagines that he's actually Othello. The left-wing dude who tries to assassinate Republican office-holders or shoots a Trump supporter isn't just a little deeper into the Resistance mind-set than the average activist; he's the guy who totally *misunderstands* the Resistance, who listens to all the online talk about treason and Fascism and thinks that he's really in 1940s France and his online allies are actually the Maquis instead of just the cosplay version. The guy who shows up at the Comet pizza parlor in Northwest DC with a gun because he thinks that prominent liberals are running a pedophile dungeon downstairs, or the guy who parks his truck on the Hoover Dam and demands that certain imaginary indictments be unsealed isn't just a little bolder and action oriented than the typical "Pizzagate" or "QAnon" conspiracy theorists; he fundamentally *misunderstands* the meaning and purpose of those labyrinthine theories, taking them as literal claims about the world rather than as what they are for their creators (a sport, a grift, a hobby) and for most of their participants (political entertainment and an odd form of virtual community).

This doesn't excuse the grifting or the rage stoking, especially Trump's presidential grifting and rage stoking; far from it. But it's important context for thinking about whether online politics is destined to unleash the furies in the real world. Lies and propaganda are normal features of revolutionary movements, but there is usually true belief woven in as well; Joseph Goebbels propagandized like Satan, but he believed absolutely in his Fuehrer and his cause. But Alex Jones just believes in selling supplements, Donald Trump just believes in selling Donald Trump, and a remarkable amount of online extremism is a mix of irony memes and pranks and playacting, with anonymous trolls competing with very public grifters to exploit an aging society's anxieties and an adrift youthful population's appetite for stimulation.

The reason that Steve Bannon achieved—for a brief spell—so much celebrity was that almost alone among Trumpian figures, he seemed to have a coherent philosophy beyond grifting. And I emphasize that "seemed" because, especially now that he's been arrested for a literal grift, there's a possibility that all his name-checks of Fascist intellectuals were just a con as well.

Similarly, one reason that the Antifa kids favored masks long before the coronavirus made them universal is that an awful lot of them are playacting their revolution, and they don't want to put their names and faces to something that's fundamentally just a game. And you can tell that it remains a game because nobody wants to play once the stakes turn to life or death. The famous "CHAZ" in Seattle, the Capitol Hill Autonomous Zone established to model the left's no-cop utopia, did not exactly eclipse the Paris Commune in ferocity or zeal. It lasted weeks only because of the left-wing city government's forbearance, it took exactly two murders in its precincts to bring the cops back in, and they met no resistance whatsoever.

Or take the most extreme and briefly terrifying example: the 2017 rally in Charlottesville, Virginia, that promised to "Unite the Right," and brought white supremacists of the old-school skinhead and new-model "preppy dudes with tiki torches" varieties together for a weekend of marching, networking, and phony brawls with their Antifa equivalents. When one of their numbers took the Weimar playacting literally and drove his car through a crowd of counterprotestors, killing a woman outright, did it invigorate the nascent movement, inspiring organized violence, and bring in new recruits eager for a chance at real mayhem? Not really: the movement rapidly disunited, dissolving into finger-pointing and disavowals, and by the time the one-year anniversary of Charlottesville rolled around, the attempt to host a similar rally in Washington, DC, produced the indelible image of a few pathetic-looking white nationalist leaders huddled together in their special DC Metro car—generals abandoned by their foot soldiers at the first whiff of real violence, outnumbered by the gawking journalists.

Baudrillard's America

In March 2017 *Foreign Affairs* asked Keith Mines, a State Department excerpt on developing-world civil strife, to assess the risk of a second civil war here in the United States. He gave America a 65 percent chance of falling into such a conflict in the next ten to fifteen years; the other academics he assembled for the exercise came up with a slightly lower consensus of a 35 percent. After Charlottesville, the *New Yorker* highlighted Mines's work and interviewed him: "We keep saying, 'It can't happen here,'" he told the reporter Robin Wright, "but then, holy smokes, it can."

By the autumn of 2020, Mines's fear of looming civil conflict was an increasingly popular anxiety. But it was still difficult to discern who exactly would be fighting it. The absolute numbers of anarchists, black nationalists, Boogaloo Boys and white supremacists could fill a Reddit chat room or a city square but not a battlefield. For most of our partisans, real violence is unlikely to suddenly become more appealing than the virtual alternatives—not least because some of our most polarized factions are distinguished by their extremely comfortable late-modern lives. The fiercest anti-Trump resisters were well-educated suburban liberal moms; the staunchest MAGA folk were seventysomething retirees in the Villages. Who among them is supposed to take up arms?

Overall, the United States has a polarized politics and a radicalized online discourse, but few of the other normal historical ingredients for civil war. Our democracy is long-established rather than a Weimar-style novelty, our military is resolutely depoliticized, our warring factions don't have unified control of their own regions (many Southern states are trending Democratic, California's hinterland is filled with Republicans), and our central state even in its decadence retains a clear monopoly on violence.

When the former Yugoslavia descended into civil war in the 1990s, it was difficult for the warring factions to find soldiers to fight the actual battles, to a point where the Serbian nationalists ended up relying on soccer hooligans and convicts. That was a society that still remembered World War II and was riven by still-more-ancient hatreds. Our own hatreds burn hot in their own way, but not obviously in *that* way—the old way, the way that once persuaded young men that *dulce et decorum est* to die for a country or a cause, the way that gave Europe its 1930s and the pre–Civil War United States its anti-slavery and pro-slavery forces killing one another in Bleeding Kansas.

In the age of online frenzy, there is an understandable fear that some kind of cultural-political cascade will carry our society downward into a similar kind of civil strife. But it may be that the nature of our decadence, our comfortable civilizational old age, makes that scenario unlikely, and that our problem is a different one: that our battles are sound and fury signifying much less than in the past; that even as it makes them more ferocious, the virtual realm also makes them more performative and empty; and that online rage is often a safety valve, a steam-venting technology for a society that is misgoverned, stagnant, and yet ultimately far more stable than it looks on social media, or under the extremely unusual conditions created by the pandemic.

Recall that Barzun wrote that decadence could be a "very active time" and "peculiarly restless" despite its tendency toward fatigue and repetition. That combination—restlessness and even frenzied activity that ultimately just recycles and repeats—was also predicted by Jean Baudrillard, famous for his pre-Internet emphasis on simulated reality as the default experience of late modernity. The French theorist answered Fukuyama's "end of history" argument by suggesting that a society facing the closing of its historical frontier would not, in fact, suffer the sleep of a museum docent, the "centuries of boredom" that Fukuyama feared, because of the great "postmodern invention of recycling":

> We shall not be spared the worst—that is, History will not come to an end—since the leftovers, all the leftovers—the Church, communism, ethnic groups, conflicts, ideologies—are indefinitely recyclable. What is stupendous is that nothing one thought superseded by history has really disappeared. All the archaic, anachronistic forms are there ready to reemerge, intact and timeless, like the vi-

ruses deep in the body. History has only wrenched itself from cyclical time to fall into the order of the recyclable.

Combine Baudrillardian simulation and Baudrillardian recycling, and you have the strange experience of political radicalism under decadence. Step inside the matrix of online political debate, and it feels like all of history is coming back. Socialists and Marxists, again! Catholic monarchists and white supremacists, again! Step outside, into the unhappy tranquility of everyday middle-class life, where drugs and suicide are still far more serious temptations than political radicalism and revolutionary violence, and it feels like you've been inside a Violent Passion Surrogate—all the tonic effects of living in the 1930s, but with a lower body count.

If you want to feel like Western society is sliding into the abyss of civil war, there's an app for that, a YouTube clip of rioting to watch, a convincing simulation waiting. But in the real world, it's possible that Western society as a whole is still leaning back in an easy chair, hooked up to a drip of something soothing, playing and replaying an ideological greatest-hits tape from its wild and crazy youth, all riled up in its own imagination and yet, in reality, comfortably numb.

6

A Kindly Despotism

In the summer of 2018, a body was discovered in a car parked in the East Village in New York. The dead man, identified as Geoffrey Corbis, had been inside the automobile for a week before anybody noticed.

After some investigation, it turned out that his real name was Geoffrey Weglarz and that his life story traced a particularly depressing variation on the larger baby boomer arc. Born one of seven children in Florida in the 1950s, he was a space-age obsessive as a kid—he and a childhood pal "would spend hours rehashing the details of each expedition," the *New York Times* reported in an obituary-cum-analysis of his death. Later he became a software designer in New York City, married and had one child—but his personal and professional lives seemed to peak around the millennium and decline thereafter. There was a particularly big setback after the financial crisis, when he left jobs twice; after he quit the second one, because it required trips to Texas that strained his joint-custody arrangements, he couldn't find a new one. Eventually he became an exemplar for late-middle-age unemployment, appearing on a *PBS NewsHour* documentary to describe his bottoming-out finances, his personal anxiety.

But around this time, in 2013, something else happened: Weglarz sinned against his neighbor and the social fabric, and his punishment was permanent and severe. He went through a McDonald's drive-thru, received the wrong fast-food order, and returned to complain, leading to an altercation in which he threw the sandwich at the McDonald's employee—who was pregnant. The legal penalty was minimal—a disorderly conduct charge against Weglarz that was ultimately dropped. But the pregnant-worker detail earned the incident a brief flare of mass-media attention, which in turn earned Weglarz a permanent record in a place that matters more to many people's life prospects than the legal system: the etched-in-granite record of his Google search results, as available to any prospective employer as to any potential friend or date.

Thereafter, what had been a difficult job search became impossible, forcing Weglarz to assume a different name and live under the "Geoffrey Corbis" alias for the remainder of his life—a life that ended with the acquisition of poison from the Internet five years after his online notoriety, and a final good-bye by text message from the car where his body lay rotting for a week.

The grisliness of that discovery finally did what Weglarz was powerless to do himself: if you Google his real name today, the headline that helped push him toward his suicide, "Enraged Fairfield Man Throws Food at Pregnant McDonald's Manager" is at last no longer the top search engine result.

The Age of "Social Credit"

The same summer that Weglarz took his life, on the bullet train that runs from Beijing to Shanghai, the loudspeakers began playing the following announcement: "Dear passengers, people who travel without a ticket or behave disorderly, or smoke in public areas, will be punished according to regulations, and the behavior will be recorded in the individual credit information system. To avoid a negative record of personal credit, please follow the relevant regulations and help with the orders on the train and at the station."

A social credit system is hardly the most terrifying experiment in totalitarian control ongoing in the People's Republic of China. (That distinction belongs to the cultural genocide being imposed on the Uighurs in the Chinese west.) It's a relatively gentle form of supervision and manipulation, which applies the logic of credit ratings to all kinds of potentially antisocial behavior—on trains and airplanes and, increasingly, in China's cities. Urbanites and travelers covered by the system may find themselves with scores that rise when they donate to charity and fall when they run a red light. Or jaywalk. Or walk their dog without a leash. A high score comes with perks, such as renting bikes without a deposit, fast-tracking visa applications. Let your score fall far enough, though, and you may find yourself barred from buses, trains, and airplanes, denied the right to make certain purchases, stripped of access to social services, publicly shamed on government billboards or online.

Because these systems are still experimental, there are variations in different cities (a dedicated points system just for dog owners, for instance, where a low-enough score will bring animal welfare to your door to take the pooch) and informal versions run by private companies that overlap with the governmental version. But the Beijing government hopes to have an integrated China-wide social credit system running very soon. If it succeeds, it will be the capstone on a larger project of digital-age adaptation, in which China's Communist Party, which was supposed to go the way of all flesh under the radical pressure of the Internet, has instead bent the technologies of the virtual age to serve the cause of political stasis and social stability: censoring the Internet so that it becomes a machine for encouraging consumption and delivering distraction rather than a haven for dissent; harnessing surveillance technologies and facial-recognition software to ensure that Chinese citizens have even less privacy than before; and relying on the popularity of Chinese Internet companies' social media apps to track movements, financial transactions, conversations, and more.

And if you regard the coronavirus as the first great test for this still-emergent system, you would have to say that so far it succeeded.

A disease that at first seemed like it would shake the pillars of the Communist-ruled order was ultimately suppressed more ruthlessly, and also more effectively, than in the liberal West. Yes, some of China's disease statistics were probably deceptive, but that doesn't change the basic reality of the United States and Western Europe enduring wave upon wave on infections while Beijing quashed its outbreaks. If you don't mind the tyranny, the Chinese surveillance state worked exactly as intended.

In the last chapter, we considered how a stable decadence might be something chosen freely rather than imposed—how the inhabitants of a wealthy, aging, comfortable society might prefer to stagnate amid virtual distraction, costume-party politics, and pharmaceutical comforts rather than working to remedy, renew, reform, or revolutionize the real world. But preferences are malleable, "free" choices are conditioned, pleasures blur into addictions, and both corporate and governmental exercises of power help determine which choices seem natural and which ones don't. So this chapter is about the strategy of control that the authorities in a decadent society might use to keep order, the structure of incentives, of rewards and punishments that already partially define life under decadence and—if our system is to be sustainable—will necessarily become more effective, pervasive, and fully realized over time.

Compared with China's social credit system, the version of this strategy visible in the Western world is much more decentralized and haphazard, more circumscribed and civilized by the residual liberal traditions of the West, less designed and more evolved—and less ruthlessly effective in a crisis, as the year of the coronavirus demonstrated.

But to appropriate the famous description of Deng Xiaoping's vision as "capitalism with Chinese characteristics," the emerging system of social control in a decadent West might be usefully described as "a police state with liberal characteristics." Both its rules and its ruthlessness will be shaped and checked by the West's cultural individualism and its political emphasis on human rights. But it will still have an authoritarian edge—a gently despotic aspect—under a banner that isn't the red of Communism or the black and brown of fascism, but a friendly, helpful, cheerful color. The color of a nurse, of a caregiver, of the kindliest possible inquisitors: the gentle, childlike color *pink*.

The Pink Police State

The phrase "pink police state" belongs to James Poulos, an eccentric Californian philosopher-pundit who distilled it from a Marilyn Manson music video for the 1998 single "The Dope Show," in which the riot police then being deployed to antiglobalization protests were portrayed (as Poulos describes it) "dressed head to toe in pink, drawing one another close in an amorous embrace." The use of this image by Manson, a figure who was then supposedly the "most dangerous and threatening person in pop music," might seem like a subversive vision, an attack on the authority of cops. But Poulos saw it instead as a tacit celebration of a social order just coming into being, one in which public authority was "aggressively intervening in the intimate details of everyday life as a *friend* to some kinds of civil liberties but an *enemy* of others."

The civil liberties to be protected and encouraged in this new order are the liberties of pleasure and consumption, and the freedom to be "safe"—broadly defined—from threats to bodily integrity, personal expression, and psychological well-being. The liberties to be limited are the liberties that enable resistance, both personal and political: the freedoms of religion and speech, and the ability to participate fully in the culture without sacrificing your privacy, without having your life be a kind of open book.

In effect, Poulos argues, the pink police state partially erases the idea of a public/private divide, replacing it with alternative binaries of health/disease and safety/danger instead. Social problems in this landscape are increasingly medicalized, with the language of treatment rather than moral exhortation a default response to any kind of disruption or unhappiness. Private conduct is freer in the variety of acts that are allowed, but more closely regulated in any case where there is a possibility of not just physical but also psychological harm. And certain older political and religious liberties fall more on the "harm" or "danger" side of the new binaries, because religious exclusion or moral discrimination might wound the individual's sense of well-being, and political speech might likewise express an antipathy that becomes hateful, therefore damaging, therefore unacceptable.

The most fully realized version of this regime exists on certain American college campuses, which have groped their way to the pink police state out of a kind of commercial necessity. In the last few decades, our universities have distinguished themselves by promising seemingly incompatible things to their two customer bases: to the parents footing the bill, they promise safety, supervision, and an environment where the precious children of the upper-middle class will be tended with all the care that helicopter parents expect; to the kids actually making the choice, they promise a long *Rumspringa*—a four-year holiday from both childhood rules and adult responsibilities, in which the debauchery of *Animal House* or *Old School* is supposed to be included with tuition.

Harmonizing those two promises is the task of the ever-expanding college bureaucracy, whose mission is to protect the health and well-being of its student body without resorting to oppressive moral virtues such as chastity and temperance that might bring the party to a halt. Instead, the bureaucracy offers counseling and pharmaceutical treatment for the depression that turns out to be commonplace in a social environment supposedly devoted to carefree hedonism, free contraception to prevent the harm of STDs and the still-graver danger of pregnancy (the pink police state is particularly hostile to unplanned, unsafe conception), mildly repressive rules for campus speech that gently discourage anything that might upset students educated into left-liberal assumptions about the universe and their own identities, and the strange emergent phenomenon that the law professors Jeannie Suk and Jacob Gersen have dubbed the "sex bureaucracy"—a system intended to prevent rape and sexual assault that turns campus administrators into "bureaucrats of desire, responsible for defining healthy, permissible sex and disciplining deviations from those supposed norms."

This system is strikingly self-regulating, with little sign (despite a thousand think pieces about a "higher education bubble") of slackening demand—though declining birthrates may soon have some effect on its sustainability. The absence of due process in the sex bureaucracy sometimes perpetrates injustices against young men, which in turn produces some anxiety and backlash from parents and donors, but the constituency likely to rally in defense of *a privileged dude accused of rape when he actually just acted like a creep* is inherently limited, and most kids experience the sex bureaucracy as a soft despotism rather than an active one. The conformism imposed by politically correct rules of discourse provokes a certain kind of backlash from right-leaning students and alums—but that backlash usually is itself so extreme (inviting Milo Yiannopoulos to freak out the squares!) that it only confirms the campus consensus that right-wing speech can be reasonably excluded without any intellectual cost. Meanwhile, the more prevalent form of protest, from the social-justice left, exists in symbiosis with the pink-police-state apparatus: protestors take offense at some campus-specific controversy or at the residua of vanished white male patriarchy (a statue, a title, a song), and the administration responds by promising to establish yet another layer of caring bureaucracy devoted to identitarian forms of personal empowerment—one in which, upon graduation, a certain type of protestor can immediately find work.

Nothing quite like this system exists in the world that awaits outside of college. But a similar health-and-safety culture dominates the neighborhoods and workplaces into which many college graduates matriculate, and especially the planned campuses in which the most technically proficient among them work. Mayor Michael Bloomberg's dream of a New York purged of Big Gulps and loosies and handguns, in which traffic cameras and ubiquitous stop-and-frisk policing makes Brooklyn safe for brunches and boutique bondage dens, is the pink police state applied to urban policy. The Silicon Valley offices where young programmers are offered vast workout centers and polished yoga spaces but no child-care options (save a company incentive to freeze one's eggs), and where right-wing engineers are occasionally fired for wrongthink *pour encourager les autres*, is the college model extended into adult professional existence. And much of western Europe has its own distinctive version, aimed at policing the tensions between natives and new arrivals, secular post-Christians and Muslim immigrants, which keeps the Continent's theme-park streets as safe as possible for tourists with surveillance and crackdowns on civil and religious liberties that would make Dick Cheney blush.

All of these examples are limited in their aegis as well as their oppressiveness, of course. College lasts only four years, you can move out of Brooklyn, nobody is forcing you to work for Google, and with sufficient effort, you can even escape France or Belgium for the as-yet-more-libertarian USA. But at the same time, one of the features of early twenty-first century America is a growing conformity and consolidation in upper-class life, with the norms of college campuses extending in varying ways through media enterprises and cultural institutions and corporate HR departments. Elements of both the #MeToo and anti-racist movements can be understood in this light—as attempts to shape, strengthen and expand the incipient pink-police-state order, with more particular rules for relations between the sexes and the races, more expansive definitions of what constitutes harm and discrimination and what forms of speech should be regulated or excluded from elite spaces.

And these ambitious regulatory projects aren't bounded by specific institutions, because they can imagine themselves writing rules for a much larger sphere: Namely, the Internet, which many of its disillusioned inventors increasingly acknowledge functions as a universal surveillance system—one that records your every move, your every transaction, your every utterance and photograph and e-mail, for purposes that are primarily corporate and commercial (to borrow from the novelist Walter Kirn, in an *Atlantic* essay on his Internet-age paranoia: send a text saying "don't let the bedbugs bite," get an e-mail ad for a commercial exterminator service the next morning) but that inevitably add up to a system of surveillance and control.

As the security expert Bruce Schneier once put it, the issue isn't that the Internet has been penetrated by the surveillance state, by the National Security Agency or the Central Intelligence Agency. It's that the Internet, in effect, *is* a surveillance state: the virtual fulfillment of Jeremy Bentham's Panopticon, where Big Brother doesn't have to watch everyone because everyone is always watching everybody else.

Learning to Love the Panopticon

This dystopian possibility haunted the online experience early on: witness paranoid Clinton-era movies such as *Enemy of the State* and *The Net,* in which innocents found themselves digitally hunted, surveilled, and erased. But the early Internet was far more anonymous than enfleshed experience—a world of chat rooms and comment sections, aliases and handles and screen names, whose spirit was encapsulated by a famous *New Yorker* cartoon's promise that "on the Internet, nobody knows you're a dog."

If all you want to do online is leave anonymous comments, then this experience still persists, to a point. But for most people, what the Internet really offers is the *illusion* of privacy, the *feeling* of communicating unobserved—and because of that feeling, most Internet users don't feel the need to shroud themselves in pseudonyms, preferring to communicate online the way they do at parties or in living rooms, texting and e-mailing and DM-ing in the same casual style that one would once have used in a letter or a phone call, and engaging in social media as though their tweets and posts are only going to be read by intimates and pals instead of the world entire.

Which means, inevitably, that they are actually much more exposed—to strangers and enemies, ex-lovers and ex-friends, hackers and stalkers—than human beings ever would have been before their social lives migrated online. And they are exposed, above all, to a novel kind of persecution and harassment, because the ability to see so many half-formed, poorly thought-out ideas and opinions issuing all over has tempted people to do what people do best: to go after their enemies or perceived enemies, to dox them and drag them and ideally get them fired, to invent new crimes to describe tweets or Facebook posts that they find offensive, and to generally act, without being hired or paid to do it by any central authority, like *cops*.

What Freddie deBoer, a man of the left, writes about his own part of the political ecosystem applies to the entire Internet, not just the progressive portions:

> The woke world is a world of snitches, informants, rats. Go to any space concerned with social justice, and what will you find? Endless surveillance. Everybody is to be judged. Everyone is under suspicion. Everything you say is to be scoured, picked over, analyzed for any possible offense. Everyone's a detective in the Division of Problematics, and they walk the beat 24/7. You search and search for someone Bad doing Bad Things, finding ways to indict writers and artists and ordinary people for something, *anything*.

Now, it is at least possible to participate in online culture while limiting your horizontal, peer-to-peer exposure to the mob. But it is practically impossible to protect your privacy vertically—from the big online businesses and service providers and social media networks and (through them) the security agencies that can easily access most people's every click and text and e-mail. As Poulos notes, this is "not a police state in the sense that George Orwell would be familiar with, but one . . . woven into the fabric of trillions of transactions online and off." And every new information-technology breakthrough, every new form of tech (the Alexa in your house, the computer in your car, the Slack chat as the office social scene), promises to make our every move and download and even utterance a little easier to track. In the surveillance state, everybody knows you're a dog.

The good news is that this "state" is not a unitary (or semiunitary, at least) entity like the Chinese Politburo, which necessarily limits its oppressiveness. But it is an interlocking directorate of institutions, corporate and governmental, that are populated by like-minded people with a desire to share information and a similar basic incentive to use their power to keep the system stable, to keep themselves securely in power at the top. There's a reason that the Internet companies have been happy to cooperate with European governments in cracking down on extremist speech, just as they've been willing to cooperate with China's rather more severe restrictions. There's a reason that there's been so much tacit cooperation (despite official denials) between those same big Internet concerns and the NSA. There's a reason that Silicon Valley big shots talk about privacy in roughly the same paternalist language favored by government spokesmen. "If you have something that you don't want anyone to know," Google's Eric Schmidt told an interviewer in 2009, "maybe you shouldn't be doing it in the first place."

That kind of language frightens privacy advocates, but most people in the developed world don't seem to mind it. There are periodic exposés detailing what the NSA can know about you, or all the ways in which Internet giants are effectively spying on you to monetize your data, but with some exceptions, people seem to get really upset about privacy issues only when it affects their bank accounts directly—when there's a hack that lets somebody steal their credit cards or befoul their credit history. The *general* loss of privacy simply isn't a big political issue, no matter how many magazines run anguished essays and how many civil libertarians sound alarms. The public's attitude toward this new reality tends to look less like the anxiety you hear from chin strokers and book writers, and more like the online *pensées* collected by a Twitter account called "Nothing to Hide" in 2015, after the news broke that the NSA had been helping itself to data from just about every major American Internet company. Here are a few reactions from the vox populi:

> If it can save people from another 9/11-like attack, go for it. My e-mails/phone calls are not that exciting anyway . . .

> This sort of thing was bound to happen. We live in the information age. Besides, I have nothing to hide.

> If you share your whole life on social media, who cares if the government takes a peek?!?

This unconcern reflects the extent to which the pink police state simply hasn't been experienced by most people as oppression, at least up until recently. Yes, it has granted extraordinary knowledge and potentially tyrannical powers to Silicon Valley and Washington, DC. But following the health-and-safety-and-entertainment logic of the system, most citizens have been monitored without ever feeling persecuted or coerced. Instead of official requirements to participate and conform, they've faced soft pressure, constant nudges, and the general knowledge that their every move could be caught on a surveillance camera or simply on someone's smartphone and then shared as widely as social media can reach. Instead of an explicit program of political repression, there has been a haphazard mob-based enforcement of social and political norms and occasional Big Data–enabled abuses that keep everyone on his or her toes. And instead of people jailed for nonparticipation or nonconformity, there have been cautionary example of men and women rendered unemployable by a YouTube video or Twitter lapse or—like Geoffrey Weglarz—a real-world altercation whose Google residue they can never wash away.

It's possible that as the more overtly ideological and left-wing aspects of the pink police state come to the fore—as the rules of wokeness, broadly defined, become more entrenched in American institutions—there will be more resistance and backlash, more anxiety about the fate of free speech, and eventually more (mostly but not exclusively right-wing) political resistance to the new surveillance state. On the other hand it's also possible that the spate of firings and defenestrations in elite institutions in 2020 were mostly about forcing a generational change of the guard in a few highly competitive spaces, and once that change has been accomplished the pink police state will continue to function gently for most people, for whom a certain degree of conformity will seem like a price worth paying for the sake of social peace.

In this atmosphere, certain forms of public misbehavior will become rarer even as certain forms of paranoia will be more reasonable. But because genuinely dangerous people will often be preempted or caught more swiftly, because the system comes down hard only on young men interested in joining ISIS, or devotees of Alex Jones, or the occasional luckless idiot who riles up the Twitter mob, the privacy-for-security swap will remain acceptable to most Westerners—especially when there is no obvious alternative short of disconnecting from the Internet entirely.

From Hidden Violence to Social Peace

Moreover, the system may be accepted not only because the Internet seems like a necessity but also because it genuinely increases certain kinds of peace. Just as virtual entertainment draws people away from real-world danger, technologies of mass surveillance can plausibly claim to discourage criminality and violence without some of the harsher costs usually imposed by law-and-order politics. Just as porn and pharmaceuticals promise to deliver pleasure without the risk of disease, pregnancy, and pain, the pink police state can promise to protect pleasure through its nudges and regulations without the downside costs that libertinism traditionally imposes.

In the essay quoted above, deBoer discusses the irony that the "everyone's a cop" quality of Internet discourse is advancing even as the United States finally begins to turn away from the mass-incarceration policies imposed in response to the crime wave that ravaged American cities from the 1970s through the 1990s. But this is not an irony, nor is it even a coincidence. It's just the evolution of elite strategies of control, elite responses to the potential downsides of a hyperindividualist, hedonistic culture. Mass incarceration as practiced by politicians of both parties was the first stage of that evolution, a desperate and flailing and often-brutal attempt to use state power to deal with the anarchic consequences of the 1960s, the sexual revolution and the drug culture and the decline of moralistic institutions. To be maximally cynical, it was a way for affluent suburbanites to protect *their* right to get divorced and sleep in on Sunday morning and smoke a little weed, by making sure that the increasingly fatherless sons of the demoralized underclass were locked up for dealing crack. Who needs churches and two-parent families and the old American puritanism, in other words, when you can have a culture that preaches "If it feels good, do it," and then puts the people who take that message too literally in prison?

Extending that cynicism to the present era, you might say that mass incarceration became less necessary once virtual entertainments were invented to keep kids from broken homes indoors and take the edge off their physical and sexual aggression—and also once a surveillance state developed that made crime less likely to pay, escape from law enforcement more difficult, the outlaw life much harder to sustain.

A similar point can be made about sex and pregnancy and childbearing as well. Just as we used mass incarceration as a strategy for managing crime, beginning in the 1970s we used abortion to manage teen pregnancy and out-of-wedlock births, substituting the vacuum pump for shotgun marriages and sexual restraint. Tellingly, both incarceration and abortion are *hidden* forms of violence, one imposed through a distant archipelago of prisons and the other in the darkness of the womb, both creating an illusion of peace sustained by a denial of the reality of what happened in a cellblock, what the abortionist dealt out. But, also tellingly, both have become less necessary to the system over time: as the pink police state has come of age, abortion rates have fallen alongside both crime and incarceration rates—both because virtual sex no less than virtual violence takes the edge off real-world desire, and also because the system relies increasingly on chemical solutions that are kinder than abortion, such as the temporary sterilization of Depo-Provera, to make sure that the poor don't have too many kids. And then it also relies on pharmaceutical abortions, so that the violence that remains is even more secret and private than before.

You might also extend this argument to foreign policy, and to the way our system deals with the threat of terrorism, Islamic and otherwise. The wars that immediately followed 9/11, the invade-and-occupy-and-nation-build strategy that came to grief in Iraq and Afghanistan, were an analogue to the mass-incarceration era's blunt-force approach to the dangers unleashed by late-modern discontents. The turn toward drone warfare and surgical assassinations from the Obama era onward, meanwhile, is a lower-cost and less-violent approach, and therefore perhaps a more sustainable one—using technological breakthroughs, virtual warfare (for the soldiers at our end, not the targets at the other), and the awesome power of surveillance to hunt down enough terrorists that even if their deaths encourage new recruits, their organizations are too harried to ever bring their war back to our shores.

The watchword in all these cases is sustainability. A system of control that requires huge prisons and 1.5 million abortions annually will inspire outrage, activism, and protest. But a system of control that relies on constant surveillance, technologically abetted house arrest, virtual entertainments and pharmaceutical sterilization and prescription abortions will fade more into the background of everyday life. The underlying problems that require these responses may worsen or just languish unaddressed, but they won't trouble the nation's conscience nearly as much as in the recent past.

Likewise, a foreign policy that requires permanent occupations and large ground armies and thousands of combat deaths will quickly unmake presidencies. But a foreign policy conducted with satellites and drones, and sometimes fighter jets and special forces, a foreign policy that promises to minimize civilian casualties even though it never quite eliminates them—well, even if such a national security strategy never *wins* its wars, even if it just keeps them sufficiently stalemated in order to keep the homeland reasonably safe, it can still command permanent public support because the violence seems sufficiently distant and hidden and virtual as to be a price worth paying, or simply worth ignoring, for a general age of peace. Thus, the present antiwar dilemma: as the Yale law professor Samuel Moyn writes, "The containment and minimization of violence in America's wars . . . have only made it harder to criticize America's use of force in other countries." The more surgically precise the intervention, the more sustainable it becomes. With enough technique, the forever war can last forever.

Rebels in the Machine

It's not that nobody objects to this system or that nobody rebels. Poulos insists that unlike the World State in *Brave New World*, which tries to bring almost everyone (save a few "Savages" and exiled malcontents) into the system of health and well-being and soma and euthanasia, the "danger" and "illness" portions of the pink police state's map will always be populated: "The horizon of transgression always recedes from the reach of officialdom, however unprecedented in its scope." Alongside all the good behavior, there are still trends that run the other way: the kids are having less sex and fewer babies, for instance, but in defiance of the culture of "safe" sex, they are acquiring more STDs. And politically, as the horizon of transgression recedes, the transgressive ideas percolating there have the potential to become more radical, which is also part of the story of the Internet: alongside conformism-inducing mobs and wrongthink-policing "cops," it also offers spaces in which radicals and reactionaries can find one another, encourage one another, radicalize one another, meme one another into joining ISIS or embracing Marxist-Leninism or operationalizing the Unabomber's manifesto or reviving Catholic integralism or otherwise threatening the late-modern order at its roots.

It also offers space for figures such as Donald Trump, who would never have appealed to many people if he didn't constantly enact precisely the kind of transgression that the kindly Panopticon is supposed to shame, to cancel, to rule out. The mere fact of Trump's presidency is proof that the system we are discussing is not *inherently* stable in the way of Huxley's World State. By regulating dissent and chasing it to the margins, it's always possible for the pink police state to invite it to come roaring back as populism, radicalism, revolution—and more so, presumably, if anything happens to reduce the pleasures of consumerism, the system's cushioning of wealth.

But the Panopticon is also adaptable. It creates in-between spaces where people can be exiled from elite institutions without being driven all the way to full rebellion: The writer who loses a job at a major magazine can set up camp on Substack, the exiled academic can find a podcast audience, and banishment from core institutions feels like a comfortable exile rather than a spur to further radicalism. And the system draws even rebels back into its matrix of playacting and performance—or perhaps it encourages and elevates forms of rebellion that are well suited for that matrix, that emerge from within its rules, its simulated realities, and can be reabsorbed.

Trump is a case study insofar as he became president because he was the reality-television version of a Great Businessman, and he governed (to use the word very loosely) as a Baudrillardian simulation of the Great Demagogue, playing different versions of his part in different regions of the media ecosystem—the racist heel on CNN; the pop-ulist hero on Fox—and constantly seeking validation from within the simulated realities of cable news and Twitter. What Trump wanted, more than power—which he gained without knowing how to use—was *attention*, retweets, televised and online validation. And much of the right-wing revolt against the system has a similar attention-seeking quality: conservative populists talk about overthrowing what they see as left-wing structures of surveillance and cultural control, but their specific demands often circle back to a desire for their own place on the system's outskirts—a space to monetize their YouTube videos and to circulate their pro-Trump memes, free from fears of shadow ban-ning and deplatforming and true banishment.

In other words, Trump-era populism draws a certain kind of en-ergy from moving back and forth across the safety/danger line, but when pressed, it prefers to appeal to the system as a client demanding services, or as a subject demanding its rights, rather than accepting the options for exile—understandably enough, since most of the extrapan-optical options are crawling with white supremacists, and the provo-cateurs who actually get banished from the social media monopolies soon find themselves unable to monetize their provocations.

This means that the war between the populist right and Silicon Val-ley ultimately fits the pattern described in the last chapter, in the sense that the populists are fighting primarily for the right to entertain and monetize, and their performance of political incorrectness and loud complaints when that performance inspires brushback is less a real rebellion than a validation of the larger system, the outskirts of which they are content to occupy so long as there is money to be made. In this, the media populists are playing the same game as Trump himself, who remained part of the Fake News Complex that he was suppos-edly at war with—desperate for the attention of the *Washington Post* or CNN even as he attacked them, whining about his Twitter numbers to anyone who listened, well aware that he was driving ratings and subscriptions higher among his supposed "enemies" and willing to take the deal because he wanted to be in their headlines, whatever the cost.

Which is why you could make the case that a true radicalism, a true threat to the Panopticon, would not be visible online at all; the rebellions that we can see percolating are, almost by definition, codependent with the system, constrained and pushed constantly toward entertainment by their choice to depend upon and negotiate with an order they supposedly abhor. And this too is a reason to regard the new populism and its weaker left-wing analogues as challenges that the system might be able to handle, haphazardly but effectively, without either revolution or reform.

The problems of the late-twentieth century would become permanent fixtures of the twenty-first, in this vision of our future. Underclass fatherlessness, working-class disarray, drug abuse, out-of-wedlock births, loneliness, childlessness, suicide, general postreligious anomie, terrorism, and radicalization of all kinds—these would all persist without resolution. This persistence wouldn't pass unnoticed; indeed, it would regularly inspire political rebellions. But the rebellions from the left would lead to elite reshufflings framed in the language of revolution without any revolutionary action, while those from the right would be swiftly reabsorbed into the entertainment portion of the Panopticon, their leaders drawn into negotiations over their audience share and their right to monetize their antiestablishment message— and meanwhile, the underlying problems would continue to be managed, and managed, and managed, by screens and drugs and drones for some indefinite period of time.

But still, one might respond, if the rebellions allow someone as manifestly unqualified as Trump to claim the powers of the presidency, if politics as entertainment accelerates polarization and confirms gridlock, then even if the system is internally self-stabilizing, how can it possibly deal with the impingement of crisis from outside? How can a decadent society hope to avoid being challenged by more vigorous rivals, and ultimately—like so many of history's sclerotic empires—being subverted, dismantled, overthrown?

One answer is that it can't, and doom is closer than we think. But another possibility, for the next chapter, is that the decadent society doesn't have to fall, if all its plausible external rivals and challengers are either too weak, too unready, or too close to decadence themselves.

7

Waiting for the Barbarians

In 2016 the French novelist Michel Houellebecq capped a career spent penning acidic, pornographic critiques of hedonism and consumerism with a novel that imagined his longtime target—late-Western liberalism—actually being overthrown. The book, *Soumission* (*Submission*), extrapolated the polarization of French politics forward to an imagined near-future presidential election in which the top two vote getters were the real-world far right leader Marine Le Pen, and the invented leader of a nascent Islamic party, Mohammed Ben-Abbes. Fearing the far right above all else, part of the liberal establishment throws its weight behind Ben-Abbes, who wins and ushers in a slow-motion Islamicization of French society—in which men and women, right and left, gradually submit to the religion of the Prophet and join a new trans-Mediterranean Islamic empire.

The book is a dystopia but not, as the casual reader might expect, a cautionary tale about political Islam, a version of *The Handmaid's Tale* about shari'a law. The fact that it was published the day of the *Charlie Hebdo* massacre, and the weird coincidence that Houellebecq himself was being satirized on the magazine's pre-massacre cover, led people to link him to all the European conservatives warning against the peril of Islamist extremism. But while Houellebecq is certainly a reactionary of some sort, that was not exactly what his book was doing. Rather, as in his other novels, *the actual dystopia is the contemporary*

West, and the imagined French turning to Islam is portrayed as a possible step forward, a return to vitality and health, a path that might lead out of decadence.

To this end, everything French in the story is satirized, as Houellebecq depicts the different ways that different contemporary groups weakly make their peace with the Islamic order: feminists welcoming punitive laws against male misbehavior, Catholic reactionaries discovering common ground with their erstwhile Muslim foes, a sophisticated Nietzsche scholar deciding that the manly vigor of Islam answers his complaints about Christianity's soft and feminine side. And the satire is sharpest in the case of the Houellebecq-esque narrator, a scholar of the nineteenth-century "decadent" writer Joris-Karl Huysmans who yearns to imitate Huysmans's reversion to Catholicism but simply can't make the leap of faith, and who ends up seduced into the new Islamic order by the promise of polygamy.

Islam, however, is not satirized. Ben-Abbes, the offstage Napoléon of the new Islamic France, is portrayed as a kind of political superman, and his religion and civilization are treated with a distant, careful sort of admiration and respect. This choice gives the novel a dreamlike power entirely absent in most right-wing rants against jihadism. The Islamic world exists in a distant austerity that throws Western decadence into sharp relief, offering itself as an alternative that promises some sort of forward movement rather than just a nostalgic revival of Christendom. Islam in *Submission* isn't a reaction or a return, the way the reversion to Catholicism that Houellebecq's protagonist contemplates might feel; it's reactionary futurism, a revived Dar al-Islam as the natural successor of the exhausted Western project.

But if that dreamlike quality is novelistically effective, it's also telling for the sustainability question with which this book's middle chapters are concerned. Because if *Submission* feels rooted in the real world when it satirizes the decadent French but dreamlike when it depicts their Islamist successors, doesn't that suggest that there might *not* be a genuine alternative to decadence in the real, nonnovelistic world? That the late-modern West's existing rivals, as opposed to its imagined enemies or inheritors, have too many challenges and weaknesses of their own to effectively exploit our torpor and stagnation? That our various fears of apocalypse, left and right, reflect a kind of cultural death wish that everyone secretly knows will not be imminently satisfied, a weary desire for a coup de grace that isn't actually on its way, a fear that our alternative to catastrophe is W. H. Auden's description of the late Roman Empire, a civilization lasting for centuries "without creativity, warmth, or hope"?

Perhaps "death wish" is too extreme. But at the very least, there is a natural human desire to see history as a morality play in which virtue leads to strength and decay to destruction. For that play to work, though, there has to be some force capable of delivering the just comeuppance, of surging over the palace walls after the writing appears upon them, of bringing Babylon low as it deserves. Some of the threat inflation of our own era may be driven by a desire to discover or invent such a force, because the only thing more frightening than the possibility of annihilation is the possibility that our society could coast on forever as it is—like a Rome without an Attila to sack its palaces, or a Nineveh without Yahweh to pass judgment on its crimes.

There's a famous poem from 1904 called "Waiting for the Barbarians," by the Greek poet C. P. Cavafy, that gets at this peculiar psychological-cultural predicament. Cavafy envisions a Roman-style city where everyone expects the Huns to roll in at any moment:

What are we waiting for, assembled in the forum?

The barbarians are due here today.

Why isn't anything happening in the senate?
Why do the senators sit there without legislating?

Because the barbarians are coming today.
What laws can the senators make now?
Once the barbarians are here, they'll do the legislating.

Why did our emperor get up so early,
and why is he sitting at the city's main gate
on his throne, in state, wearing the crown?

Because the barbarians are coming today
and the emperor is waiting to receive their leader.
He has even prepared a scroll to give him,
replete with titles, with imposing names.

Why this sudden restlessness, this confusion?
(How serious people's faces have become.)
Why are the streets and squares emptying so rapidly,
everyone going home so lost in thought?

Because night has fallen and the barbarians have not come.
And some who have just returned from the border say
there are no barbarians any longer.

And now, what's going to happen to us without barbarians?

They were, those people, a kind of solution.

In the spirit of Cavafy, this is a chapter about why the barbarians—meaning not howling savages, but any force capable of overthrowing the liberal order and inheriting the world—may not be on their way.

Waiting for the Barbarians

The Fourth World War That Wasn't

Let's begin with Houellebecq's candidate for an inheritor: a new Islamic order that converts and conquers and sweeps the once-Christian West into a twenty-first-century form of dhimmitude, the subservient status that past Islamic empires once imposed on their non-Muslim subjects. This was how history was supposed to return after 9/11, according to some of the more imaginative, eager-for-the-fight Western intellectuals—neoconservatives on the right and would-be Orwells of the left. Where once fascism and Communism had challenged the liberal order, now some kind of Islamic ideology would do the same. Call it Islamism, or Islamofascism, or (for the more paranoid or Islamophobic) just Islam itself; pin it on Osama bin Laden or Sayyid Qutb or the Wahhabis or the mullahs or the Prophet Muhammad; however you defined it, a new sort of religion-infused ideology was on the march, and a great war for civilization was upon us. The age of Fukuyama was over; the world of Samuel Huntington's "clash of civilizations" had arrived, and the struggle would happen everywhere: along the borders between Islamic civilization and its neighbors, within Islamic societies where liberal ideas might yet take root or be imposed by Western intervention, and within those European cities where Muslim immigrants had created de facto Islamist colonies, islands of extremism that might yet expand to forge Eurabia.

This post-9/11 vision recognized something fundamental: that Islam is not really assimilated to the order I'm describing as decadent, that Islamic civilization is the West's most immediately visible Other, and that the Islamic world's internal conflicts are creating off-the-map spaces where not only young Muslims but also young Westerners seek radical alternatives to the feeling of civilizational exhaustion.

But those truths are not sufficient to sustain the larger claims of sweeping civilizational conflict or Cold War 2.0 or World War IV. Such claims require imagining an Islamic world that's expanding rather than convulsing; that's consolidating rather than being consumed by civil wars; that's winning converts within the West's elite rather than primarily among its dropouts; that's dramatically exceeding Western fertility rates rather than converging with them. And all these imaginations are just that: fancies that bear no relationship to the actual state of Islamic alternatives to Western liberalism.

The Houellebecq fantasia offers a useful way to think about the difference between the threat inflators and reality. In Houellebecq's world, the genius of Ben-Abbes creates a France-led Islamic imperium that extends south to encompass North Africa; in our world, the actual EU is struggling to prevent refugees from collapsing North African states from crossing the Mediterranean, building walls against an Islamic world that's threatening only because of its dysfunction. In Houellebecq's world, Qatari and Saudi moneymen compete to buy up French universities and subsidize French intellectuals; in our world, they're bribing Western governments, certainly, but they're mostly spending money trying to influence the region-destabilizing, intra-Islamic civil war next door to their own fiefdoms.

In Houellebecq's world, Islam is enough of a coming thing to seduce high-profile academics the way Marxism and fascism won over portions of the intelligentsia in days gone by; in our world, with rare exceptions, it's conspicuously not. Those older ideologies carried an air of world-historical confidence, projecting an image of technological proficiency and industrial progress, which is almost entirely absent among Islam's revolutionaries and would-be caliphs. The various Islamist experiments, the Islamic Republic of Iran and the soi-disant Islamic State and, of course, Saudi Arabia's gangster theocracy, are dangerous to the West but not really seductive to Westerners; a few deluded anticolonialist writers flirted with Khomeini-ism in 1979, but that affair died quickly, and today no Western observer visits Tehran or Riyadh and announces that he has seen the inevitable future. Movements such as Al Qaeda and ISIS can exploit Western anomie to seduce and recruit, but their targets are hapless, marginal, even deplorable. There are no Islamist Rosenbergs or Kim Philbys, no Islamist analogue to Alger Hiss, and while Muslim intellectuals in the West sometimes engage in double-talk about the illiberal aspects of their faith, there is simply no Islamic equivalent of the Marxists who once populated Western academia and openly expected to undo the liberal capitalist order from within.

Finally, Houellebecq imagines a French Islam whose adherents are numerous enough to build a powerful Muslim Brotherhood–style political party in the heart of Europe; in our world, that scenario still seems relatively remote. Alarmists predicting the West's imminent fall to an Islamic successor often concede that, yes, Islamic countries aren't powerful or geopolitically ascendant, but that doesn't matter because Muslims in Europe are having babies and non-Muslims aren't, so by simple demographic momentum, the Islamic crescent will eventually rule Britain and Germany and France. But while the fertility differential is real, and the Syrian refugee crisis demonstrates that demographic change can accelerate suddenly, it's also the case that Middle Eastern birthrates have been tumbling for a generation, headed for the same below-replacement levels as the West. What's more, birthrates for Muslims within Europe are higher than for natives but dropping steadily as well. So while assimilation is clearly a serious problem for Europe, a source of ongoing tension, violence, and political disruption, it's still a leap from that trend to something more culturally existential—some future that transforms restive minorities into majorities; something that drives Islamicization outside the banlieue and the ghetto. (A true demographic transformation in Europe would require massive *sub-Saharan African* immigration, much of it Christian—but that's a topic for part 3.)

In the end, the convergence in fertility between the Middle East and western Europe, and between immigrants and natives on the Continent itself, may suffice to limit Europe's Islamicization—absent, again, some kind of larger intellectual and cultural revolution, some as-yet-unseen ascent of Islamic practices and ideas. Such an ascent is possible; Islam's encounter with the secularized version of its ancient Christian rival is the kind of strange collision in which unexpected futures might be forged. But the form of Islam that could imaginably replace liberalism hasn't been invented yet.

The Phantom of Illiberalism

Some of this analysis of Islam's weaknesses applies to other potential rivals to the liberal world. First, there is the ideological problem: the fact that the West's would-be rivals lack the mix of zeal, coherence, mysticism, and futurism that tends to propel challengers to established world pictures. (I'm thinking not only of Communism and fascism but also, before them, liberalism in its challenge to the ancien régime, and before liberalism, Protestantism, early Islam, early Christianity.) Indeed, Islam is stronger on this count than others. For all its civilizational weaknesses, the Muslim world picture does inspire stringent zeal and real belief—whereas elsewhere in the non-Western world, there is a lot more intellectual fraudulence where conviction ought to be.

Take the case of Vladimir Putin's Russia, which has lately sought to return to the ideological role that Moscow played under the czars—as a rallying point for traditionalists worldwide, as a religious-conservative bulwark against the West's revolutionary liberals. Putin has obviously enjoyed some success with this gambit: he has admirers among Europe's far right parties, authoritarian friends around the globe, and his interventions in Ukraine and then in America's 2016 election prompted a surge of liberal Russophobia, with talk of a renewed Cold War.

But as a worldview, a system, an alternative civilizational architecture, Putinism is mostly smoke and mirrors. The czars' traditionalism was in defense a still-extant ancien régime, a still-potent traditional Christianity, an order rooted in a deep historical inheritance even when its days were numbered. Today's Russia, brutalized by Communism and then taken over by oligarchs and grifters, is not a traditional society in any meaningful sense of the term, and the only thing it has in common with many of its potential developing-world allies is a contempt for democratic norms. Under the Romanovs, the throne-and-altar idea still had a real claim to political legitimacy. But there is no comparable claim Putin can make for his own authority, and no similar mystique around his client dictators, be they Central Asian strongmen or Syria's Bashar al-Assad. And there is no obvious mode of transmission for his system once he dies or retires: his successor will either take power by brute force or claim the pseudolegitimacy of a rigged election, the tribute that even its enemies pay to the norms of the liberal era. Either way, there will not be a clear alternative to liberalism at work, only violence or parody or both.

Perhaps there is something embryonic within the "illiberal democracy" being practiced in various ways by various strongmen from Moscow to Istanbul that could *develop* into a serious ideological challenger to the West. But unlike the totalitarianisms of the 1930s, or, for that matter, unlike the Islamic Republic of Iran or the Kingdom of Saudi Arabia, none of these regimes has actually claimed an alternative source of legitimacy; an alternative vision of where sovereignty resides. "Illiberal democracy" in practice is either just liberal democracy with somewhat more nationalism than Western bien-pensants prefer, or pseudodemocracy dominated by a dictator who doesn't want to own up to his own authoritarianism—because, again, he's still tacitly accepting the legitimacy of the late-modern Western liberal order. Let Putin be crowned czar of all the Russias, let Turkey's Recep Tayyip Erdoğan revive the caliphate under his own personal rule, let Poland or Hungary remake themselves as Christian monarchies, and we can begin to talk about the fall of the Fukuyaman, end-of-history world. But what exists in the so-called illiberal democracies now is just a more nationalist or conservative or degraded form of what exists in "normal" Western countries—a somewhat different variety of decadence, most likely, rather than a postliberal inheritor.

Nor is it even necessarily new. How is Viktor Orban's officially democratic but one-party-dominated Hungary all that different from the de facto one-party system that prevailed in Mexico for most of the second half of the twentieth century? From the de facto one-party rule that often characterized mid-to-late-twentieth-century South Korea and Japan? It's quite normal for democratic systems to produce powerful parties that bend the rules to keep themselves in power, and nobody thinks that Mexico when it was dominated by the Institutional Revolutionary Party (PRI) represented an ideological challenge to liberal democracy. For all the sound and fury about so-called illiberal democracy under Orban or Poland's nationalist party, Law and Justice, the same may be true of eastern Europe today.

Doubting the Chinese Century

China is a more complicated case. In one sense, it mirrors the Russian situation, since it still bills itself as a Marxist-Leninist state, but nobody believes the official rhetoric, making its formal ideological self-presentation an exercise in sustained mendacity. At the same time, you can see in the Chinese system something closer to the form that a postliberal order might take: a system where technocracy is formally elevated over liberal norms and democratic principles; a system promising that a modernized Confucian bureaucracy, a twenty-first-century version of China's past experiments in meritocracy, can deliver growth and order and (perhaps especially) technological innovation more effectively than liberalism can.

It's for this reason that, unlike Islamism, the Chinese system has soft admirers among the Western elite. Not admirers of one-party rule, precisely, but pundits and businessmen who are at least impressed by the way that Beijing can push ahead with big policy changes and big projects without the snarls of democratic debate. And unlike Putin's Russia, China has enjoyed a rate of economic growth that's both an advertisement for its system and a source of growing global soft power. So the elites in developing nations—in Africa especially—who see its one-party meritocracy as a model worth imitating are closer to constituting a nascent postliberal order than are the illiberal client states of Moscow.

The possibility that Chinese civilization will really inherit the earth will be considered further in part 3. But China's future also might illustrate a different hypothesis, which is that the near future will see a kind of *convergence-in-decadence* between the world's rising great powers and its existing empires, in which growth and progress in the non-Western world levels off and political futility increases, and it turns out that the problems discussed in part 1—the stagnation and sclerosis of an aging society—are waiting to greet China (and India and Brazil and Turkey and Nigeria . . .) as well.

In this future, the reality of decadence as I've described it would be compatible with a lot of the boosterism about the "rise of the rest," and the arguments about dramatic recent global progress associated with liberal optimists like Harvard's Pangloss, Steven Pinker. On the surface, the almost-everything-is-getting-better arguments that Pinker has made in books like *Enlightenment Now* and *The Better Angels of Our Nature* seem in tension with my thesis, but not necessarily or completely. Pinker's optimistic take could be accurately describing the very real gains to human welfare that are achieved by developing nations as they follow Europe, the United States, and East Asia down the liberal-capitalist path. But then *decadence* would be accurately describing what waits for those nations at the end of their journey.

In other words, instead of the kind of leapfrogging that happened when the United States of the late-nineteenth and early-twentieth centuries surged past Great Britain to claim global mastery and technological dominance, in the twenty-first century we would see only convergence, as today's rising powers and developing economies succumb to the same aging, the same torpor, that have afflicted the richest economies since the 1970s. This is especially likely to be the case if the more pessimistic reading of our recent technological stagnation is correct, and we are really hitting ceilings on world-changing break-throughs, not just experiencing a temporary lull. The technology writer Timothy Lee, for instance, has suggested that if the great modern leap was produced by a few nonreproducible breakthroughs—the exploitation of fossil fuels, above all, with a last boost offered by the invention of the transistor—then we should expect not an Asian-dominated future of continued rapid growth, but a future in which "the living standards of mature post-industrial civilizations . . . converge on a sustainable level," taking different paths to the same prosperous stagnation.

We already saw a version of this when Europe's economies, which had grown so rapidly in the 1950s and 1960s, didn't actually pass the United States after the 1970s, when our current era of stagnation began, but instead stagnated in their turn. In the same way, China and India and others might see their own growth level off as the low-hanging fruit is plucked, the easy gains are made, and the pressures of demographic decline begin to make themselves felt in Asia as well.

And those pressures are likely to be, if anything, stronger in the economies that are supposed to dominate the "post-American world" than they have been in the developed West, because the transition to low birthrates has happened more swiftly in many of those countries—sometimes prodded along, as in China, by ruthless population-control programs—and created a situation where the new powers may end up growing old before they finish growing rich. If economic growth rates in East Asia and South Asia level off, it's easy to see still-darker versions of the decadent world's problems besetting Asian societies: the loneliness of a postfamilial society's middle-aged and elderly worsened by the relative weakness of the social safety net, the West's male-dropout problem worsened by abortion-induced male-skewing sex ratios and millions of surplus young men.

Disappointing growth is hardly a hypothetical. In Brazil and South Africa, often touted as potential great powers of the future, the economic growth rates of the last ten years have been indistinguishable from growth rates in America and Europe. India has done better, and the absence of one-child totalitarianism means that it isn't growing old as fast as China. But in the last few years, there has been an unexpected Indian deceleration, linked in part to the ham-fisted way that Prime Minister Narendra Modi's government imposed currency and tax reforms. The joke often applied to Brazil, that "it's the country of the future, and it always will be," recurs with similar-situated countries for a reason: it's (relatively) easy for poor, misgoverned countries to grow rapidly for a time when misgovernment diminishes, but it's a lot harder to achieve an acceleration that carries them past the pacesetters and into the new economic territory that the escape from decadence requires. In this sense, the story of globalization might turn out to be both a Pinkerian story of rising standards of living *and* a story of ultimate stagnation—because the trains are all headed toward the same destination, and nobody's found another line of track to take instead.

Perhaps this won't be true of China; perhaps it's already on a different railway line. But at the very least, there should be doubts around the edges of the Chinese story. Its growth statistics are remarkable but not entirely trustworthy. There is a particularly suspicious stability since 2015, when the GDP growth rate fell to 7 percent from its once-consistent high of more than 10 percent per annum, and some measures of activity suggest that, in fact, the real growth rate has been much lower than the official numbers for the last five years. Even the official numbers show a deceleration that is taking China off the trajectory achieved by Japan and South Korea—a consequence, the *Wall Street Journal*'s Greg Ip suggested in a recent analysis, of China's rapid aging, its reliance on state-driven infrastructure spending, and its substantial overhang of debt.

Meanwhile, even if China's police state looks frighteningly effective at the moment, the degree of repression exerted against religious minorities and dissidents is itself a signifier of internal divisions, fault lines that might shift destructively should growth begin to really fail. President Xi Jinping's recent consolidation of power at the expense of the party elite that elevated him shows how easily a meritocratic-technocratic model of legitimacy can decay back into autocracy. The Chinese network of client states is more a patchwork than any kind of NATO in the making, with plenty of anti-Chinese resentment at work behind the scenes. And China's approach to diplomacy during the window of influence granted by its suppression of the coronavirus and the West's struggle to do the same has been swaggering and often counterproductive, encouraging its own encirclement rather than wooing prospective allies away from the American-led order.

And for the leaders of the world's soon-to-be dominant power, China's elite can appear rather pessimistic. Capital flight keeps rising, a near majority of wealthy Chinese would like to emigrate, and those who do leave the country warn of darker times ahead: when Chen Tianyong, a real estate developer, decamped for Malta in early 2019, he published a long manifesto (which quickly disappeared from the Chinese Internet) describing China's economy as "a giant ship heading to the precipice. . . . Without fundamental changes, it's inevitable that the ship will be wrecked and the passengers will die."

The Chinese government seems all too aware of the potential structural pressures on its system and the possible limitations on future growth. This 2015 analysis from Peter Thiel might be an overstatement, but it's worth pondering:

China is probably the most definitely pessimistic place in the world today. When Americans see the Chinese economy grow ferociously fast (10 percent per year since 2000), we imagine a confident country mastering its future. But that's because Americans are still optimists, and we project our optimism onto China. From China's viewpoint, economic growth cannot come fast enough. Every other country is afraid that China is going to take over the world; China is the only country afraid that it won't. . . . China can grow so fast only because its starting base is so low. The easiest way for China to grow is to relentlessly copy what has already worked in the West. And that's exactly what it's doing: executing definite plans by burning ever more coal to build ever more factories and skyscrapers. But with a huge population pushing resource prices higher, there's no way Chinese living standards can ever actually catch up to those of the richest countries, and the Chinese know it.

This is why the Chinese leadership is obsessed with the way in which things threaten to get worse. Every senior Chinese leader experienced famine as a child, so when the Politburo looks to the future, disaster is not an abstraction. The Chinese public, too, knows that winter is coming. Outsiders are fascinated by the great fortunes being made inside China, but they pay less attention to the wealthy Chinese trying hard to get their money out of the country. Poorer Chinese just save everything they can and hope it will be enough.

Now, disaster may not actually arrive, and if it doesn't, Chinese power will be greater in a generation than it is today, and there will be necessary global political adjustments that follow from that fact. But a powerful China is not the same thing as a hegemonic China, or a China that's seen as a cultural or political model for the world. If China ends up as another rich-but-stagnating economy with a distrusted elite relying on surveillance and other technologies of control to maintain its hold on power, then it won't have pioneered an alternative to Western liberalism that the rest of the world will leap to follow; it will be another case study in convergence, of liberal democracies and pseudodemocracies and would-be meritocracies all ending up in the same kind of place, as de facto oligarchies trying to manage stagnation and its discontents.

Decadence Defends Itself

The desire for flight from China, the desire among the very people who seem poised to guide the West's great rival to instead decamp for New York or London or Vancouver, points to still another way that decadence is well defended: the Western order is still pretty good at weakening potential rivals through recruitment.

The system that we call meritocracy, with its promise to build an elite by finding the best and brightest in every corner of society—and in a global society, every corner of the globe—advertises itself as a way to build the most talented possible upper class, the most intellectually deserving elite. The actual record of the Western elite over the last generation offers reasons to doubt this claim of talent and desserts. But even if it is false, meritocracy may still shore up and protect even an ineffective elite, because it drains the talent from the provinces and the peripheries and deprives potential rivals and potential rebels of the leaders who otherwise might challenge its hegemony.

This talent-draining, rival-co-opting scenario is not some outlandish conspiracy theory. It appears in the first clear description of modern meritocracy; indeed, in the book that coined the term: Michael Young's *The Rise of the Meritocracy*, a work of fiction published in 1958 that masqueraded as a work of history and political analysis written in the year 2034. The fictional author of the text, a smug sociologist who believes absolutely in the new order and the "brilliant" elite created by privileging standardized tests over the social register, explains near the end why, unlike the prior ruling class, the meritocracy will never be overthrown: because it co-opts exactly the kind of people who might do the overthrowing:

> The last century has witnessed a far-reaching redistribution of ability between the classes in society, and the consequence is that the lower classes no longer have the power to make revolt effective.

For a short moment, they may prosper through an alliance with the odd and passing disillusion of a section of the upper classes. But such déclassé people can never be more than an eccentric minority—the Populists have never been more than that as a serious political force—because the élite is treated with all the wise distinction that any heart can desire. Without intelligence in their heads, the lower classes are never more menacing than a rabble, even if they are sometimes sullen, sometimes mercurial, not yet completely predictable. If the hopes of some earlier dissidents had been realized and the brilliant children from the lower classes remained there, to teach, to inspire, and to organize the masses, then I should have had a different story to tell. The few who now propose such a radical step are a hundred years too late.

A footnote to the text reveals that the author of this arrogant analysis was murdered by a populist mob soon thereafter. But Young doesn't reveal whether the mob was able to prove the author's smugness wrong by doing more than rioting, leaving open the possibility that the basic reality of meritocracy is what he both embodies and describes: a cognitive elite whose arrogance and insularity match the pedigreed aristocrats of old, but who are graced with populist enemies too disorganized, self-defeating, and easily deceived to do more than riot and react.

Two brain drains sustain this balance: one global and the other national. The global brain drain happens through high-skilled immigration, the one kind of immigration that still has something like bipartisan support in the polarized West. And for good reason, if you think of it as a process whereby the skilled professionals or would-be professionals of Latin America and Africa find their way to Europe and North America—there might be more Ethiopian doctors in Chicago than in Ethiopia, to pick a particularly arresting example—and try to help their children find their way into the West's elite, while the countries that they leave behind get remittances in exchange for losing their natural leadership class to Western cities. The deal's efficiency is blessed by practically every professional economist, but it's political consequences are also notable: it's a pretty good way to make the Western world's potential rivals a little bit richer but a lot less talent rich, by siphoning away their most ambitious citizens, offering them membership in an elite that they might otherwise supplant.

Something similar happens domestically as well. The most feared "barbarians" in the Western world today aren't invaders from the distant steppes; they're the Rust Belt deplorables voting for Trump, the *gilets-jaunes* burning shops on the Champs-Élysées, the little Englanders forcing their country into an unexpected Brexit. A great deal of anxious elite commentary about our decadent order assumes that these internal rebels might pull down the system from within, that populists "inside the gates" (assisted by Russian bots and selfish, short-sighted plutocrats) are the existential threat that Western institutions last faced when the Soviet Union was still in business; that the European Union and NATO and America's Pacific alliances could all be pulled apart by nationalism, and the jungle world of the 1930s could suddenly return.

But as we saw in chapter 3, there is very little to suggest that the populist movements are prepared to wield power in any effective way. Instead, they resemble the description of the "mercurial" working classes offered by Young's pompous civil servant: they are disorganized, poorly led, conspiratorial and anti-intellectual in a way that undercuts their own effectiveness, vulnerable to con men and manipulators, and swing wildly from far right to further left without finding talented leaders or a clear program. The shambolic progress of Brexit, the feckless governance of Donald Trump, the inchoate protest politics roiling France—these are disturbances, but they are not exactly transformations, and they still resemble Jacques Barzun's reference to "the deadlocks of our time" far more than they do Vladimir Lenin's ride to the Finland Station or Mussolini's March on Rome. And the mix of anxieties and aspirations involved seem querulous, irascible, nostalgic—a populism of the Western twilight, a nationalism of civilizational old age, a reaction to stagnation that's stagnationist itself.

Again Houellebecq's dreamworld is a useful contrast. In his novel, the Islamist president is an empire builder, like European nationalists in the 1930s. But in our world, Marine Le Pen is not going to reconquer Algeria or bring back the House of Bourbon—she just wants to throw out immigrants and redistribute wealth to pensioners and provincials. Even the nationalists of eastern Europe, the most politically effective Western populists, don't actually want to leave the European Union. They mostly seem to want to roll back the clock to the degree of national independence enjoyed by member states circa 1975, with less immigration and more domestic cronyism than EU norms allow. The promise to "make X great again" thus cashes out as a more ethnocentric way to experience sclerosis, a little more self-determination amid stagnation, plus a dose of corruption on the side. It might be bad; it isn't yet the counterrevolution.

Perhaps our populists just await the right leader, the right crisis, the right combination of the man and the moment to become agents of actual regime change. But it is also possible that meritocracy really does protect elites from effective challenges, and that our current spasm of populism is just that, a spasm, after which the establishment will return unchastened to power as it already has in the form of a center-left septuagenarian in the United States. In which case the convergence between the unstable powers of the developing world and the stagnating leaders of the developed world could universalize a pseudorepublican form of oligarchy, as in the populist-friendly intellectual Michael Lind's vision of what the later-twenty-first century might hold if populism is defeated:

> The other possibility . . . is that today's class war will come to an end when the managerial minority, with its near monopoly of wealth, political power, expertise, and media influence, com-

pletely and successfully represses the numerically greater but politically weaker working-class majority. If that is the case, the future
North America and Europe may look a lot like Brazil and Mexico,
with nepotistic oligarchies clustered in a few fashionable metro-
politan areas but surrounded by a derelict, depopulated, and despised "hinterland."

You can spin a still-darker, global version of the Lindian scenario
if you weave in the challenge to sustainability that this chapter hasn't
considered yet: the challenge of climate change, and the possibility
that decadence will end in fire and flood. The more apocalyptic scenarios for climate crisis will be taken up in the final section of this
book, but the less apocalyptic possibilities—which are also the more
likely ones, the core Intergovernmental Panel on Climate Change
projections—suggest a future in which climate change is mostly a
manageable burden for wealthy countries, imposing discomfort and
requiring adaptation and mitigation, but not, in fact, the end of civilization as we know it. On the other hand, rising temperatures are more
likely to be a seriously destabilizing force in poorer countries, in the
global South, in Africa and the Middle East and India—more likely to
limit economic growth, more likely to overwhelm efforts at mitigation,
more likely to encourage yet more of those regions' elites to decamp
for London or New York and more likely to simply kill the people left
behind.

In which case, it's possible that strictly as a matter of Machiavellian
self-interest, unmoored from moral debt or humanitarian obligation,
climate change will prop up Western or developed-world dominance.
A crisis created unintentionally by Western industrial development
could, in one of history's cruel ironies, help a decadent West hold off
challenges from its rivals because it imposes greater ecological costs
on the formerly colonized, the formerly defeated, than on the countries that led the first industrial wave and first began to warm the world.

Therefore one can imagine a future shaped by climate change

that's like the present, but more so. Every rich place on earth would be more like every other rich place, every poor place more like every other poor place, and the national-level political order would seem like a fractal of the international-level political order. There would be an elite that seems interchangeable from country to country, a restive impotence and a lot of human suffering wherever that elite is hated or opposed, zones of chaos and disorder that don't really threaten the metropole, and no nation or civilization charting a radically different course. That's a useful distillation of what it would mean for decadence to continue despite recent disturbances, and, indeed, to gradually become universal; that might be what sustainable decadence would mean.

Why this sudden restlessness, this confusion?
Because night has fallen and the barbarians have not come.

And it's more likely than you think.

8

Giving Decadence Its Due

Now I want to briefly answer the frustration that has probably been building, among the more normal and well-adjusted and unfanciful sort of reader, with the tone of the preceding chapters. The world I am describing as perhaps "sustainably decadent" is, after all, as wealthy and healthy and long-lived as any society in human history, with many cruelties removed, various inequalities substantially reduced, the hand of tyranny lighter on most people than in many prior epochs, the chances of horrifying tragedy diminished. Of course there are problems, unhappiness, difficulties, territories of suffering and exile and despair. But given the range of possible options and the possible apocalypses that always lurk ahead, shouldn't we *want* the current order to be sustained, decadent or not? And if so, then instead of bemoaning the inevitable flaws of our present situation, shouldn't we work harder to celebrate its virtues and, in the process, resist and marginalize the death wish—the sense of romantic regret at the end of history, the dangerous yearning for high purpose, the suicidal yearning for a barbarian invasion?

Obviously, I think such celebration is a mistake, or this book would not exist, because it would suffice to read a Pinkerian panegyric to modernity and then go take your Zoloft and binge-watch yourself to sleep. But I would go this far with the skeptical reader: if it's essential not to simply treat a prosperous stagnation as the highest of human aspirations, it's also important for a decadent era's critics to give decadence its due.

The Risks of Antidecadence

That due starts with the reality that complaining about decadence is, almost by definition, a luxury good—a feature of societies where the mail is delivered, the trains and planes are running on time, the crime rate is relatively low, and there are plenty of entertainments at your fingertips. Neither I nor most of this book's likely readers have known the kind of fear endemic to the human condition in less privileged and prosperous eras, under chronically unstable political conditions, or simply under the kind of tyrannies that make a "pink police state" or a "soft despotism" look, well, soft and easily endured. The dose of existential fear occasioned by the coronavirus has been quite enough, thank you, to teach us to appreciate the gifts of health and life and order. A general peace and a relative stability are not the highest goods, but they are still important ones—and their despisers sometimes find themselves gravely punished when they get the more dynamic world they crave.

Not every attempt to escape decadence leads to such a punishment. But the last hundred-odd years of Western anxieties about the subject offer plenty of examples of a disastrous style in antidecadent politics—in which a craving for Meaning and Action leads to the piled corpses of Verdun and Passchendaele; or a desire to escape political deadlocks and stalemate leads to the Führer and the thousand-year Reich; or a nostalgic yearning for the great ideological clashes of the Cold War leads to post-9/11 hysteria, a military quagmire in Middle Eastern deserts, an imaginary World War IV with casualties that are all too real. If the motto of a decadent civilization might be the English Catholic essayist Hilaire Belloc's couplet "always keep a-hold of Nurse / For fear of finding something worse," the politics of antidecadence has a way of finding that "something worse" with disquieting regularity.

Which makes it perfectly rational to cast a cold eye on decadent societies, to recognize their disadvantages and disappointments and secret sins, to point out the way their trajectories can bend toward a comfortable corruption, a rotten sort of peace—and yet also provisionally prefer their frustrations and stalemates to many of the possible alternatives. Especially since Adam Smith's line that "there is a great deal of ruin in a nation" also applies to decadence; many elements in a society can turn stagnant, there can be many intimations of dystopia, before the possibility of human flourishing is in any way extinguished.

It is not always easy, but human beings can still live vigorously amid a general stagnation, be fruitful amid sterility, be creative amid repetition, and build good and fully human lives that offer, in microcosm, a counterpoint and challenge to the decadent macrocosm. And the decadent society, unlike the full dystopia, allows those signs of contradictions to exist, which means that, under decadence, it always remains possible to imagine and work toward renewal and renaissance. This is not always the case, to put it mildly, when you gamble on a revolution, or hasten a crisis, or open the doors to barbarians from outside or within.

Of course, one of the recurring critiques of the decadent society is that its stability is an illusion, that sustainable decadence is a contradiction in terms, and that decadence always makes a civilization uniquely vulnerable to crisis, invasion, destruction—in which case it's better to gamble on the revolution, risks and all, than just sit waiting for the inevitable coup de grace. But giving decadence its due also requires noting that dynamic societies are perfectly capable of bringing destruction upon themselves, when they hit some ecological limit without realizing it (there was nothing decadent about the Easter Islanders, nobody more dynamic than the Once-ler in Dr. Seuss's *The Lorax*) or gain some technical mastery they are ill-equipped to handle. It was not decadence but the dynamism of the atomic age that almost destroyed the world in 1962 and in a few close calls thereafter. It will not be decadence but dynamism—the dynamism of the still-developing world, where carbon emissions are rising even as they dip in the slow-growth West—that gives us a climate catastrophe, should one ultimately come. As a thousand Faustian tales attest, destruction can easily be the unexpected punishment for Promethean ambition.

Stewarding Stability

With this peril in mind, one can even build a case for sustainable decadence not as a falling-off or disappointing end but as a case of the human race finally achieving a healthy balance between the misery of grinding poverty and the dangers of growth for growth's own sake. From this perspective, the rich world's present stagnation, for all its discontents, is actually the best way to balance humanity's material needs against its tendency toward self-destruction. Sustainable decadence offers the ample benefits of prosperity with fewer of the risks that more disruptive eras offer to a species as capable of self-slaughter as our own. Indeed, pending the discovery of a nearby Earth-2 ready for human habitation, we should be grateful if growth and innovation stall out. The richest countries should be content to stay roughly where we are, enjoying ever-more-immersive leisure pursuits that GDP doesn't measure, the developing world should be content to aim for convergence—and stagnation beyond that point shouldn't bother us too much, because it means that we'll avoid all kinds of risks. Technological stagnation means that robots won't kill us all or even take our jobs; intellectual and religious and ideological stagnation means fewer fanaticisms and utopian follies; demographic decline is defusing the population bomb; and economic stagnation could be the only force capable of limiting carbon emissions and keeping climate change manageable.

The crucial task for twenty-first-century humanity, in this view, would be making the most of a prosperous stagnation: learning to temper our expectations and live within limits; making sure existing resources are distributed more justly; improving institutional functioning at the margins; using education to lift people, especially young men, out of the prison-and-virtual-reality nexus and into the sunlit uplands of the creative class; treating the chronic conditions of old age more humanely; and doing everything we can to help poorer countries transition successfully into our current position. This would require accepting that the postwar boom isn't coming back, accepting that the space race was mostly just Cold War posturing, accepting that we're an aging society that can't afford vast socialist experiments or growth-chasing supply-side fantasies, accepting that we aren't going to spread democracy by force of arms—accepting, in other words, that the discontents motivating idealists of the center and populists of the right and left are just differing forms of nostalgia, which can be managed but never satisfied, and which are ultimately just impediments to achieving contentment in our civilization's old age.

I think it's fair to see this view, however underarticulated, as one of the important premises of the last American presidency's policy making. Like Trump and Bernie Sanders eight years later, Barack Obama ran for president in 2008 as a critic of decadence, as a yes-we-can idealist promising a return to the 1960s New Frontier, and he certainly made forays into liberal utopianism during his eight years in office. But his real temperament was technocratic and managerial, and the management of decadence—a "Don't do stupid shit" approach to everything from financial capitalism and globalization, to China and the Middle East—was an essential feature of Obaman governance.

Which his enemies and critics recognized. Conservatives called it "managing decline," the left called it "neoliberalism," and the Trump-Sanders populist efflorescence emerged from those critiques. But Sanders lost the primaries twice, Trump lost the popular vote twice, and in 2020 the American people opted for the closest thing to an Obama restoration by installing his vice president in the White

House. So perhaps it's too soon to declare that this kind of managerial stewardship is doomed to political defeat and that populist rebellions will inevitably overthrow its cautious competence. Perhaps with the right leaders and a little luck, managerialism will make a comeback. Perhaps the technocrats will learn some lessons from their recent failures. Perhaps the task of sustaining decadence is the task that we—we the fortunate, we the long-lived, we the spoiled—should want our leaders to pursue.

This is the optimistic answer to the Michael Lind scenario with which the prior chapter closed. In this revision of his pessimism, it holds that it would be a *good* thing for the "managerial minority" to suppress populist revolts and rule from its creative-class enclaves and meritocratic hubs, because simply preserving our "fully grown" economy (to borrow a phrase from the economist Dietrich Vollrath) is the most important task of statesmanship. And for all its faults, our technocratic elite—the Romney-Republican variation as well as the Obamanauts and Bidenites—has strong incentives to make sure that our in many ways enviable situation lasts as long as possible and can be enjoyed by as many people as possible while it does.

Accepting rule by technocrats doesn't mean that we shouldn't also want reforms to help the people who aren't enjoying decadence, who are suffering economically or physically or emotionally—we should! But those reforms should take the (centrist, neoliberal, technocratic) form of better schools or better opioid treatment programs or better incentives for corporate investment in the heartland; they should be incremental, meliorist, and cautious. Not because meliorism can cure every ill, but because the more revolutionary alternatives are too dangerous, and a simple greatest-good-for-the-greatest number calculus requires that we keep the existing system running and seek its stability against fantasies of utopia or risky schemes for limitless expansion.

I am describing this view and not endorsing it, but I should admit that I did endorse a version of it, in effect, by declining to cast a presidential vote for Donald Trump, in elections—especially, perhaps, the election of 2020—where he faced off against candidates who embodied exactly the kind of sustainable-decadence liberalism I've just described. Sure, Trump is a phony and ineffective scourge of decadence, but I didn't decline to vote for him because of his phoniness; I declined because I feared the unknown dangers that his promise of disruption carried in its train, with the case study of how he handled the coronavirus as confirmation of those fears. So I, too, followed the logic sketched above: despite believing that the populists have a point, despite having enough critiques of decadence to fill this book, when offered the chance to risk the return of history, I declined to take the gamble, preferring the technocrats and their stewardship of stagnation because I'm afraid of what might inherit power should they fall.

The experience of being a very young writer during the post-9/11 moment, when many conservatives and some liberals romanticized the return of history and then regretted the war that followed, probably shapes my caution here. That experience offered me a milder version of the lesson that waits at the end of Evelyn Waugh's story of English Catholic aristocrats in the 1940s, the Sword of Honour trilogy, which follows the romantically inclined Guy Crouchback through his disillusioning years of military service during World War II. Near the end of the third book, *Unconditional Surrender*, Crouchback has the following exchange with a Jewish escapee from the war's savagery while he's working to save refugees in the Balkans:

> "It is too simple to say that only the Nazis wanted war. These Communists wanted it too. It was the only way in which they could come to power. Many of my people wanted it, to be revenged on the Germans, to hasten the creation of the national state. It seems there was a will to war, a death wish, everywhere. Even good men thought their private honour would be satisfied by war. They could assert their manhood by killing and being killed. They

would accept hardships in recompense for having been selfish and lazy. Danger justified privilege. I knew Italians—not very many, perhaps—who felt this. Were there none in England?"

"God forgive me," said Guy. "I was one of them."

So now, as in prior eras, a decadent world does not need a surfeit of Guy Crouchbacks, hastening off in search of their longed-for crusade and finding only blood and death and disappointment.

The Shadow of Dystopia

Yet decadence still needs critics, because the case for sustainability carries you only so far. Even if the dystopia never quite arrives, the longer a period of stagnation and repetition continues, the more the "futility" and "absurdity" that Barzun describes as characteristic of such eras will crowd out essential human goods, and the narrower the space for fecundity and piety, memory and invention, creativity and daring. If attempts to lurch upward from decadence can risk disaster, the unresisted drift of decadence leads, however slowly and comfortably, into a territory of darkness, a posthuman landscape as barbarous as it is posh, whose sleekness covers over a sickness unto death.

And without critics, without resistance, this drift can carry things a long way without anyone fully noticing how far. True dystopias are distinguished, in part, by the fact that many people inside them don't realize that they're living in one, because human beings are adaptable enough to take even absurd and inhuman premises for granted. There's a reason that only Aldous Huxley's Savage, raised fully outside the World State, can articulate a full critique; the other characters in *Brave New World* achieve at most an unsettlement, an allergy, a personal resistance. Likewise if we feel that elements of our own system are, shall we say, dystopia-ish—from the reality-television star in the White House to the addictive surveillance devices always in our pockets and our hands; from the drugs and suicides in our decaying hinterlands to the dogs-over-kids sterility of our rich cities—then it's possible that a true outsider would look at our decadence and judge it even more severely than I do. A time traveler from the past, say, who spent an hour on our porn sites or our social media networks or an evening watching cable news or a day in an opioid clinic might report back that the future is simply dystopian, full stop.

So to embrace decadence as a destination is to always risk becoming, without ever realizing it, the equivalent of Mustapha Mond, Huxley's World State steward—a smooth defender of stability for its own sake, of "civilization" as the abolition of human nature for the sake of human comfort, who condescends to his dystopia's critics with a litany of all the ills that his brave new world has cured. A version of that condescension informs every defense of our present situation (*I suppose you want to bring back smallpox. . . . I bet you miss the plague. . . . Nostalgic for the witch trials, are you?*), and it's a voice that will still be there, smug to the very last, if our dystopian elements become more universal but our wealth and stability remain.

So it must be met, not by fantasies of ennobling world wars, not by Tyler Durden from *Fight Club* planning to blow up all credit card companies and Ikea living rooms sky-high, but by the hope that where there's stability, there also might eventually be renewal, that decadence need not give way to collapse to be escaped—that, instead, it can be transcended, that the renaissance can happen without the misery of an intervening dark age.

Meanwhile, it's also a mistake to overrate the influence of a civilization's critics. Generally, the dark age comes—the war or the catastrophe or the apocalypse—whether the critics of decadence welcome it or not. Nothing lasts forever: not the cruel decadence of the last world empire, and not our own version of the Roman peace. And it's to the potential deaths of our decadence, the ways our Rome might fall or change or be reborn, that this book's final section turns.

PART 3

The Deaths of Decadence

9

Catastrophe

In Mel Gibson's *Apocalypto*, a feverish 2006 movie made by a man descending into his own personal inferno, we are given a vision of an imaginary Mesoamerican civilization, a pastiche of Aztec and Maya, just before the Spanish conquest. The story is told through the eyes of a hunter named Jaguar Paw, who lives an Edenic life with his tribe in the forest primeval before he is kidnapped, and his clansmen murdered, by a party of warriors from the capital. Dragged from the jungle into cultivated fields, through suburbs, and up to the pyramid-shadowed city where he's destined to be a human sacrifice, he witnesses a civilization in decay—beset by disease, social dissolution, and environmental ruin, with its political system turning to the superstitious wickedness of ritual murder in a desperate attempt to escape the cost of its own sins.

Since we know that the Spanish are lurking just offstage, this portrait of Mesoamerica before the fall fits the epigraph that Gibson gives the film, a line from the historian Will Durant: "A great civilization is not conquered from without until it has destroyed itself from within."

The movie is great, but the epigraph is wrong, and the real history of pre-Columbian America is a counterpoint rather than an example of Durant's claim. There were problems in the great Native empires, of course, weaknesses and corruptions and internal divisions that Hernán Cortés and Francisco Pizarro were able to exploit. But there is no certain proof that the Aztec or Inca empires were at maximally decadent phases of their existence overall, no sense that the fall of either Montezuma or the Great Inca was somehow predictable given just the evidence of what was happening within their pre-Columbian domains.

Instead the Native empires fell because of what *couldn't* be predicted or expected just from extrapolating the trends of, say, 1350 to 1475. Even if an educated futurist in Tenochtitlan in the years before Cortés had somehow imagined the possibility of a technologically proficient invader arriving from distant shores, given the state of knowledge at the time (on both sides of the Atlantic), nobody could have foreseen the world-historical role played by the armies of microbes that came with the conquistadores, devastating indigenous societies and preparing them to crumple before the military blows that followed. The lesson of 1492 and its consequences isn't that misgovernment and human sacrifice invite conquest and guarantee destruction. It's that any civilizational order, decadent or otherwise, is sustainable only until the right black-swan development arrives, at which point it might be doomed in a way that no simple extrapolation, no sociological analysis, could have possibly predicted.

The Columbian encounter is a particularly stark example, but human history offers plenty of case studies in unexpected apocalypses, which arrive with little regard for the internal situation of the society, and overwhelm the resilient and decadent alike. Just as our Aztec futurist would have failed to see European microbes coming, an analyst of Roman politics in the age of the Antonines couldn't have predicted the impact of devastating plagues on the later empire, and a pundit in thirteenth-century Paris wouldn't have seen the worst of the Black Death coming and with it the collapse of the high-medieval order.

Our own era knows much more about the causes and risks of plagues, and we've just received an object lesson in their recurrence even in the antibiotic age. So it's somewhat less likely that a sudden assassin for our civilization would be entirely invisible in the way that certain past assassins were. But it could certainly be unexpected—a trend only now gathering unseen, a mutation that hasn't happened yet, a catastrophe that in hindsight will seem essentially random, noncontingent and unrelated to any specific feature of our age.

Or, alternatively, our age could end with an apocalypse that's contingent on our technological proficiency, but that still happens entirely accidentally or as an act of terrorism or interstate sabotage that gets wildly out of hand. This is a danger that the Aztecs and Romans didn't face, but we do: our achievements mean that even under conditions of stagnation, even without the leap toward the kind of world-destroying artificial intelligence feared by certain Silicon Valley worriers, we have many different civilizational murder weapons lying around waiting to be used or to go off by themselves. We have built and aimed weapons at one another that could wipe out millions or billions in an instant. As we've just seen, our planes and trains and automobiles create endless vectors for deadly diseases to move more swiftly between societies than ever before. Our way of life depends on a technological infrastructure that various disasters could put to an existential test. And the longer the time horizon for sustainable decadence, the more likely it becomes that the whole thing accidentally goes bang—in a Y2K-type meltdown, in a nuclear exchange that happens because the early warning systems misfire and some nuclear line officer fails to keep his cool, in a Stephen King-esque Captain Trips outbreak, or the Skynet endgame feared in Palo Alto.

Or, of course, the meteor. Were the dinosaurs decadent? Alas, their books have not survived.

A Path to 1929

With that important preamble, let's try to predict a few scenarios for catastrophic change; the scenarios that follow trend lines rather than landing on the beach in conquistador's armor or erupting like a zombie epidemic. This means talking about three possibilities in particular: the possible economic unsustainability of an aging world's deficit-financed prosperity, the grimmer scenarios for climate change, and the unique nondecadence of Africa.

The first possibility inspired what was, in hindsight, unwarranted anxiety during the aftermath of the 2008 financial crisis, when "as goes Greece, so goes the entire West" was a common fear among deficit hawks, and everyone from German bankers to Tea Party Republicans were preaching the absolute necessity of austerity. This style of thinking had a lot of intuitive power but foundered on the facts—specifically the total absence of the inflation that it predicted would follow from stimulus spending and quantitative easing. So today, including on the Trumpified American Right, the consensus has turned over. The smartest thinking holds that central banks were too tight after the crisis rather than too loose; that the real constraint on deficits is the inflation rate, not some arbitrary debt-to-GDP ratio; and that Greece foundered as much because of Germany's inflation paranoia as because of its own profligacy. Meanwhile, the fear that we're printing and spending our way to disaster is confined to a dwindling band of deficit hawks and goldbugs and professional prophets of catastrophe— the sort of people who have successfully predicted thirteen of the last three recessions.

If the smart thinking is correct, then Western fiscal and monetary policy, far from pushing us toward disaster, is part of the system that might sustain our decadence indefinitely. If some deep structural force such as population aging is keeping inflation in check even when unemployment falls, there's no reason why our technocrats can't manipulate the money supply to avoid another recession even though we might never get another dramatic boom. If interest rates are destined to stay low everywhere, there's no reason why the United States can't more or less eternally monetize its debt—with our Treasury bonds functioning, as the University of California at Berkeley economist Brad DeLong suggested, as a kind of modern version of the old

Medici Bank: a safe and stable place to park your money even if you aren't getting some immense return. If long-assumed constraints on deficits and the money supply don't apply to an aging, stagnant economy, then our stagnation can be subsidized indefinitely—and even economy-wide crises like the one occasioned by the coronavirus can be managed through swift injections of liquidity.

But smart thinking can be wrong. The United States is in uncharted territory with its deficit spending, with a debt-to-GDP ratio that has passed 100 percent in peacetime for the first time ever, and with the costs of paying for an aging population destined to rapidly increase. The combination of private-sector borrowing and public-pension liabilities add to the economy's debt dependency, the gap between what is earned or taxed and what is owed. We are only thirteen years removed from a global economic crisis that wasn't supposed to happen, one touched off by the unexpected consequences of private debt obligations undertaken recklessly by home owners and banks. That the deficit hawks were wrong about the response to that crisis does not necessarily mean they will be wrong forever.

And if they are right someday, we may not have the information we need to see the crisis coming. "Greek interest rates were low right up until they weren't," the conservative economist John Cochrane wrote recently, in a post warning against blitheness among deficit doves. "Interest rates did not signal the inflation of the 1970s, or the disinflation of the 1980s. Lehman borrowed at low rates until it didn't. Nobody expects a debt crisis, or it would have already happened."

Moreover, everything I wrote in earlier chapters about how the mix of performative radicalism and practical gridlock is more politically stable than many people think has not been tested in an economic downturn as bad as the Great Recession, let alone a true depression. And while central bank action and federal relief prevented 2020 from recapitulating 2008, the scale of the disturbances under coronavirus conditions suggested plenty of ways in which performative radicalism can become more real and deadly under trying circumstances. If the aftermath of the last Great Recession gave us the new socialism and the new Far Right, and the pandemic gave us the George Floyd protests, it's certainly possible that another crack-up would take the ridiculous elements of today's extremisms and make them terrible instead.

So, imagine, as one scenario, a near-future test that resembles 2020 but with more destructive variables. Like the coronavirus this crisis could begin in China, perhaps with another virus that's slightly more lethal and less easily contained (and that kills children in large numbers, a panic-sowing factor that we were spared this time), or perhaps with a major environmental disaster or a similarly destabilizing event. This stalls out the Chinese economy more completely and permanently than the Wuhan outbreak, and the crash then interacts with China's rapidly worsening demographic balance and the repression and discontent in places such as Xinjiang and Hong Kong, creating a mix of economic and fiscal pressure that destabilizes the regime in Beijing (while also perhaps making it more bellicose).

Then as the contagion (literal or simply economic) spreads from China, and the rest of the world stumbles toward disastrous recession, imagine that in Washington, DC, the Congress is even more polarized and gridlocked than it was in 2007 to 2009 or 2020, the conflict between (say) a Democratic president and a Tea-Party Redux G.O.P. more intractable, and none of the various bailouts and stimulus packages can get through the legislature this time. So instead of the flawed but somewhat effective response that mitigated the Great Recession, you get something more like the flailing and folly that followed the Crash of 1929, with many more debt-leveraged enterprises and public programs failing in its wake. And then, when the Federal Reserve acts to fill the breach, it turns out that we've reached Cochrane's tipping point, and suddenly inflation starts galloping, and an American debt crisis finally arrives.

Likewise, when the contagion spreads to Europe, the Continent is more divided than in 2009 to 2010, the pro–European Union consensus weaker, and instead of Berlin and Brussels forcing the periphery to accept their economic terms, you get failed governments everywhere, Grexit and Italexit and then even a French departure. This in turn deepens the economic downturn, with trade barriers going up as economies contract, which feeds political turbulence in North Africa and the Middle East, which generates another refugee crisis, which further empowers the Far Right even as the economic crisis further empowers the Far Left.

Then all of these developments, in Europe and the United States, interact with the Internet and its extremist element in a way that resembles the summer of 2020 but with more violence, and on a more disastrous scale—proving that when youth unemployment climbs high enough, YouTube and Twitter can be genuinely radicalizing even in an aging society, and cities and campuses can fill up permanently with protestors and rioters even when there's endless entertainment on their screens. Bombing campaigns proliferate, riots spread, the American Left finds its Hugo Chavez while the American Right finds a more effective version of Trump. Fascists and Marxists compete for power in Europe, China goes to war with its neighbors to escape domestic turmoil. Put it all together and suddenly we're no longer experiencing a virtual 1930s, an online or reality-television simulacrum of the past, but the full return of history, and the expiration of decadence in fire and authoritarianism and human misery.

The Uninhabitable Equator

That's an attempt to imagine catastrophe, or at least another 1929 and its ideological aftermath, with only political and economic variables (and the experience of 2020) in the mix. But the variable that's more likely to put an end to decadence isn't fiscal or political but climatological. Poll most educated Westerners about how their particular civilization ends, and they'll cite rising global temperatures, rising sea levels, spreading fire and melting ice, flooded cities, and heat waves that just become the weather. In an earlier chapter, I briefly made the case for the manageability of the problem—the extent to which the actual expert consensus, while not vindicating "denialists," points to a future in which the costs of climate change are expensive but bearable for rich countries, with enough paths to mitigation and adaptation to make rising temperatures a source of developing-world instability and suffering but not global calamity.

But there are clearly climate scenarios that would threaten catastrophe on a scale that doesn't fit within the sustainable-decadence paradigm. A world three degrees Celsius hotter in 2100—the current IPCC mean projection—looks very different from a world where emissions and climate feedback systems interact to give you six or seven degrees of warming. The latter scenario might not drown Manhattan, but it would probably dramatically expand the earth's uninhabitable or barely habitable zones, elevating heat stress in warm regions beyond air conditioning's ability to compensate, while simultaneously wrecking the ecology of food production along the equatorial belt.

And not only there: in his pessimistic book *The Uninhabitable Earth: A Story of the Future*, David Wallace-Wells argues that elevated warming will generate "unprecedented droughts, and unprecedented flood-producing rains across the world's food-producing regions," including "some of the most densely populated parts of Australia, Africa, and South America, and the breadbasket regions of China." Food production couldn't simply shift north under this scenario because the soil in Siberia and Canada wouldn't support current levels of agricultural production. So absent further technological revolutions that a decadent society may not be able to produce, this would guarantee that the massive famines that sixties-era alarmists claimed would follow from overpopulation, and that the Green Revolution helped forestall, would arrive a century or so later as the result of impossibly high temperatures instead.

People would die in these famines, but they would also move—

the way they are moving already, but more so, out of the equatorial zones and into the richer, cooler countries to the north. The fullness of Wallace-Wells's dire title need not come to pass to create an essentially uninhabitable *portion* of the earth—a belt stretching the length of the equator, a Greater Sahara that swallows regions where many hundreds of millions of people live today. And the consequence would be what Bill McKibben, one of the most eloquent climate alarmists, calls the "shrinking" of the planet: "Until now, human beings have been spreading, from our beginnings in Africa, out across the globe—slowly at first, and then much faster. But a period of contraction is setting in as we lose parts of the habitable earth."

At a sufficient scale, that contraction would accelerate mass migration to a point where it ceases to be politically manageable. In the Syrian refugee crisis, in which drought played a supporting role, you had a preview of how migration can upend political normalcy in the developed world. If that one crisis helped give us Brexit and Trump and various populist victories across the European continent, it's not hard to see how a rolling, decades-long pattern of climate-driven migrations could put stresses on the developed world that our sclerotic institutions and political coalitions simply aren't prepared to bear. In other words, even if most rich countries are capable of mitigating and adapting their way through the climate crisis (an "if" that someone watching California's struggle to handle its wildfires might reasonably doubt), with sufficient devastation in the rest of the world, the crisis will come home to them regardless, carried by the northward march of millions of refugees.

Such a rolling crisis, such stresses and pressures, would not be distributed evenly across the societies that I'm calling decadent. The United States would still have oceans to protect it, and it would still share its hemisphere with Latin America, where population growth has leveled off and demographic decadence is setting in. Climate catastrophe in the Caribbean or the Amazon would doubtless send many more people toward El Norte, in the same way gang violence in Central America has spurred refugee movement lately. But there would still be some geographic and demographic limits on that migration, which would protect North America and the United States from the fiercest sort of challenge to their systems.

But Europe is in a very different position, because its version of decadence is in a much more unstable equilibrium with its neighbors. And not just with the Muslim Middle East, the source of so much current anxiety, but, above all, with the place where the future of humanity is being born, day by day, child by child: the continent of Africa.

The Greatest Migration

In a world where every culture and society can seem to be converging, Africa is the outlier: relatively poor in a world of affluence, still war-torn in a world more at peace than in the past, increasingly religious rather than secularizing, youthful in a graying world, and fertile in an age of sterility and demographic decline. The continent's situation is far more complex and hopeful than Western cliché often suggests, with growth, industrialization, and political progress coexisting with corruption, decay, and civil war. This means that its exceptionalism could make Africa a source of renewal, or a place where a genuine alternative to contemporary modernity takes shape; that possibility will be considered in the next chapter. But that same exceptionalism could also create a permanent crisis, with the continent where humanity originated playing a crucial part in a period of developed-world collapse.

The numbers alone guarantee some kind of major African role in whatever form the human future takes. In 2004 the United Nations projected that Africa's population would level off by 2100 around two billion, a bold prediction of convergence, of full African participation in demographic decadence, the swift graying of the world. But Africans did not cooperate, and that prediction has been revised upward ever since; by 2018, the UN was projecting that Africa's population will reach four and a half billion by the turn of the next century instead.

Overall, by 2100, two out of every five human beings could be African—but they will probably not all be *in* Africa. The continent is large and in certain respects underpopulated; a billion-person march northward isn't likely if the worst climate scenarios don't come along. But *something* will happen as Africa adds billions of people and the population of Europe, rich and aging, shrinks by a hundred million or more. In the late 1990s, Europe and Africa had about the same population; a hundred years later, there could be seven Africans for every European. Even with the Mediterranean between them, and the Sahara as an impediment, that kind of equilibrium cannot be plausibly sustained. In some form or another, manageable or not, Eurafrica is coming.

In the more manageable scenario, helpfully calculated by Noah Millman for *Politico* magazine in 2015, migration from Africa to Europe would resemble Mexican immigration to the United States from the 1970s to the early 2000s. During that period, Millman wrote, "The Mexican population doubled, growing by about 60 million people," and "an additional 10 million (on a net basis) migrated to the United States. Applying comparable ratios to Africa and Europe, between now and 2050, nearly 200 million Africans would be expected to migrate to Europe. Between one in four and one in five Europeans would be African immigrants."

Can Europe integrate those kinds of numbers successfully, without political breakdown, authoritarianism, ethnic violence, civil war? Let's stipulate that the answer might be yes, whether under continuing conditions of unhappy but stable decadence or amid some sort of Eurafrican renaissance in which mass immigration reinvigorates the West.

But now consider that those Mexican numbers belong to a period when Mexico itself was fairly calm politically, and any natural disasters or ecological problems were localized rather than general. Whereas in our catastrophic scenario, African migration into Europe (and westward migration from the Middle East and South Asia) wouldn't be driven just by economic incentives; it would be part of a dramatic re-treat from the hottest portions of the world—a desperate migration seeking not opportunity but survival.

At a certain scale, that kind of migration becomes a true world-historical event, a hinge from one age to another. Imagine the world south and east of Italy and Greece reduced to a state of general an-archy, in which gruesome conflicts like the Congolese Civil War or the recent agony of Syria and Libya and Yemen become the tem-plate for state collapse almost everywhere, famine and disease and ethnic cleansing—with northward movement a constant throughout the growing anarchy. Imagine the economic consequences for the wider world, as stagnation gave way to a spreading crisis, a cycle of failing crops, falling consumption, failing markets in an interlocking world. And, finally, imagine the possible developments in Europe: either a breakdown in political authority, a retribalization pitting na-tives against immigrants, new megacities against the countryside, or else a kind of rapid adoption of the techno-authoritarian model being pioneered in China, in which liberal democracy ceases to decay and simply falls, replaced by the bureaucratic surveillance state that ex-ists already within the liberal carapace but might, under these circum-stances, break out and become the government in full.

The Neo-Medieval Future

If something like this happens, we will look back on Trump-era dis-turbances and recognize them not as the playacting that they often seem to be but as a kind of dress rehearsal for a looming tragedy—Karl Marx's dictum about history repeating as tragedy followed by farce, but in reverse. And more even than in the first scenario, the sce-nario of economic crisis, in the climate crisis/mass migration scenario, impulses that today belong (at least officially) to the disreputable ex-tremes will become near universal. In a landscape of rolling calamity and constant migration, the concepts of reform, renewal, and renaissance will lose their salience entirely, and what will be sought, quite understandably, is a kind of Augustus or Diocletian option for the West: a figure or figures capable of imposing order, guaranteeing public safety, and ensuring continuity of government when all else seems to be melting into swiftly warming air.

In the scenario I am imagining, that desire will be stronger in Europe, since the pressure of migration will be heaviest there—but that pressure will make the task of the would-be Augustus more difficult, and preexisting European divisions still more so. So Europe might experience a kind of hyperfragmentation, a vertiginous return not just to the pre-EU national order but to the regional and local order that centuries of nation-building subsumed—a thousand Brexits, if you will, except with open warlordism this time instead of social media chest-thumping. Meanwhile, immigrant communities and enclaves might be large enough to pursue Brexits of their own, turning today's ethnic strongholds into the basis for tomorrow's Eurabic and Eurafrican microstates.

Eventually, over a long-enough time horizon, new or new-old nation-states or a new European empire might be formed out of these fragments. But they will look as different from the sprawling decadence of the European Union as the Frankish kingdoms of the early Middle Ages looked from the fourth-century Roman world. In the meantime, the only unifying force in such a disunited Europe, the equivalent of bishops and monastics taking over for Roman governance in late antiquity, might be corporate powers—the tech companies above all, based in the United States or China, which would continue to hang the necessary satellites and extract the necessary Bitcoin or Libra payments from natives and migrants alike, maintaining a kind of virtual connection to a former world that had otherwise passed away.

Meanwhile, other world powers would endure the way Byzantium endured the twilight of the classical world—as a redoubt, a fortress, in which the forces driving state collapse are held at bay by walls both figurative and literal, and perhaps by the power of surveillance above all. The United States would find its Augustus or see the establishment of a kind of enlightened Politburo, merging the power of the two remaining nondecadent institutions in the country—Silicon Valley and the military—in a system that retained republican forms the way China currently retains Marxist ones, as pleasant illusions and rhetorical gestures that nobody believes. China would extend its empire, while India, too close to the uninhabitable belt, would fall into the same warring-states chaos as Europe; Japan and Australia would become refuges but also clients of the rival American and Chinese empires. Despite the persistence of smartphones, technological stagnation would give way to regress in much of the world, while the only major advances in the authoritarian empires would be in surveillance and monitoring, in attempts to prevent global anarchy from penetrating the fortresses of the wealthy—the places where decadence was still sustained.

Out of the lawless, stateless realms, new things would come—as Islam came out of the desert to transform the post-Roman Mediterranean; as the beginnings of Europe were made by jumped-up chieftains in post-Roman France and Germany.

The collapse would not last forever; the dark age would be temporary. But the catastrophe would still be real, not merely virtual. There would be dead beyond counting, much of what we take for granted would be lost, and, depending on the unpredictability of climate change, there might be more blows every time human civilization seemed to be getting back upon its feet. Whatever succeeded, whatever inherited, the historians of the future would draw a line—blurry, debated, a moving target, but still generally agreed upon as real—and say: "Here late modernity ended, here the West's autumn gave way to winter, here the attempt at a universal civilization was broken on nature's wheel."

The Writing On the Wall

If this is how the story of our decadence ends, there will be a morality-play element to it after all, a sense in which our fall fits the Durant quote and the Gibson vision strangely well. Because climate change and population imbalances and mass migration are not problems dropping like European invaders out of a clear blue Mesoamerican sky, nor are they accidental Y2K or nuclear-launch disasters that can be feared but not exactly predicted. Instead, they are challenges that follow from long-term technological and economic trends, long-term patterns of human behavior—which in turn means that they're the kinds of trends that a vigorous, nondecadent, advanced civilization should have been able to cope with and head off before they led to some dégringolade.

If mass migration ultimately overthrows the Western political order, there will be a cautionary story told by reactionaries ever after, in which the foolish elites of America and Europe couldn't see that their relaxed attitude toward immigration and their indifference to the most basic aspect of human flourishing imaginable, the birthrate, were both species of decadence, which richly merited the destruction that followed. But then, if that mass migration is actually driven by climate changes that render the global South semihabitable, the technocrats of the future will have a strong case that, in fact, the decadence that really counted was the political stalemate—the institutional irresolution, the policy gridlock—that made it impossible for Western governments to act on climate policy together or alone. (They will especially argue that it was the decadence of conservative institutions, conservative political parties, and conservative intellectuals in the United States that helped bring about the unnecessary catastrophe.) And somewhere between the two perspectives would be the Cassandras of technological stagnation, arguing that the problem wasn't political decadence so much as the too-slow pace of innovation, the failure of promised clean-energy breakthroughs or geo-engineering technologies to emerge in time—a different kind of decadence than the political or cultural sort, or an additional element in the mix that laid late-modern civilization low.

I think it is precisely the history-as-morality-play element in all these narratives that makes me skeptical that the catastrophe will come, or that it will come in the semipredictable *high temperatures plus population imbalances plus migration equals fatal political and economic crisis* that this chapter has described. But perhaps that is my own fatal participation in decadence at work—the extent to which, as a member of a decadent American conservatism, I have imbibed too much climate change skepticism over the years, and the extent to which, as a member of a decadent society, I cannot lift my eyes to see the truth: that "Mene, mene, tekel, upharsin" is already written on the wall.

10

Renaissance

In the summer of 2017, Donald Trump gave a speech in Poland defending Western civilization. "The fundamental question of our time," he orated, "is whether the West has the will to survive. Do we have the confidence in our values to defend them at any cost? Do we have enough respect for our citizens to protect our borders? Do we have the desire and the courage to preserve our civilization in the face of those who would subvert and destroy it?" If so, he told his audience, "we must work together to confront forces, whether they come from inside or out, from the South or the East, that threaten over time to undermine these values and to erase the bonds of culture, faith, and tradition that make us who we are."

Needless to say, the speech was not universally admired. Immediately, Trump's critics denounced it "as a statement of racial and religious paranoia," a betrayal of the American commitment to universal values, a dog whistle to his alt-right supporters. The problem was the speech's particularism and chauvinism: to revive talk about "the West" in an age when once-European ideas such as liberalism, democracy, and capitalism flourish globally is to link yourself decisively to a racial or religious definition of what it means to be a Westerner—a reactionary move, typical of Trump, and a cultural and political dead end.

In a certain way, both the speech and the denunciations were important; in another way, they were entirely useless. Important, because they distilled one of the deadlocks of our time—between people who imagine that the resources of a fading past can revitalize Europe and America, and people who think that the only possible problem with our cosmopolitan society is that it isn't cosmopolitan enough. Useless, because of the essential emptiness of each side's posturing—an empty traditionalism championed by a heathen reality-television opportunist, set against a thin cosmopolitanism that's really just the extremely Western ideology of liberal Protestantism plus ethnic food.

No renaissance is possible so long as this deadlock endures. On one side, a defense of the West's historical Christian and European character that reduces that civilization to a #MAGA bunker; a preservationist project steeped in nostalgia for the dynamism of the past. On the other side, a vision of a civilization with no common memory, no religious roots, no distinctives beyond its political procedures, and no self-awareness about its establishment's vaulting arrogance and historical illiteracy. A conservatism with no vision of how to revitalize itself and, therefore, no defense except the wall, the moat, the rampart. A liberalism that doesn't recognize how little it satisfies the human heart; how vulnerable it would be to real challenges if ever they arose.

Visions of Eurafrica

Around the same time that Trump was giving a speech about a civilization whose decadence he embodies, an African cardinal went to southern France to celebrate a Mass honoring the martyrs of the Vendée—the thousands of Catholics, mostly peasants, killed by French revolutionary armies in the 1790s when they rose against the dictatorial Parisian government and its Reign of Terror. The cardinal, Robert Sarah, was born in Guinea in what was then French-ruled West Africa in 1945, and he rose from rural poverty to become a priest, a bishop, and then a leader of the African episcopate, before rising further to become a cardinal of the Roman Catholic Church and a leader of the Church's traditionalist wing.

But the conservatism of his homily for the Vendée memorial made a fascinating contrast with the conservatism of Trump's speech. Where Trump offered a vision of the West that seemed to belong to Sarah's youth, and portrayed Europe as a redoubt potentially besieged from "South and East," Sarah, a man of the global South, told a story in which the French martyrs of the Vendée were bound by ties of faith to Christians of Africa and the Middle East, who were in their turn beset by both Islamist persecutions and a new cultural imperialism from secular European governments, which seek to impose Western sterility on the fecundity of Africa. But Africa, Sarah said, "like the Vendée, will resist! Christian families everywhere must be the joyful spearheads of a revolt against this new dictatorship of self-ishness!" And not Africa alone, but also African Christians and European Christians together: "You, people of France, you, people of Vendée, when will you rise with the peaceful weapons of prayer and charity to defend your faith? My friends, the blood of martyrs flows in your veins, be faithful to it! We are all spiritually sons of *la Vendée martyre!*"

Instead of the binaries of populist conservatism and secular cosmopolitanism, in other words, Sarah proposed a vision of the future in which his own faith, Catholic Christianity, effectively embraces the Eurafrican scenario that, in the last chapter, we considered primarily as a destabilizing threat. He imagined his fellow Africans leading a reinvigoration and enrichment of a *portion* of the Western inheritance— the Christian part—even as he asked European Christians to join him in defense of *African* cultural distinctives against Western leaders (including France's current president, Emmanuel Macron) who are frightened by African birthrates and would prefer the continent to converge with European decadence. He envisioned the links between north and south neither as a threat to the north, nor as a chance to simply remake the south in the north's image—but as an opportunity for entirely new, pan-racial configurations that would reach back into Europe's past to reshape both continents' third-millennium future.

Since the new configuration that the cardinal has in mind involves a vigorously traditional Eurafrican Roman Catholicism, the more secular reader might prefer stalemate and stagnation. But the Sarah template isn't applicable only to traditional religion. If the greatest danger to the stability of decadence involves mass migration from the global South, the global South also holds the key to many scenarios of renaissance. It may be that a decadent West can imagine non-Westerners only as perfectly assimilated modern liberals, or else as terrorists, theocrats, and exotic threats. But perhaps something else can be imagined by people such as Sarah, who effectively stand on both sides of the European-African divide. Perhaps the visions of the once colonized can save both their own people and the erstwhile colonizers from a chaotic, disastrous collision, and point the way to something that is new and *good* instead.

There are other examples, besides Sarah's Catholic vision, of this Eurafrican imagination. After World War II, in the waning days of the old European empires, the would-be leaders of the then-colonized world argued over what kind of relationship an independent Africa or Caribbean might ultimately have with its former European rulers. Most were in favor of simple separation, but not all: two of the dissenters were Aimé Césaire of Martinique and Léopold Sédar Senghor of Senegal (the subject, together, of a fascinating book called *Freedom Time: Negritude, Decolonization, and the Future of the World* by the historian Gary Wilder), both politician-intellectuals who combined anti-imperialism with a desire for some kind of continued political union with the French Republic, some kind of "federal" political project that would enable Africans and Europeans to live as equals under the same government and flag.

This project technically succeeded in tiny Martinique, which remained a French *département*, but in the wider colonial world, it was foredoomed, rejected by the colonizers because it asked them to surrender too much of their own sovereignty and by the colonized because it stopped short of the promised liberation. Yet the doomed project was also potentially prophetic, imagining as it did the inevitable reconvergence of Europe and its former colonies, and the need of a synthesis of north and south, white and black, that neither the West's postcolonial critics nor its conservative defenders have aspired to since.

Césaire and Senghor embodied that synthesis culturally by being Francophones who loved the European canon and believed in the "miracle of Greek civilization," even as they argued for a distinctively African civilizational genius—a *negritude* that turned the old derogatory label into a celebration of both ancient Africa and Afro-futurism. (When Senghor ruled Senegal, he spent his presidency translating Gerard Manley Hopkins, T. S. Eliot, and W. B. Yeats into French.) They imagined that synthesis politically by being Marxist-leaning French republicans who argued that the West's universalist ideals, never adequately lived up to by actual Western governments, could someday create a republican canopy capable of covering the races of both Africa and Europe, beneath which humanity would become (to quote Césaire) "more than ever united and diverse, multiple and harmonious."

This dream has not been fulfilled. The transnational institutions we have are weak and corrupt, and the global culture that binds Europe to its former colonies is a lowest-common-denominator culture of pop stars and superhero movies, not the mix of Goethe and *negritude* envisioned sixty years ago.

On the other hand, the dream did not fail completely. For instance, certain traditional Western artistic forms, no less than the traditional Western religion of the African Robert Sarah, have retained life and vigor under decadence only because of the syncretistic genius of ex-colonials: from Chinua Achebe to V. S. Naipaul, to cite the novelistic case. And even in pop culture, what is the most successful and dramatically interesting of the endless superhero movies, *Black Panther*, if not a superficial but still fascinating paean to Afro-futurism—one that found a clamorous audience in the West?

The example of Wakanda is particularly interesting because Marvel's fictional sub-Saharan hidden kingdom is so resolutely *different*. Different from the stereotypes of African backwardness that it was invented to rebuke, obviously, but also strikingly different from the modern liberal order as we know it, with technologies that exceed our own but a politics and culture that are proudly illiberal—indeed, monarchical and theocratic.

So it isn't just that *Black Panther* in, yes, the inevitably superficial way of a blockbuster, with the inevitably play-it-safe conclusion—taps into a yearning for an out-of-Africa renaissance, for an African-shaped future that's dynamic rather than dystopian: Make Africa Great, and then Make the World Great Again As Well. The different facets of Wakandan exceptionalism also suggest the different ways in which a renaissance might ultimately come about, the different trajectory-altering transformations—technological, political, and religious—that might lead our civilization or its inheritors *up* from decadence.

The Return of the Future

Let's start with the technological solution to decadence, because it's the one that our culture, and particularly our elite culture, is conditioned to expect. This solution would involve the end of the technological lull or slowdown or stagnation and the arrival of some set of major breakthroughs, either just around the corner or possibly in development right now, that kick-starts economic growth, leads to sweeping cultural change, and creates an entirely new set of political and ideological debates.

The examples are easy to imagine because they've been confidently prophecied for as long as I've been alive. An energy revolution that both radically cheapens transportation and radically scrambles the politics of the world's energy-producing regions (and everywhere else, eventually). A robotics revolution that radically reduces the amount of human labor required to pile up wealth, with both utopian consequences (Keynes's vision of a short workweek becomes a reality, leisure becomes the default state of life) and destabilizing ones (the rich keep working for reasons of status competition, mass unemployment stalks everybody else). A revolution in medicine and biotechnology that changes the way we do, well, just about everything, by extending life spans (starting with the long-promised cures for Alzheimer's disease and cancer), rewriting reproduction (today, CRISPR, the next day artificial wombs), and enabling genetic engineering on a species-altering scale. A revolution in space flight that gives us real space tourism, moon bases, and eventually a colony on Mars. A revolution in artificial intelligence and the study of consciousness that does the same, only more so, by enabling human beings to escape the physical plane altogether.

Despite the disappointments of the last few decades (or perhaps because they don't fully acknowledge them), the default assumption of most futurists is that one or more of these scenarios are inevitable. When you go looking for people in our culture who still talk like Victorian-era utopians, you'll often find visions that fold together all of these possible breakthroughs. In 2014 Kevin Kelly, a founding editor of *Wired* magazine, asked his Twitter followers to compose a "100-word description of a plausible technological future in 100 years" that they or he would want to live in. The responses he published had a certain commonality, envisioning a postscarcity, leisure-rich economy and a society trending toward some form or another of transhumanism. One example:

> 2030: The last of the unsustainable energy and fiscal policy edifices crumbles just as embedded intelligence emerges. We've got the wind in our sails. Billions of people rapidly move from wage slaves to participating in a decentralized, sustainable, opt-in economy which affords them the time to innovate and crowdsource a tsunami of solutions. 2060: Biodiversity blossoms. Conscious-

ness comes under direct control. You can physically live on Mars, Antarctica, New Atlantis, or in the asteroid belt. Many choose life in distributed mind servers and live centuries in a week. 2090: Boredom unthinkable. Conscious population: 10^{20}. Biome restored. 2114: Begin Second Earth.

Another:

Immortality had shifted the focus on short-term thinking to long-term goals. A new era of responsibility had dawned. Body modifications and rejuvenation were only a virus away (new exotic options were available on the free market), and many people changed appearance weekly, to keep up with the latest trends. This invalidated the past trends of judging by gender and race [and] meant we distinguished entities by expertise and experience only. Since robots harvested the food we needed and built our houses in self-chosen tribal groups with independently chosen government structures, humans were free to imagine and create utopian worlds with more art and research than ever before.

One of the themes of this book has been the narrowing of ideological horizons, the way that both political utopianism and religious idealism have lost their grip on the contemporary imagination. But a kind of pure techno-utopianism, infused with secularized religion, plainly still exists among the people who work at the existing technological cutting edge: they don't believe God or politics can save us, but some of them still think that science alone will suffice to do the trick; that we can be as gods through the power of digital technology alone, and that if they just hang on long enough to see it, their bodies will be transformed, their minds uploaded, and their very selves freed, empowered, and near-permanently preserved.

One can be skeptical of this utopianism and still see it as a possible seedbed for some of the technological breakthroughs that Kelly's correspondents envision. Maybe we have simply been in a kind of bottleneck for the last few generations, achieving important scientific breakthroughs that don't (yet) translate into society-altering changes. At a certain point, we'll clear the bottleneck, and it will become clear that our era was a necessary prelude to renewed acceleration—eventually giving us self-driving cars courtesy of a finally profitable Uber, a Mars colony courtesy of the Elon Musk–Jeff Bezos space race, and radical life extension courtesy of Google's longevity lab or some other zillionaire investor who can't imagine shuffling off this mortal coil.

As I noted earlier, perhaps the trauma of the coronavirus, and the extent to which it exposed the reality of state incapacity in so many Western countries – as well as a gulf, at least in one particular form of decadence, between the sclerosis of Western Europe and the United States and the adaptability of the Pacific Rim—could turn out to be an experience that helps push or pull us through the bottleneck, into the post-decadence future on the other side.

"This monumental failure of institutional effectiveness will reverberate for the rest of the decade," the tech CEO Marc Andreessen wrote in widely-quoted essay early in the pandemic, "but it's not too early to ask why, and what we need to do about it." His answer: We need to *build* again. "Our nation and our civilization were built on production, on building. Our forefathers and foremothers built roads and trains, farms and factories, then the computer, the microchip, the smartphone, and uncounted thousands of other things that we now take for granted, that are all around us, that define our lives and provide for our well-being. There is only one way to honor their legacy and to create the future we want for our own children and grandchildren, and that's to build."

The building that he envisions—the investments in "new products, in new industries, in new factories, in new science, in big leaps forward"—could theoretically happen on a world-altering scale without having the truly utopian scenarios come to pass. Terraforming Mars and becoming a multiplanetary species may be unattainable for now—but just going to Mars would be a bigger leap for mankind than anything we've accomplished since Neil Armstrong. The hard problem of consciousness probably isn't solvable by brain scans and increases in processing power, and so you and I probably won't actually be uploading our very selves to the cloud—but that doesn't mean that Artificial Intelligence and robotics can't radically transform the economy, the labor force, the built environment. No Silicon Valley mogul is likely to live forever in his current body—but in a world that remains stable and wealthy and scientifically proficient, someone or someones may figure out how to achieve substantial life extension, genetic selection for unusual strength or speed or appearance, and other scenarios that have belonged for years to the realm of "just around the corner" science fiction.

If some of these innovations happened in the kind of cascade that defined the industrial revolutions—with innovation in transportation, biotech, and automation happening concurrently, as innovation often happened prior to the 1970s—then other rapid transformations would inevitably follow. Human social institutions would change dramatically, to put it mildly, if babies could be grown in vats and people lived to be 125. Our political and economic debates would be scrambled if the rich suddenly began availing themselves of technologies and treatments that seemed to call a shared human nature into question. If an incremental process of automation that pushes 5 percent or 10 percent of the workforce into idleness has given us today's populist disturbances, imagine what the kind of automation that renders 40 percent of the human workforce redundant would do to the existing Western order.

Then further imagine what it would do to the geopolitical order if these innovations were all emanating from the People's Republic of China. There is a possible future where it becomes clear that the real bottleneck—the real source of temporary technological decadence—

wasn't technological proficiency so much as a dearth of societal ambition and centralized incentives and unsqueamishness about moral considerations. In this scenario, it would be Chinese scientists, subsidized and encouraged by an ambitious government and unencumbered by residual Christian qualms about certain forms of experimentation, who take the great leap from today's CRISPR work to tomorrow's more-than-human supermen—and suddenly the world would enter a scenario out of the original *Star Trek* timeline and its predicted Eugenics Wars, with a coterie of Khan Noonien Singhs in power in Beijing and the rest of the world trying to decide whether to adapt, surrender, or resist.

For the resisters, the word *renaissance* wouldn't naturally apply to a world that seemed by our lights to be trending in a dystopian direction . . . but if we lost the Eugenics Wars, the superhuman winners might happily describe their rise and victory that way. And even the resisters would need a word besides *decadence* to describe the genetically engineered future: we might be moving in a dangerous, even wicked direction, but we would be moving; stagnation, drift, and repetition would no longer be the defining features of the day.

Indeed, nothing is more characteristic of a dynamic society than a new moral conflict driven by some sort of technological and economic change. So, in that sense, a war over what to do with a new eugenic science would demarcate the end of decadence even more clearly than a less morally complicated scientific leap.

Is There Life After Liberalism?

But if technological acceleration would inevitably create new political and ideological conflicts, what if the up-from-decadence process ran the other way, and a dramatic political or ideological change came first? As we have seen, it's easier to declare a crisis in the liberal-democratic order than to actually discern viable alternatives to liberalism or democracy or capitalism. Yet as with technological and scientific progress, maybe we're in a period of preparation, of necessary ground laying, in which postliberal alternatives are gradually being theorized, and in a generation or so, they will begin to reshape the world outside of blogs, tweets, and books.

One possibility is suggested by Patrick Deneen's *Why Liberalism Failed*, perhaps the most prominent Trump-era diagnosis of our political decadence. Like most such texts, it is longer on critique than on prescription, but Deneen ends with a vision for a new postliberal politics that might be described as *local revolution*, in which the oligarchic sclerosis of developed-world institutions is escaped by a refounding of virtuous communities on a more human and organic scale.

These communities would not fit a simple ideological pattern. They might encompass everything from new versions of the utopian communes of the 1960s and the nineteenth century, to libertarian experiments such as charter cities, to attempts to re-create the monastic communities that arose under Rome's imperial decay, to simple revivals of town-meeting democracy and other vanishing Tocquevillian forms. Describing the trajectory of these "intentional communities," Deneen suggests that at first they could coexist with the broader liberal order and benefit from its sustainably decadent protection. But over the long run, they might supply a full alternative to our own era's sense of lost possibility:

> [Initially,] they will be regarded as options within the liberal frame, and while suspect in the broader culture, largely permitted to exist so long as they are nonthreatening to the liberal order's main business. Yet it is likely from the lessons learned within these communities that a viable postliberal political theory will arise, one that begins with fundamentally different anthropological assumptions not arising from a supposed state of nature or concluding with a world-straddling state and market, but instead building on the fact of human relationality, sociability, and the learned ability to sacri-

fice one's narrow personal interest not to abstract humanity, but for the sake of other humans. With the demise of the liberal order, such countercultures will come to be seen not as "options" but as necessities.

If Deneen is right, then it makes sense to look for a political renaissance in places far from the centers of official power. The resilient religious communitarianism of Mormon Utah, for instance, might be more relevant to the world's future than anything happening in London or Paris or Washington, DC. The success of a city-state such as Singapore might offer a political model for the next century that's more relevant than today's groaning national and imperial institutions. The oft-mocked libertarians who tried to make New Hampshire a "free state" via ideological in-migration, or the Silicon Valley billionaires imagining "seasteading" as a way to build new political institutions on land reclaimed from Poseidon, might actually be visionaries. Small might be beautiful; exit and internal exile might eventually make the world anew.

But it's also possible that local experiments can't really work in a mass society and a globalized world absent a revolution from above. Their size might remain too small to scale, their constant vulnerability to larger forces and powerful enemies might be too immense. Deneen's critical depiction of the liberal order suggests that it ultimately brooks no rivals; my own account of the decadent society suggests that decadence is perpetually seductive even to its critics. In which case, any alternative would need to begin with institutions that have more power and more scale; it would need to be a *nationalist renewal*, not just a local one, because only the nation-state has the scale and potency to experiment with different political forms without being dissolved or crushed.

This is the political right's clearest answer to decadence at the moment, embodied not only in the various attempts to provide intellectual scaffolding for Trumpism, but also in documents such as the Paris

Statement of 2016, in which a group of the Continent's right-leaning thinkers united to argue that the "true Europe is a community of nations," not the officially cosmopolitan EU, and that only through the kind of national community that both "competes with other nations" and "takes pride in governing itself in its own way" can European culture be renewed.

In this theory, nationalism resupplies many of the things that are dissolving under decadence: the historical and religious memory required for real artistic greatness, the communal support required for marriage and family and ordinary human flourishing, the sense of competition and common purpose required to spur technological progress, and the common bonds that enable good government to triumph over factionalism and gridlock. In which case nationalist experiments of the kind cropping up around the world, however crude some of their leaders and demagogic their tactics, might eventually be shaped into political vehicles for a renaissance.

The implicit model here—strikingly, given the right's history with anti-Semitism—is the nation of Israel: the last bastion of nineteenth-century nationalism, an ethno-religious Western republic in a secular and cosmopolitan age, and a country whose combination of high birthrates and resilient religiosity and technological proficiency makes it undecadent in certain interesting ways. The leading theoretician of nationalist renewal is an Israeli intellectual, Yoram Hazony, who in his recent book *The Virtue of Nationalism* makes an audacious attempt to construct a kind of Jewish-Protestant-Anglo-American tradition of nationalism that he claims has been buried by the lapsed-Catholic imperialism of the current European project. (The German aggressors who destroyed Europe in the twentieth century, in Hazony's account, are imperialist rather than nationalist figures, thus quarantining the Hitlerian nightmare—supposedly—from his nationalist project.) These arguments are the intellectual correlative of the unexpected friendliness between eastern Europe's nationalist governments and Benjamin Netanyahu's Israel, with the former looking to the Israeli model as they try to grope their way toward an effective, possibly post-liberal form of nationalist democracy.

That sort of unexpected crosscurrent has something in common with the Eurafrican scenarios with which this chapter opened, in the sense that it carries intimations of a very different set of alignments, interactions, and conflicts than you see in the deadlocks of our times. But it's also understood by the political left as a new alignment of authoritarianism, chauvinism, and cruelty to outsiders, which, from the vantage point of left-intellectuals, is where nationalism always leads, even if you get some nice statues and architecture along the way. In which case, a "renaissance" driven by nationalism would be like a "renaissance" driven by Chinese eugenics: a transformation, no doubt, but one unworthy of the name.

Hence the left's political answer to our decadence, which isn't a rejection of globalism and cosmopolitanism but a deepening of both: *a new socialist internationalism*; a revolution in economic and political solidarity that transcends the evils of capitalism and the moral limitations of the present liberal order. If our globalist elite has failed and produced nationalist backlash, the answer must be a more left-wing governing class, a more active mass politics, and more effective and integrated forms of transnational government—whether at the scale of the European Union or the larger scale required to tackle climate change—rather than a return to nationalist myths. If neoliberal economics has produced too many losers, too much disappointment, the answer isn't to throw up walls and harden borders but to bring the market—just as the Marxists have always wanted—more completely under rational control, and subject it more thoroughly to the moral logic of redistributive justice. If people seem unhappy and adrift in late modernity, unable to form families and connections and find real happiness, the answer isn't to return to dead religions or to surrender anew to patriarchal control, but to clear away all the economic obstacles to human flourishing—to save human beings from the destructive values that capitalism inevitably teaches and requires.

As a politically active theoretician of this perspective, the closest left-wing analogue to Hazony or the Paris Statement's intellectuals might be Yanis Varoufakis, the Greek politician-intellectual and the leader of his country's populist party of the left. His answer to the Paris Statement is the Democracy in Europe Movement 2025, DiEM25, which envisions a Europe renewed by becoming more integrated, unified, and democratic, rejecting the nationalist "cocoon" in favor of stronger instruments of continentwide government that are accountable to every European, not just Brussels and Berlin. This internationalism carries more than just a whiff of the old socialist *internationale*; Varoufakis argues explicitly that for all the errors of their disciples, the authors of *The Communist Manifesto* set the agenda that should still guide the contemporary left:

> While we owe capitalism for having reduced all class distinctions to the gulf between owners and nonowners, Marx and Engels want us to realise that capitalism is insufficiently evolved to survive the technologies it spawns. It is our duty to tear away at the old notion of privately owned means of production and force a metamorphosis, which must involve the social ownership of machinery, land, and resources. Now, when new technologies are unleashed in societies bound by the primitive labour contract, wholesale misery follows. In the manifesto's unforgettable words: "A society that has conjured up such gigantic means of production and of exchange is like the sorcerer who is no longer able to control the powers of the nether world whom he has called up by his spells." The sorcerer will always imagine that their apps, search engines, robots, and genetically engineered seeds will bring wealth and happiness to all. But . . . only by abolishing private ownership of the instruments of mass production and replacing it with a new type of common ownership that works in sync with new technologies will we lessen inequality and find collective happiness.

It is the collective happiness that is essential to the power of this case. At one level, the neo-Marxist alternative presents itself as a practical-minded remedy for today's discontents: only by taming capitalism can we lessen inequality, only by taming capitalism can we restore democracy, only by taming capitalism can we avert the climate catastrophe, only by taming capitalism can we fund useful innovations rather than all those "apps" and "search engines." But at another level—the level at which it more plausibly answers the challenge of decadence—the new socialism presents itself as a means to moral and cultural renewal, an answer for the same end-of-history discontents that Hazony and other nationalists want to answer with memory, tradition, and identity.

Thus a representative socialist blueprint, in an essay from Australia's *Guardian* newspaper imagining life in 2050 "after the failure of capitalism," starts out with the economic structure of the new order: the free education, the community-run credit unions, the thirty-hour workweek, the replacement of corporate jobs with public-sector work, the guaranteed income. But soon it moves on to the communitarian and aesthetic aspects of the imagined socialist society, the newfound ease of balancing work and family, the proliferation of "community groups" dedicated to arts and ideas. A similar intention informs the spate of recent essays arguing that whatever the difficulties with Soviet domination, women under Eastern European socialism were more sexually and romantically fulfilled than their Western counterparts are today; patriarchy and capitalism together have given us the polarization of the sexes, but the socialist vision will reconcile them.

Like Marx himself, imagining that a man set free from capitalism might become a cosmopolis unto himself—a fisherman, hunter, or farmer by day and an intellectual by night—today's critics of capitalism envision setting human beings free from the tyranny of work and seeing them blossom into happy dilettantes, with time for all the humane pursuits that in our own society seem to be decaying, and time as well to achieve a full discovery of their own true identity within the race-and-gender tangle that occupies so much attention on the left. And like their conservative and reactionary rivals, the radicals of the left ultimately see problems of solidarity and meaningfulness as the essential problems of our age: the Green New Deal will save us from global warming, but, more importantly, it will bring us together in common labor, give each man and woman and nonbinary person a dignified purpose, and redeem us from division, confusion, and decadence itself.

The Religious Solution

As described, such a political regeneration sounds almost religious. And however anticlerical its leaders, a successful socialist revolution *would* be religious, at some level, because every culture has some religious sentiment at bottom, and even "secular" political revolutions tend to either feed off religious sentiments (as the liberal revolutions of the eighteenth and nineteenth centuries often fed off varieties of nonconforming Protestantism) or else seek to supplant religion with an alternative metaphysic, an alternative account of capital-H History and the eschaton.

Indeed the aspect of left-wing ideology that has the most power in our society today—not socialism but the social-justice attitudes described with the resonant term "woke"—has a palpable spiritual dimension, with its rhetoric of conversion and self-scrutiny, its communal liturgies, its distinctive mix of iconography and iconoclasm, and of course its witch-hunting dark side.

But might it not be simpler, then, to straightforwardly imagine a religious revolution rather than a political one as the likeliest pathway out of decadence—whether at the level of a Great Awakening, the level of a Reformation or a Counter-Reformation, or even the level of Christianity's beginnings, and the transition from the pagan world of Rome to the age of monotheism?

The simplest means to religious revival would be a slow-motion one: a transformation through demographic change, with culture shifting downstream from differential birthrates, as secularism and attenuated forms of faith gradually die out. There are recent, if modest, precedents for such a change. A significant part of the shifting religious dynamics of 1970s America—the decline of the Protestant mainline and the increasing vigor of evangelical Protestantism—can actually be traced to a divergence of liberal Protestant and conservative Protestant birthrates in the 1920s and 1930s, during the fundamentalist-modernist controversy. Likewise, in American Judaism today, the extraordinary birthrate differential between the Orthodox and their Reform and Conservative cousins is ensuring that Judaism's future will be more devout than would have been expected two generations ago.

These are trends at the margin, though. A truly transformative religious revival would require a more significant fertility divergence, not only within religious traditions but between religious populations in general and the secular and lukewarm. But some version of the gap exists already; a widening over the next few decades, with major cultural consequences for the 2070s, is hardly unimaginable. Indeed, entire books have been written by anxious secularists making the case that, for just this reason, the religious could inherit the modern world. "In effect," writes one such author, Eric Kaufmann, "secularism must run"—in terms of attracting converts from its fecund religious rivals—"to stand still and sprint in order to succeed."

But as someone who moves back and forth between secular and religious worlds, I have enough respect for the pull of nonbelief, the tendency toward attrition among the children of the devout, to suspect that differential birthrates could be the way that *religion* ends ups running to stand still. Indeed, that's mostly been the story of the last few decades. Religious conservatives have been having more children for many generations, and yet they have achieved at best a provisional resilience in a world where almost every institutional faith is weaker in the developed world than it was before the 1960s.

So probably something else would be needed—some significant

catalyst or intellectual shift—to really change the religious landscape, be it a sudden weakening of the hold of what the philosopher Thomas Nagel calls the "materialist neo-Darwinian conception of nature" on the Western intelligentsia, or some unexpected development, political or scientific, that reshapes the way modern man thinks about either society or the universe. Or (as in American revivals past) it could just be the influence of some particularly charismatic and determined group of religious leaders, preachers, and church planters on a society that turns out to be a more fertile mission field, more spiritually hungry and desperate for community, than it seems to be right now.

Or, of course, something stranger still could happen, since both major and minor religious revolutions in Western history have proceeded from events—visions and revelations and miracles—well outside the bounds of "normal" historical patterns. One can come up with reasons, in hindsight, to explain why Christianity emerged in the Roman Empire, or why Islam came to dominate the Middle East, but nobody this side of eternity could have possibly foreseen the shape of those transformations in advance. And the likelihood of something along those lines happening again—of some entirely new religious faith emerging to end our current end of history, and open a chasm between our era and whatever age succeeds it that is as "vertiginous," as the great historian of late antiquity Peter Brown puts it, as the "the drop" between the classical and Christian worlds—well, those odds are known to God alone.

The Return of Paganism

But here are a few scenarios that do not necessarily require the arrival of some new revelation. One would be the reversal of the Roman-era Christian revolution and the consolidation of a fully post-Christian form of religion in the Western world.

Already there is a strong post-Christian religious *tendency* that's visible in various places in our culture but hasn't taken on a fully coherent, culture-shaping form. It might usefully be described as an inchoate neo-paganism—meaning not the literal worship of Osiris or Odin (or not necessarily), but a general belief in the immanent divine, in a supernatural reality that's interwoven with the material world rather than standing outside it as a Creator God.

This pagan tendency presently takes several different forms. There is the highbrow tradition of intellectual and aesthetic pantheism, which includes figures as various as Spinoza and Nietzsche, Emerson and Whitman, and which shows up among a lot of contemporary writers who are spiritual but not religious, gnostic but not Christian, pantheistic but not theistic—from Sam Harris, to Barbara Ehrenreich, to the late Harold Bloom, to the former Yale Law School dean Anthony Kronman, the author of a long religious apologia called *Confessions of a Born-Again Pagan.*

Next, there is the more middlebrow embrace of New Age spirituality and self-help religion, which emphasizes the pursuit of spiritual experience as a means to health, wealth, and happiness in this life: the Oprah Winfrey, *Eat Pray Love*, Deepak Chopra style of late-modern religion, which draws from a mélange of religious sources, Western and Eastern, but mostly emphasizes a therapeutic form of faith, in which the purpose of prayer and meditation is here-and-now happiness through harmony with the universe and the God Within. (The Jungian masculinism of Jordan Peterson may play a similar role for his devotees.)

Then there is the most overt and literal form of neo-paganism: the booming business in horoscopes and astrology, the psychics and mediums doing a brisk trade in communication with the spirit realm, and the people (overrepresented on the online extremes of left *and* right, interestingly) who simply self-describe as Wiccan or neo-pagan, and whose numbers are growing fast enough—even if their literal belief in the spirits and deities they worship is somewhat variable—to make overt paganism a rival to some of the shrinking mainline Protestant churches in Europe and the United States.

Finally, there is the influence of the civilizations, Asian especially, where polytheism and pantheism never lost the battle with monotheism—of the Hindu and Shinto and Buddhist and animist traditions that still predominate in the Indian subcontinent and East Asia, all of which have some increasing influence in North America and Europe, however altered in transmission.

These various strands are not yet woven together into something one could describe as a new religion. For that to happen, not only would there have to be some syncretistic convergence at the popular level between Oprah devotees, practicing Hindus, and would-be druids and shamans, but the highbrow pantheists—the intellectuals and tastemakers—would need to embrace a clearer cultic aspect for their faith, a set of public rituals of the kind we associate with, say, classical Roman devotions, as opposed to just private experiences with 'shrooms or meditation. (Burning Man almost gets you there, but not quite. . .)

Maybe that's impossible; the Western intelligentsia tiptoed in that direction in the spoon-bending, "What's your sign?" days of 1970s religion, but nowadays our intellectuals seem embarrassed by anything too frankly supernaturalist, and our Silicon Valley overlords prefer to launder their religious impulses through techno-utopianism rather than New Age rituals. Moreover, the last extended elite flirtation with neo-paganism reached a horrific apotheosis in Nazi Germany, and today's elite is justifiably frightened of releasing those dark forces—meaning that they might cling to the egalitarian aspect of Christianity even if it's part of a strained and incoherent world picture, rather than risking the aristocratic, decidedly inegalitarian temptations that can creep in when you make the natural world your moral standard.

Still, the range of different forms of paganism means that the raw materials are there for something more dramatic—if the philosophers of pantheism became a little less secularized and a little more mystical, and the New Agers and neo-pagans became a little more organized and centralized, and the convergence interacted with the spiritual aspects of progressive politics to create a new kind of widespread public worship, complete perhaps with the construction of new sacred spaces, new temples, in the heart of the world's cities. To the extent that Western decadence is shaped by Western Christianity's mix of weakness and resilience, its internal stalemate in the debate over its confrontation with modernity, its preservationist but not dynamic position in the culture, then it's hard to imagine a more decisive way to end this phase in history than with the full revival of the religious tradition that Christianity once displaced.

A Western Islam? A Christian China?

But, of course, Christianity has other rivals. If the return of paganism is one end-of-religious-decadence scenario, another obvious one would be the spread of Islam, in Europe especially, out of its current position as the ghettoized Other, and into the role of cultural inheritor that both radical and merely ambitious Muslims envision for their faith.

As I argued in chapter 7, this is not presently happening: Islam is growing in the West through migration rather than conversion, and to outsiders it's defined more by its ongoing convulsions and civil wars— and, of course, the threat of terrorism—than by its potential allure as an alternative to an incoherent secularism and a faded Christianity.

But if the Houellebecqian scenario is therefore *presently* a fantasy, it need not be one permanently. A million words have been written about whether Islam can escape from the medieval fundamentalism of ISIS and adapt, like Christianity, to modernity. But these frameworks impose clichés on the Islamic world that don't actually fit. First, because the fundamentalism of contemporary Islam is itself extremely modern, invented in reaction to Islamic civilization's weakness and decline—and the rejection of certain kinds of fundamentalism is precisely what medieval Muslim civilization accomplished, meaning that a model for the Islamic future might already exist in the Islamic past. And second, because the entire category of secular modernity is shaped and stamped by the Christian civilization it overthrew, and the church-state struggles from which modern liberalism emerged. There is no reason to assume that a religion with a different theology and history would simply follow Christian pathways—Reformation, revolution, secularization—in its development or transformation.

Instead, the thing that makes Islam a "problem" in the current Western context, the fact that it hasn't participated in the Christendom-Reformation secularism dialectic that still defines the Western world, also raises the possibility that it could develop or appeal anew in ways that seem to escape the stalemates of belief and secularism, liberal and conservative Christianity. One could imagine—hypothetically!—an Islam that induced post-Christian intellectuals to turn from their incoherent agnosticism to a non-Western form of Unitarianism, an Islam that offered the decaying Western working class an abstemious and purpose-driven and family-centered social order, an Islam that attracted some of the lost boys drawn to far right politics (a few far right European figures have actually made that leap; "a moderated form of Islam is probably the West's only hope," the famous MAGA personality Mike Cernovich tweeted recently), an Islam that somehow adapted the faith's puritanical tradition to the puritanical late feminism of #MeToo. In all of these cases, the relevant model would be the Houellebecqian character who turns away from his ancestral Catholicism because it seems to have no future, but embraces Islam because it does. It could prove easier for a society that has lost its sense of metaphysical purpose to rediscover the transcendent through a religion that seems at once similar to *and* different from the religion of its ancestors, when the latter seems to have dead-ended or decayed or otherwise become too far a leap for even faith to make.

Of course, believing Christians, like myself, would dispute that their own faith has actually dead-ended. The story of Christian history is one of unexpected resurrections, of what G. K. Chesterton called the "five deaths of the faith" (the fall of Rome, the Muslim challenge, the crisis of the Reformation, the Enlightenment, the march of Darwinism) giving way to unlooked-for renewals and rebirths. So if we imagine religious decadence ending with a new paganism or an Islamic renaissance, we should also imagine it ending with a Christian revival—especially since, for all its weaknesses, Christianity remains institutionally significant, at least for now, in America and Europe on a scale no rival faith can match. In the event that there were a renewal of interest in Christianity within the developed world's elite, or a grassroots Great Awakening that fills the yawning social void where populism currently flourishes, it would still find a vast preexisting Christian infrastructure, which it might reclaim and fill with newfound zeal, like empty wineskins with new wine.

But perhaps, to go back to Robert Sarah's Vendée speech, the next resurrection of Christianity is already happening outside the West, and the fate of Christianity in Europe and North America will be shaped by forces external to the Christian faith's old heartlands. If it's possible to imagine a late-twenty-first-century world remade by African numbers and Chinese power, it's also possible to imagine a religious landscape remade by African and Chinese Christianities. The former is a peripheral force for non-Africans for now, but a dynamic, continent-reshaping force south of the Sahara; the latter is a persecuted minority faith but one that's arguably the strongest non-Communist worldview in China, with the potential to take over the Middle Kingdom much as Christianity once took over the Roman Empire: slowly, and then all at once.

Imagine a Eurafrica in which black Christians fill the Gothic churches of the Old Continent—something that happens already if you look in the right Parisian neighborhood—and then gain enough power and influence to build new ones, in new-old styles, in both Nantes and Nairobi. Imagine a Chinese empire circa 2100 that's more Christian than its secularized or paganized American rival for global power, and that's governed by a Confucian-influenced version of the old throne-and-altar integralism that liberalism overthrew. Imagine a global renaissance of Christian art and architecture, philosophy and literature, in which American and European Christians are, at best, bit players. Or imagine a reversal of the scenario I conjured earlier, in which some Chinese breakthrough in genetic engineering leads to a global Eugenics War; imagine instead that it's a suddenly Christian-izing China and its African allies resisting the secular West's genetic engineering, its attempted *Homo Deus* leap.

Indeed, just about any scenario for a religious revival could be linked to backlash against some dehumanizing technological development. You could call this the "Butlerian Jihad" possibility, after the future rebellion against artificial intelligence imagined by Frank Herbert's science-fiction classic *Dune*. Indeed, you wouldn't necessarily need the huge AI or biotech leap: even a refinement of existing virtual reality, one that draws more people more fully into the violence and pornography of unreal playgrounds, would seem to demand a religious response, even a dramatic one. Perhaps not quite a jihad . . . but at the very least an effort to tame and humanize the new technologies of simulation that escapes current culture war categories sufficiently to usher in a different—at long last—religious era than the one the baby boomers made.

Not One Renaissance but Many

The potential entanglement of religious revival and technological change is a good place to conclude this chapter, because one of the themes of this book is the essential entanglement of decadence—meaning the way that the economic, demographic, intellectual, and cultural elements of our predicament are all connected, so that you can't just pick out a single cause or driver of stagnation and repetition, or solve the problem with a narrow focus on one area or issue.

If that's the case, it makes sense that the same would be true of any renaissance, any plausible escape. Instead of a single primary cause—life extension! #fullsocialism! a religious awakening!—driving all the secondary ones, a real renaissance would look more like the birth of the modern world, when the Renaissance and the Reformation and Counter-Reformation and the scientific revolutions and the age of discovery were happening on top of one another, influencing each other and driving each other forward in ways that historians have been unpacking and repackaging, explaining and reexplaining ever since.

The real answer to the question "What might end decadence?" isn't actually one thing or another; it's a lot of things happening all at once. The political rise of China and the cultural rise of Africa *also* changing the shape of global religion. A technological breakthrough leading to a reinvigoration of capitalist growth—which then *also* creates the material foundation for a new birth of socialism. A genetic-engineering or AI breakthrough leading to a new culture war that *also* reinvigorates existing religions or forges a new faith. A leap into space that *also* inspires poets, philosophers, religious visionaries, and statesmen back on earth. A period of migration that involves war and instability and cruelty but ultimately invigorates decadent societies rather than undoing them, leading to cultural transformation *and* demographic revival *and* new technological innovation *and* faster economic growth *and* new forms of political order . . .

This "everything together" phenomenon holds, perhaps above all, for two things that certain modern prejudices assume can't be joined together: scientific progress and religious revival. It isn't just that some technological advance could, as suggested above, act in creative tension with religion by provoking a moral crusade or jihad in response. It's also that scientific and religious experiments proceed from a similar desire for knowing, a similar belief that the universe is patterned and intelligible and that its secrets might somehow be unlocked. Which is why in periods of real intellectual ferment and development, there is often a *general* surge of experimentation that extends across multiple ways of seeking knowledge, from the scientific and experimental, to the theological and mystical, to the gray zones and disputed territories in between.

Thus the assumption, common to rationalists today, that religion represents a form of unreason that science has to vanquish on its way to new ages of discovery, is as mistaken as the religious reflex that regards the scientific mind-set as an inevitable threat to the pious simplicities of faith. In fact, early modern scientists were fascinated by scriptural prophecies, the Victorians read Darwin while organizing seances, and the space age was awash in strange religious ferments. The rocket science of the 1940s had an occultist, hermetic side, embodied in figures such as Jack Parsons, the founder of the Jet Propulsion Laboratory and a disciple of Aleister Crowley, who recited Crowley's "Hymn to Pan" during rocket tests and conducted rituals with L. Ron Hubbard aimed at bringing the female divinity "Babalon" to earth. The moon landing itself, of course, coincided with the dawning of the Age of Aquarius on earth. And the larger Apollo project, as Kendrick Oliver argues in *To Touch the Face of God: The Sacred, the Profane, and the American Space Program, 1957–75*, was intertwined in the aspirations and anxieties of the postwar American Protestant revival—culminating in the famous Christmas Eve reading of Genesis 1 by astronaut Bill Anders as Apollo 8 orbited the earth and men wept in mission control below.

In his conclusion, Oliver makes the case that a sense of religious mission was crucial to the national commitment to space travel, and the fading of the missionary spirit, as much as any technological impediment, contributed to the closing of the final frontier:

> [Apollo] simultaneously kindled thoughts of God and the death of God. When religion was absent from the program, its absence became a point of religious concern. When religion was present, its presence meant more, to more people, than it did in any other national undertaking of the time. Only for as long as that was true did Americans live in an age of space.

Perhaps this is too sweeping. But it's a reminder that as much as the relationship between science and religion can be adversarial, there can also be a mysterious alchemy between the two forms of human exploration. And nothing will be a surer sign that decadence has ended in something like a renaissance than if that alchemy suddenly returns.

11

Providence

After that talk of God and space flight, let's end with the heavens, where we began.

Sometime in 2017, the first year of the Trump era, a strange object entered our solar system—long and cylindrical like a cigar, with features that no normal asteroid or meteor exhibits, and a curious trajectory and pattern of acceleration. Dubbed Oumuamua, the object spun like a bottle as it moved, and its strangeness inspired the chair of Harvard's astronomy department, Avi Loeb, to suggest it might actually be a piece of an alien spacecraft, a solar-sail-propelled interstellar probe.

Oumuamua didn't tarry, we couldn't give pursuit, and it probably wasn't actually the long-expected aliens; indeed, by the summer of 2019, a collection of clever astronomers had come up with enough plausible explanations to declare that the spinning cigar was almost certainly an object of "purely natural" origin.

But by then, there was a different reason to be thinking about UFOs. The Pentagon had been pressured into releasing a series of videos showing their pilots encountering genuine unidentified flying objects—footage that does not grow any less peculiar upon repeated viewings, with the UFOs displaying wild patterns of movements that clearly suggest some outlandish technological capacity, and the pilots' shared reactions testifying to the nonhallucinatory character of what they were seeing. (It was a testament to the immediate-past-erasing velocity of the Internet news cycle that stories about this footage could appear repeatedly in the *New York Times* and the *Washington Post* and each time be seemingly forgotten by everybody just a few days later.)

The caught-on-video encounters, too, probably have some explanation besides little green men come at last. But as intimations of the extraterrestrial, they help tease out the biggest question haunting a decadent and planet-spanning civilization, the cosmic issues lurking behind the themes treated in this book. We have discussed decadence as a problem of advanced economies and long-established political systems, as a technological cul-de-sac or temporary lull, as a cultural matrix in which creativity withers and repetition rules. But the question hanging over all of these descriptions, and over all the scenarios for sustainability, collapse, and renaissance, is whether some kind of decadence becomes inevitable once a world civilization arises and then finds that it has nowhere else to go.

Have We Reached the Filter?

This possibility, that decadence is an inevitable destination for a planetary species, is implicit in one of the more famous attempts to explain why, with all those endless stars and worlds beyond ours, we haven't encountered evidence of extraterrestrial civilizations more compelling than UFO videos and strange maybe-asteroids. Dubbed the "Great Filter" by its originator, George Mason University economist Robin Hanson, the idea explains our apparent isolation in the galaxy, as well as the fact that we have ascended to self-consciousness, civilization, and remarkable scientific understanding without encountering any evidence of predecessors or peers who made the same climb, by suggesting that advanced civilizations face some kind of near-universal obstacle, some extremely-difficult-to-slip-through filter, that generally prevents them from becoming the kind of star-faring species that would leave traces for our radio telescopes to find.

Having established this premise, Hanson then proceeds to the key question: Where exactly does this filter lie? One possibility, a hopeful one, is that it is already behind us, somewhere back in the early development of life itself, or in the emergence of the strange thing we call consciousness. Maybe single-celled life abounds in the universe but nothing more complex emerges save once every hundred billion years; maybe animal life abounds but the intellectual capacity to understand the laws of physics is the blackest of black swans. In which case, we are the great exception to the Great Filter, we're already through the bottleneck that keeps the universe depopulated and eerily silent, and there's no necessary limit on how far we might ultimately go.

But maybe the filter is space travel: the limits imposed by light speed, the laws of physics, the gulf between the stars. Maybe societies like ours are inescapably bound to their planetary starting places. Maybe the space-age experience will be recapitulated if we ever make it to Mars, with a brief flurry of interest followed by the realization that there's nothing for human beings on the red planet either, the costs of terraforming are far too high to bear, and every other star and planet is simply too far away to reach. Maybe exactly that kind of depressing experience has been rehearsed a thousand thousand times by a thousand thousand civilizations before us, as one by one a great array of intelligent creatures have reached a certain phase of development and then faced two options: a sustainable but depressing decadence, lasting until an unlucky collision with an asteroid or a nuclear-launch accident ends things permanently, or a destructive contest for ever-scarcer resources that eventually tears down everything to a *Mad Max* level and lets civilization start again.

If this is the inevitable pattern, it might be that nothing—not a renaissance in the arts and sciences, not religious revival, not AI, nor physical immortality—can ultimately save a species bound to a single blue dot from eventually despairing, abandoning hopes of progress and faith in metaphysical purpose, and feeling the tug of Thanatos in the French mathematician-philosopher Blaise Pascal's terror of the eternal silence and infinite spaces beyond our earthly shores. A cyclic rise and fall of planet-bound civilizations is, in that case, the literal most that any intelligent species can accomplish unaided, until their luck runs out and the ax of extinction finally falls.

This is unprovable, but to look at the Western world since 1969 is to feel the possible truth of it, which is why this book began with the moon landing and this conclusion is talking about the stars. Whether our short-term destiny is renaissance or apocalypse or just the status quo, I suspect that a truly globalized civilization cannot help tending toward decadence so long as it remains earthbound, so long as there is no hope of finding actual new worlds to leap toward, conquer, or explore. I suspect that what we see happening in our society today— the turn toward simulations and virtual realities; the declining birth-rates; the sense of repetition, stagnation, and futility—is connected on a deep level to the post-Apollo mission sense that such a hope does not exist, that there is quite literally nowhere else for mankind to go, that we are stuck here waiting to either destroy ourselves accidentally or to have nature hit reboot, via comet or a plague, on our entire up-from-hunter-gathering, east-of-Eden project.

So if we want to really escape decadence on our own, to transcend it for something longer than a season, then, absent a divine reaching down or a convenient alien arrival, we need to find a way to climb, to make a ladder to the stars, and to offer future generations of humanity a new reality to explore that's more expansive than our beleaguered planet, more extraordinary than anything that we can conjure inside our machines of simulation. We have to prove our post-Apollo pessimism wrong; we have to find a way to make the stars our destination after all. Even Elon Musk's successes have not made this future seem all that likely at the moment. But within the confines of the material world as we understand it, it's the only possibility that offers hope on the longest time horizon for what the human future holds.

When Man Can Do No More

But I would be a poor Christian if I did not conclude by noting that no civilization—not ours, not any—has thrived without a confidence that there was more to the human story than just *the material world as we understand it*. If we have lost that confidence in our own age, if the liberal dream of progress no less than its Christian antecedent has succumbed to a corrosive skepticism, then perhaps it is because we have reached the end of our own capacities at this stage of our history, and we need something else, something extra, that really can come only from outside our present frame of reference. "Fill the earth and subdue it," runs one of the earliest admonitions ever given to humanity. Well, we have done so, or come close; maybe it does not fall to us to determine what comes next.

Some of the early UFO theorists, spinning providentialist theories in the shadow of the atomic bomb, had a view like this: they believed that in splitting the atom, in making our own extinction possible, we had crossed a line that ensured some sort of extraterrestrial visitation, some reaction from the hidden forces—enlightened or otherwise—that rule beyond the limits of solar system. Was this crazy? Go ask Oumuamua. Or ask anyone who reads the Bible, a narrative in which human action often disturbs the universe sufficiently to merit an external, transformational response—be it a judgment, a chastisement, or some descent or revelation from on high.

It was in a similarly providential spirit that the early Christians cast the rise of Rome—the original known-world-spanning civilization, the ancient model for the modern world—as a divinely ordained development, a necessary precondition for the birth of Jesus Christ and the propagation of the gospel. But later Christian writers gave this argument a still-more-interesting wrinkle: it wasn't just that Rome's rise prepared the way for Christianity, it was that Rome's decadence demonstrated the need for a Messiah—that God in His providence allowed human civilization to hit a peak of wealth and political efficiency and culture, and then to experience a fallen world's limitations at precisely the moment when He sent His Son to save that world from itself.

This was G. K. Chesterton's argument in *The Everlasting Man*, his 1925 Christian outline of human history:

> . . . It is essential to recognize that the Roman Empire was recognized as the highest achievement of the human race; and also as the broadest. A dreadful secret seemed to be written as in obscure hieroglyphics across those mighty works of marble and stone, those colossal amphitheaters and aqueducts. *Man could do no more.*
>
> . . . There was nothing left that could conquer Rome, but there was also nothing left that could improve it. It was the strongest thing that was growing weak . . . it was . . . universal with a stale and sterile universality. The peoples had pooled their resources and still there was not enough. The empires had gone into partnership and they were still bankrupt. No philosopher who was really philosophical could think anything except that, in that central sea, the wave of the world had risen to its highest, seeming to touch the stars. But the wave was already stooping; for it was only the wave of the world.
>
> [With] a sense of impotence and despair . . . men shook their fists vainly at the stars, as they saw all the best work of humanity sinking slowly and helplessly into a swamp. They could easily believe that even creation itself was not a creation but a perpetual fall, when they saw that the weightiest and worthiest of all human creations was falling by its own weight. They could fancy that all the stars were falling stars; and that the very pillars of their own solemn porticos were bowed under a sort of gradual Deluge. . . . There was no God; if there had been a God, surely this was the very moment when He would have moved and saved the world.

As a historian, Chesterton was not always the subtlest or most nuanced, preferring his grand outlines to any inconvenient details, and I don't want to claim too much for this analysis of how the Romans saw themselves in the days before the Christian revolution swept their world.

But this much I will say: there were things that seemed true of Rome—that it was as large as any empire possibly could be, that it encompassed the entire world that mattered, that it was a truly universal civilization—that seem true, to many people, of our global civilization today. And a variation on the feeling Chesterton ascribes, fairly or not, to the Romans is certainly at work in our own era: that sense, to go back to my early definitions of decadence, of being *the last of a series*, without a clear sense of what comes next. So for anyone inclined to regard human history as a story being told rather than just one damn thing after another, there is something natural about the idea that certain important Authorial interventions might coincide with moments when the characters—that is, us—have reached a moment of success that is also a moment of bafflement, a long-sought arrival that also feels like a dead end.

Following this thread, it also might be seen as providential rather than tragic that our first leap to the stars didn't carry us that far, that there is for now some limit on our further expansion. Because, after all, that "Fill the earth and subdue it" admonition was given to a still-unfallen species, and the human condition under decadence raises the possibility that space travel without other forms of renewal might be less an escape from dystopia than an expansion of its scope.

This is the most plausible case against space travel, whether environmentalist or religious or both: that insofar as "modernity's drive to power over nature is a corruption of what ought to be mankind's dominion over creation," as the Protestant essayist Micah Meadowcroft puts it, we can't morally justify the expansion of that power to the stars unless we become better stewards of our planet, our societies, ourselves. This possibility resonates with cautionary themes in nuclear-age sci-fi—that we had gained power for which we were morally unready, and that greater powers needed to step in—and with themes in twentieth-century Christian science fiction, in novels like C. S. Lewis's space trilogy and Madeleine L'Engle's *A Wrinkle in Time*, in which the universe is actually crowded with sentient life that we're just too sinful to be permitted to encounter, and the real Great Filter on human expansion is our own fallen status, a kind of spiritual quarantine around our world.

In which case our present encounter with the limits of our own capacities, the seeming inevitability of decadence as a punishment for our success, might end only with better rockets or faster-than-light travel if Something Else intervenes to change things first.

To be clear: I'm not predicting the end of the world or the arrival of the millennium here, and indeed my arguments for the sustainability of decadence would cut against any crude attempt to read the book of Revelation, with all its wars and plagues and disasters, into the warp and woof of current events.

I'm just saying that if this *were* the age in which some major divine intervention happened, whether long prophecied or completely unforeseen, there would be, in hindsight, a case that we should have seen it coming. And it shouldn't surprise anyone if decadence ends with people looking heavenward: toward God, toward the stars, or both.

So down on your knees—and start working on that warp drive.

Acknowledgments

This book owes a special debt to Regent College in Vancouver, which invited me to deliver the Laing Lectures in the long-ago autumn of 2014. The path from those talks to this book was rather more winding than I expected, but a version of the arguments I made back then is in your hands right now.

Variations of many of this book's arguments have also appeared in my regular op-ed column, so I'm grateful to all of my editors at the *New York Times*, especially James Bennet, John Guida, Joe Rakowski, and Aaron Retica, for their assistance, forbearance, and support. I'm also grateful to Rich Lowry, the late Michael Potemra, and Katherine Howell for indulging my cinematic obsessions at *National Review* for many years and enabling me to professionally justify cultivating strong views on Star Wars and related matters.

My editor, Ben Loehnen, gave me the opportunity to write this book and improved it immeasurably. Rafe Sagalyn, my agent, played his usual essential role. April Lawson, James Hitchcock, and especially Adam Rubenstein and Jackson Wolford provided invaluable support.

In addition to the writers quoted in these pages, I am grateful to everyone who has argued and engaged with me, online and off, about politics, society, and pop culture, with special thanks to Reihan Salam, J. D. Vance, Elizabeth Bruenig, Michael Brendan Dougherty,

245

Acknowledgments

Rod Dreher, Alyssa Rosenberg, Sonny Bunch, Chris Orr, Kyle Smith, Adrian Vermeule—and of course my podcast sparring partners, David Leonhardt and Michelle Goldberg. Patrick Hough at the Elm Institute, Joseph Capizzi at the Catholic University of America, Samuel Moyn at Yale and Everit Street, and Yuval Levin at the American Enterprise Institute all provided institutional support and intellectual stimulation during the writing of this book.

And, as always, I'm impossibly grateful to my wife, Abigail; and our children, Gwendolyn, Eleanor, Nicholas, and Rosemary—for their love, encouragement, and support and also for giving me an urgent reason to keep writing and resist the comforts of decadence myself.

Index

Index

Index

Bundy, Ted, 119, 120
Bush, George H. W., 71
Bush, George W., 71, 80
Byzantium, 205

Caldwell, Christopher, 84
Canada, birthrate in, 50
cancer, 215
Capital in the Twenty-First Century
(Piketty), 30–31, 58
capitalism, 32, 185, 223
  neo-Marxist critique of, 223–26
  Piketty's theory of, 30–31
  rentier class and, 26, 30–31, 46
captured economies, 30
Carr, Nicholas, 108
Carter, Jimmy, 24
Carter presidency, 25–26
catastrophe, 193–208
  climate change scenario for, 199–202,
  204
  economic scenario for, 196–99, 204
  mass migration scenario for, 202–5
  unforeseen, 193–95, 207
Catholics, Catholicism, 104, 160, 187,
  232
  decline in church attendance by, 100
  lapsed, 222
  liberal, 111
  traditionalist, 210–11, 212
  Vendée massacre of, 210
Cavafy, C. P., 161–62
Central Intelligence Agency, 147
centrists, 85–86, 107, 186
  sclerosis as viewed by, 77–79
Cernovich, Mike, 232
Césaire, Aimé, 211–12
Challenger explosion, 2
change:
  perceived vs. actual speed of, 11
  see also progress
Charlie Hebdo massacre, 159
Charlottesville, Va., 2017 killing in, 134
Chase, David, 95
CHAZ (Capitol Hill Autonomous Zone),
  134

Chen Tianyong, 172
Chesterton, G. K., 14, 233, 242–43
children, of older parents, 61
Children of Men (film), 66
Children of Men (James), 47–50, 66
China, 5
  aging population of, 171
  birthrate in, 50
  capital flight from, 172, 174
  Christianity in, 233–34
  consolidation of power in, 171–72
  economic growth in, 168–69, 171
  economic slowdown in, 198
  emergence of decadence in, 169–73
  Internet censorship in, 141
  Ming dynasty abandonment of sea
  voyages by, 5
  potential limitations on growth in,
  172–73
  social credit systems in, 140–42
  surveillance in, 141
Chinese political system, 204
  as alternative to liberal order, 168–73
Christianity:
  beginnings of, 226, 228, 241
  Eurafrican revitalization of, 211–12
  liberal, 104
  predicted revival of, 104
  renewal of, as path to renaissance,
  233–34
  unexpected resurrections in, 232–33
civilizations:
  clash of, 163
  expansionism and, 3–4
civil liberties:
  colleges and universities and, 144
  "safe" vs. "dangerous" categorization
  of, 143–44
  see also pink police state
Civil Rights Act (1964), 77
Civil War, US, likelihood of second,
  134–35
class war, 177–78
climate change, 35, 206, 223, 226
  catastrophic, 196, 199–202, 204
  as consequence of dynamism,
  183–84

249

Index

Index

Index

Index

filibuster, 78

finance industry, *see* Wall Street

financial crisis of 2008, 12, 69, 80, 84, 139, 196

Finland:
 decline of sexual relations in, 55
 declining birthrate in, 53

Fire Next Time, The (Baldwin), 97

Floyd, George, protests and, 131, 198

Flynn effect, 35

Flynt, Larry, 120

food production, climate change and, 200

Ford, John, 111

Foreign Affairs, 134

Fox News, 78

France, 32
 immigrants in, 65
 pronatalist policies of, 52–53
 protest movements in, 176

Francis, Pope, 104

Freedom Time: Negritude, Decolonization, and the Future of the World (Wilder), 212

free-market policies, 25

free trade, 24, 28, 29

French Revolution, 210

From Dawn to Decadence (Barzun), 8

frontier:
 closing of, 5, 136
 New, 185
 space as, 2, 6, 236; *see also* Apollo moon program
 Turner on importance of, 3–4

Fukuyama, Francis, 12, 83, 113–14, 116, 136, 163

Fyre Festival, 17–18, 21

Game of Thrones (TV show), 95, 96

Garland, Merrick, 78

gay rights, revolution in, 99

gender, wage gap and, 100

genetic engineering, 11, 43, 215, 234, 235

Germany, 196
 immigrants in, 64–65, 85

Germany, Nazi, 230

Germany, Weimar, 129, 134

Gersen, Jacob, 145

Gharbi, Musa al-, 97

Gibson, Mel, 193–94, 207

gig economy, decline of traditional freelancing in, 27

gilets-jaunes, 176

Gingrich, Newt, 78

globalism, 223

global South:
 climate change and, 178–79, 207
 mass migration from, 212

global warming, *see* climate change

God and Man at Yale (Buckley), 97

Goebbels, Joseph, 133

Gordon, Robert, 12, 33, 34, 35, 40–41, 46

government:
 informal norms of, 78
 policy failures of, 71
 public distrust of, 75
 public expectation of action by, 75
 uncontrolled sprawl of, 72–73, 76

Government's End (Rauch), 73

Graeber, David, 12, 38, 40, 41

Gramsci, Antonio, v

Grantland, 93–94

Great Awakening, 103, 226, 233

Great Britain:
 Brexit in, *see* Brexit
 US technological mastery vs., 169

Great Depression, 30, 110

Great Filter, 238–40, 244

Great Recession, 12, 23, 27, 69, 115, 124, 197–98
 falling birthrate in, 51

Great Society, 77

Great Stagnation, The (Cowen), 33–34, 45

Greece, 84, 85
 in 2008 financial crisis, 196

Green New Deal, 226

Green Revolution, 43, 200

growth, limits on, 32–36, 46

Guardian (Australia), 225

Guinea, 210

Index

Index

Index

Index

Index

Index

Index

Index

Index

About the Author

Ross Douthat is a columnist for the *New York Times* op-ed page. He is the author of *To Change the Church*, *Bad Religion*, and *Privilege*, and coauthor of *Grand New Party*. Before joining the *New York Times*, he was a senior editor for the *Atlantic*. He is the film critic for *National Review*, and he cohosts the *New York Times*'s weekly op-ed podcast, *The Argument*. He lives in New Haven with his wife and four children.